MIGRATING
LIBRARY DATA

MIGRATING
LIBRARY
DATA

A Practical Manual

edited by **KYLE BANERJEE** *and* **BONNIE PARKS**

An imprint of the American Library Association

CHICAGO | 2017

KYLE BANERJEE has twenty years' library experience, extensive systems knowledge, and has planned and written software to support ILS, digital collections, and resource-sharing system migrations since 1996. He coauthored two other textbooks about digital libraries and has written numerous articles on library automation.

BONNIE PARKS has fifteen years' library experience and extensive metadata management experience. She served as institutional lead for consortial migration in 2014 and has taught Cataloging and Metadata Management for the University of Arizona's School of Information since 2009. Bonnie has authored several book chapters on cataloging topics, served as column editor for the "Serials Conversations" column in *Serials Review,* and received the 2016 Ulrich's Serials Librarianship award.

© 2017 by the American Library Association

Extensive effort has gone into ensuring the reliability of the information in this book; however, the publisher makes no warranty, express or implied, with respect to the material contained herein.

ISBN: 978-0-8389-1503-5 (paper)

Library of Congress Cataloging-in-Publication Data
Names: Banerjee, Kyle, editor. | Parks, Bonnie, editor.
Title: Migrating library data : a practical manual / edited by Kyle Banerjee, Bonnie Parks.
Description: Chicago : ALA Neal-Schuman, an imprint of the American Library Association, 2017. | Includes index.
Identifiers: LCCN 2016056887 | ISBN 9780838915035 (pbk. : alk. paper)
Subjects: LCSH: Integrated library systems (Computer systems) | Systems migration. | Libraries—Automation—Management. | Libraries—Data processing—Management.
Classification: LCC Z678.93.I57 M54 2017 | DDC 025.04—dc23 LC record available at https://lccn.loc.gov/2016056887

Book design by Alejandra Diaz in the Calluna, Avenir and Gotham typefaces. Imagery © Shutterstock, Inc.

♾ This paper meets the requirements of ANSI/NISO Z39.48–1992 (Permanence of Paper).
Printed in the United States of America
21 20 19 18 17   5 4 3 2 1

CONTENTS

CHAPTER SEVEN

PATRON DATA AND AUTHENTICATION   143

Nathan Mealey

SERIALS 167

Elan May Rinck

INTRODUCTION

Because no technology lasts forever, there is an ongoing need to migrate information from one system to another—each migration is a link in a chain that connects the past to the future. The pace of development is relentless. Rapid technology cycles render computers obsolete in five years and mobile devices in three. Advances create new possibilities that lead to new services, which in turn stimulate user expectations. Services and devices most people hadn't imagined a decade ago are now considered necessities. To remain relevant and to meet user needs, libraries must leverage opportunities brought about by new technologies. As a practical matter, this means most librarians will go through several migrations over the course of their careers.

Library services have changed dramatically over the past few decades. Until the end of the twentieth century, libraries served primarily as book and journal repositories. They identified, acquired, managed, circulated, and preserved books and a few other types of items. Library staff performed these tasks manually and managed operations using paper-based systems.

Computerized library systems first appeared in the 1960s, but most libraries continued to rely on paper-based systems until the 1980s. Just as moving operations from one computer system to another requires a migration process, so does converting from a paper-based to a computer-based system. The first library systems migrations were conceptually simple but labor intensive. Staff and vendors keyed information from cards into a computer or matched holdings with records that were shipped on magnetic tapes. Once the bibliographic information was in the system, copy-specific holdings and circulation information was keyed in. As acquisitions, serials management, and other functions were partially or fully converted from paper-based systems, staff manually also keyed necessary information from these modules into the system.

At least until the 1990s, Integrated Library Systems (ILSs) could be thought of as inventory-control systems built around the specialized needs of acquiring, managing, and circulating books and journals. Libraries collected other resources, such as sound and video recordings, microforms, maps, and music, but the processes developed for books and journals could be adapted for them.

These early systems were similar to the paper-based systems they replaced. The electronic catalog record looked like a card from the paper catalog. Serials modules contained check-in "cards" that looked like their paper counterparts. Following the transition from paper to electronic, business processes were still optimized for paper systems. The number of author, title, and subject access points were a function of how many would fit on a card. Newspapers, journals, magazines, and other serial publications that underwent name changes were considered entirely separate publications rather than a title change for the existing resource—a practice developed largely to avoid editing paper cards or putting more information on them than they could hold.

The Internet and cheap network computing permanently transformed library services. Although it had previously only been feasible to search representations of library resources using card or electronic catalogs, disk space, and computer power became cheap enough to allow full text searches of books, journals, and other resources.

Even more significantly, the twenty-first century marks a fundamental shift in how information is maintained and used. Historically, the purpose of a library is to preserve and provide access to resources stored in a centralized repository. But in the Internet Age, the information people need is increasingly decentralized and maintained by entities other than the library. Books, music, video, and other resources that were previously difficult and expensive for individuals to acquire are now cheaply and easily obtainable from online services provided by private companies. Given that libraries often rely on the same companies as individuals and emulate their services, it's clear that libraries have a new position in the information ecosystem that requires new service models and new systems to support operations.

Access mechanisms and processes for managing access to centralized physical resources proved ill-suited to electronic resources that lack a physical presence and change frequently. When libraries first began subscribing to electronic content, some seriously debated the best way to "check in" issues in aggregator journal databases where titles and issues are added and dropped without warning. Concepts such as "main entry," which determines whether a book is shelved by author or title endured even though electronic items can exist in many places on a virtual shelf. Cutter numbers that have no value outside shelflisting—a function unneeded for the same reasons as main entry—continued to be added to call numbers that already had little value beyond a rough tool for collection assessment. Catalogers meticulously described web pages that changed frequently and added systems notes indicating users must use browsers and connection technologies that quickly became obsolete.

Migrations are challenging because their whole point is to implement a system that works differently—and hopefully better—than the old one. This means capabilities are different. Configuration is different. The types of records and fields are different. Even when records and fields appear similar, they use data differently. Migrations change everybody's jobs as well as every procedure related to the old system. To compound difficulties, vendors and systems designers rarely prioritize developing tools to help people migrate to other systems. Migrations are complex endeavors, and it is difficult to overstate the amount of time required to prepare, organize, and communicate what is necessary to make them succeed.

People respond strongly to outward appearances, so a great amount of migration planning centers on what the system looks like to users and staff. Form and function are connected, but look and feel are relatively easy to adjust until people are satisfied after the migration, because they are controlled by configuration. As the data migration occurs only once and changes are difficult to make afterward, it is essential to dedicate sufficient energy to transferring the data on which staff and user interfaces depend.

Every service depends on a myriad of details. For example, it's easy to say we want our patrons to have access to resources owned by other libraries when they are not locally available. But for a requestable item to exist, other services to select, acquire, and manage it must be in place. If we want the patron to be able to obtain an item she wants if it's not available locally, there needs to be a way to identify which libraries own it, a mechanism for physically or electronically delivering it must be determined, copyright clearances must be obtained when required, processing fees must be paid when applicable, the patron needs to be alerted when her item arrives, and a physical item must be circulated and billed if it's not returned on time. The systems that make this and other increasingly sophisticated library services possible are complex and rely on an enormous amount of data, so migrating is technically and organizationally challenging.

To ensure smooth transitions, libraries must leverage the enormous investment they've made in existing collections, infrastructure, and staff. Thousands of configuration parameters and millions of pieces of data designed in the past must be adapted for the new system. This is a difficult task because today's cutting-edge system will someday be obsolete and we must position ourselves to meet needs that have yet to be imagined.

This book draws upon the expertise of seasoned professionals to help libraries understand how to address the technical and conceptual challenges encountered when migrating specific services, records, and types of data utilizing existing staff and commonly available technical resources. Examples are provided, but methods and tools are as generic as possible, and no programming knowledge or specific technical skills are assumed. In cases where specific expertise is required to address an issue, the conceptual issues are presented to help librarians understand what approaches will be most fruitful with IT staff and vendors.

In chapter 1, Bonnie Parks describes the migration and planning process in broad strokes. She offers insights on what must be done to prepare staff, the system, and existing data for the upcoming transition as well as useful knowledge and skills in staff and vendors.

In chapter 2, David Forero discusses formats used in migrations, technical challenges commonly presented by data, and methods for cleaning, correcting, and modifying exported data so that they function as needed in the new system. He demonstrates methods for addressing carriage returns in delimited data, mangled character encodings, invalid XML, incorrect date formats, and a wide range of other issues that prevent data from loading correctly in the new system. Because of the wide variety and complexity of problems, specific examples are used to illustrate how to break down problems into more manageable parts.

Kate Hill provides advice on handy tools staff without programming skills can use for migrating data in chapter 3. Library staff often attempt to use spreadsheet software for migrations, but it is incapable of handling large amounts of data and it often modifies information in undesirable ways. Kate offers practical alternatives for the nonprogrammer.

Many people think of MARC as obsolete, but because so much library and vendor technical and metadata infrastructure depends on it, it will continue to be a major factor for the foreseeable future. In chapter 4, Terry Reese discusses the variety of analysis, cleaning, reclamation, and data structuring tasks for which MarcEdit can be invaluable.

Kelley McGrath tackles the deceptively simple task of migrating bibliographic and item data in chapter 5. This area of library operations enjoys more robust standards support and commonality of practice than other areas, but differential record structures, handling of call numbers, access policies, material types, locations, service points, and other factors make it challenging to move this data to a new system with minimal service disruptions.

In chapter 6, Siôn Romaine offers insights on the notoriously difficult task of migrating acquisitions data, which is supported by fewer standards than any other area of library operations although directly tied to critical accounting and financial operations,

Seamless authentication is essential if patrons are to enjoy good service. Nathan Mealey walks us through a wide variety of issues that must be considered regarding authentication and migrating patron data in chapter 7. He also offers advice for those changing authentication as part of a migration, for example, switching from barcodes to Single Sign On.

Comprising eighty percent of materials budgets in many libraries, serials present a number of data and workflow challenges that must be overcome to ensure that access to some of the most valuable resources in the library continues unhindered. In chapter 8, Elan May Rinck presents many thorny issues that may occur when migrating serials data, from addressing nonstandard holdings to publication patterns.

As patrons demand more electronic resources, libraries have implemented systems designed to support the specialized data and workflows these materials require. In chapter 9, Todd Enoch describes how these complex systems that have only partial standards support can be migrated.

In chapter 10, Kyle Banerjee discusses approaches for migrating institutional repositories and digital collections. Systems vary dramatically in terms of how they are used, configured, and designed, so the focus is on commonly supported standards, methods, and what options are available for migrating critical information that is not supported by standards in the old or new systems.

In chapter 11, Al Cornish discusses the issues of migrating from individually maintained to shared systems. He walks through the benefits and drawbacks of approaches such as institutions maintaining separate records, merging records, or pursuing a master-record approach. He offers advice on options for handling local data when records are shared as well as addressing potential pitfalls.

Vendors are critical partners in migrations, but they won't understand a library's needs as well as local staff, plus they are immersed in their own workflows. In chapter 12, Kate Thornhill navigates readers through the process of deciding what work should be delegated to vendors when migrating digital libraries, how that work should be planned, what vendors can realistically accomplish, and and how to maintain relationships.

The final chapter of this book is dedicated to testing and putting the final system into full production.

In sum, this book is about more than migrating data. Rather, it is about how to extract, analyze, structure, and modify data to achieve the desired effect in a new system. It is about understanding the relationship between the system itself, the configuration, and the data. It is about understanding the migration process.

UNDERSTANDING THE MIGRATION PROCESS

Bonnie Parks, Collections Technology Librarian, University of Portland

M igrating library data from one system to another is a process that requires careful, detailed planning. Whether your library is migrating from one vendor's product to another, independently or as part of a consortia, a strong team and carefully thought-out data-migration plan are keys to success. This chapter offers advice on assembling your migration team and preparing your existing data. It assumes that your vendor of choice will provide your library with migration forms and support along the way.

ASSEMBLING THE TEAM

Your first step is to assemble your implementation team. Anyone who has worked on a project of significant magnitude (and yes, migration from one ILS to another counts as significant!) knows the first order of business is to identify a project lead. This person manages the details of the migration, navigates the team through uncharted territories and choppy waters, and at the same time keeps everything and everyone afloat.

IDENTIFY THE MIGRATION LEAD (Project Manager)

Your migration lead should possess a core set of leadership skills, namely the ability to organize your project, communicate to stakeholders, motivate the team, and delegate responsibilities. Experience with metadata or systems is helpful.

Organize

Your project manager is responsible for creating your migration roadmap. Chances are you already have a time line or a set of guidelines established by your library administration, your LMS (Library Management System) vendor, or even your consortium. Your migration lead must be organized and must also be able to work within the project framework, to set deadlines for your team, and to meet the deadlines set forth by all involved parties. The team depends on the lead to move the project along and ensure that each step in the process is clearly documented. Look at your plan as a living organism. It will change and shift as the project evolves and your outcomes become more clearly defined.

Communicate

Good communication is a critical factor in the success of your migration. Your lead must fit in with both the team members and rest of the library staff. She also needs to navigate the waters of communication among your library, IT department, and system vendors. Keep in mind that you may need to work with the vendors representing your soon-to-be legacy management system as well as representatives from the LMS you're migrating to.

Motivate

Your migration lead sets the tone and course of the project. Regardless of progress made, everyone will feel overwhelmed and maybe even a bit grumpy at some point. A sense of humor and a positive outlook goes a long way in boosting the team's morale. Your project manager should help the rest of the team look for the silver linings in the storm clouds and focus on the finished product. Celebrate small accomplishments as a team. A box of donuts can be a great attitude adjuster!

Delegate

Finally, your migration lead should be comfortable delegating responsibilities. Knowing how and when to delegate is an essential skill. Good delegation will save time, make the best use of your team's abilities, and can be a great motivator to boot. From the big-picture outlook to the minute details, projects of this magnitude will not be successful unless everyone is willing to pitch in and do her share.

ASSEMBLE THE REST OF THE TEAM

Identifying the rest of your migration team is equally as important. The size and complexity of your library determines which of these suggestions you can apply. If possible:

- Include a cataloger or metadata expert on your team. Remember, your project focus is migrating data, and both these staffers work with data all day. These staff understand the structure of bibliographic data and your current system configuration. Catalogers and metadata experts also recognize relationships among data, MARC records, and standards and generally have a good idea how these fit within the scope of the project.
- Identify a representative from each division in your library: acquisitions, cataloging, circulation, IT, and reference. (Your library may have a different organizational structure or use different terminology.) Representatives from both public and technical services are essential for providing a wide range of perspectives.
- Keep your director in the loop if she is not already a part of the implementation team. She may need to intercede with external stakeholders at some point when authoritative action and decision making are needed.
- Identify those members of your campus IT department and any other campus stakeholders with whom you'll be working. Challenges will arise, and there will be a need for technical support throughout the entire process. In many libraries, technical support lives outside the library and supports the entire campus community. Be sure to give your IT folks plenty of notice, because your project is just one of many competing projects that they may have on their plates.

DEVELOP YOUR PROJECT PLAN

Once the team is assembled and the external stakeholders have been notified, it's time to get to work. Twelve months, even six months, may seem like it's a long time away, but your migration day will arrive faster than you realize. There are several activities your team will want to consider as you're working through the planning process with your vendor.

- Establish regular meeting times and include agendas for each meeting. How often and for how long the team meets is up to your migration team.

Different-sized libraries have different needs. What's important is that your team has a dedicated time to sit down together and work. For example, my team's meetings are scheduled once a week for an hour dedicated for the entire team to meet as a group. Depending on the phase of the project, some of us scheduled additional small-group meetings to work on specific details. We also believed that it was important to keep the rest of the library in the loop, so we established once-a-month "all staff" meetings to provide progress updates and answer questions. This worked well for a library staff of eighteen employees, but you may find a different meeting schedule works better for you.

- Begin reading and digesting your new LMS documentation. Not everything will make sense at first, but once you start getting your feet wet in the new system, much of it will fall into place. Keep in mind that your new system functions differently and may use different terminology with which you're unfamiliar.

- Join the product's e-mail list. You can learn a lot about your new system just by reading the questions and answers of others. Don't be afraid to ask questions. Everyone on the list was a newbie at one point. You'll find a supportive community that is willing to help you. Keep an eye out for migration-related challenges that other users discuss. These may give you a good indication of the types of cleanup projects you may need to undertake.

- Take advantage of the training opportunities that are offered by your vendor. Al Cornish discusses more on training opportunities in chapter 11.

- If your vendor offers you a sandbox environment, utilize it. This is the best way to understand how your new system functions. Test and retest your data.

CLEAN YOUR DATA

You've assembled your team, you've set up your meetings and you've gotten your hands dirty with your new system. Now it's time to tidy up your data in preparation for the big move. Consider this an investment in your future. Your preemptive data cleanup efforts will be rewarded in the long run. Investing time in a thorough examination of the library's existing data will save everyone a great deal of work post-migration. These lists are meant to serve as guidelines and are by no means exhaustive. Each of these suggestions is optional, and the extent of their usefulness will vary depending on the type of library and system. Kelley McGrath and Siôn Romaine offer more specific instructions on how to accomplish many of these objectives in their chapters 5 and 6, respectively.

Bibliographic Data

- Weed your collection. If your library has been planning a weeding project, there is no better time. The less data in your system pre-migration, the less you will need to clean up post-migration.
- Clean up and get rid of any old data that you no longer use. Discuss with your team what data you realistically need to keep and maintain. Be ruthless. The less you have to migrate, the less time you'll spend cleaning up.
- Consolidate copy numbers to avoid confusion in the new system. Weeding that involves multiple copies does not always result in copy consolidation. For example, if your library holds four copies of a title and copies two and three were withdrawn, you're left with copies one and four. In your legacy system, it may be perfectly clear that you hold only two copies even though they are labeled copy one and copy four. This may not be as clear in your new system. Do what you can to avoid confusion.
- Identify duplicate bibliographic records. Consolidate the items and holdings and delete the superfluous records.
- Make sure all MARC fields are valid. If you use locally created fields, you may need to work with your LMS vendor to determine how—or whether—they will migrate. Some vendors allow for the use of X9X fields and 9XX fields. If you're migrating to a shared system, discuss your options with your vendor before you migrate your data.
- If you use OCLC, SkyRiver, or another bibliographic utility, make sure all your bibliographic records have system numbers and verify with your vendor whether they will migrate in their current position or will need to be remapped to another field. For example, in III's Millennium default configuration, OCLC numbers are stored in the 001 field and the OCoLC prefix is stored in the 003 field. If the library is migrating to Ex Libris's Alma product, the OCLC numbers will need to be remapped to the system control number field 035 $a with an (OCoLC) prefix.
- Make sure all bibliographic records have a title (245 $a) field. This may seem like a no-brainer, but you may be surprised with what you find if you look for it! On the flip side, make sure that each bibliographic record contains only one 245 field.
- Know where your call numbers are stored. Are they stored in your bibliographic records, item records, or some combination thereof? Are they in the correct MARC fields? Your vendor will have specific mapping protocols that depend on where and how your call numbers are stored.
- Examine your internal system codes. This is a good time to standardize, consolidate, and remove any codes that your library no longer uses. Internal codes may include location codes, status codes, and others.

- Depending on your current system, you may need to reformat any non-MARC records into MARC or MARCXML to import them into your new system. "On-the-fly" bibliographic records created at the point of circulation are often culprits. See chapter 4, where Terry Reese describes how to use MarcEdit to create and modify existing records.
- Do you currently use a single-record approach or create separate bibliographic records multiple formats of the same resource? Some LMSs require a separate record for each format. If this applies to your library, make sure you check with your vendor to determine whether you will need to change your existing records and modify your cataloging practices.
- For more information regarding problems specific to bibliographic records, see chapter 5.

Acquisitions Data

Acquisitions data and corresponding workflows are specific to each library. Your migration team should work with your acquisitions specialist to determine what data need to be retained and migrated. If your library is not under legal obligation to retain acquisitions data, purge whatever is no longer needed. Many libraries find it is easiest to determine cut-off dates for each data type.

Evaluate these independently:

- brief or suppressed bibliographic records created as part of the acquisitions workflow
- old invoices
- old and closed order records
- inactive subscriptions and standing orders
- vendor records
- check-in records
- purchase orders
- payment files

You may also want to evaluate your existing fund and ledger codes. Consolidate or delete the codes you no longer use. Chapter 6 discusses acquisitions issues in greater detail.

Holdings and Electronic Resources Data

- If your current ILS has the means, check for dead links. If the resources are no longer available, delete or suppress the bibliographic records within the parameters defined by your institution.

- Make sure all the library's physical items are associated with a location.
- Clean up and standardize your enumeration and chronology. Some systems require that holdings information be in MARC format. If your data is not in MARC, allow your staff plenty of time to undertake the conversion process.
- Make sure all locations and their corresponding codes are current. Any locations and codes in your system that are no longer used should be deleted.
- Consider a reclamation project to synchronize your holdings with your bibliographic utility. This can be especially useful in the post-migration environment to troubleshoot whether certain records failed to transfer properly.
- For more about holdings and ERM data, see chapters 5 and 9.

Item Data

- Make sure all physical items have barcodes and all bibliographic records have inventory attached.
- Review all your existing item types and codes. Consolidate and/or delete where appropriate.
- Examine your reserves. Clean up and remove any resources that are no longer on reserve or no longer used. If you do not want to remove all materials that are not currently on reserve, consider removing those resources placed on reserve by faculty who are no longer at the institution.
- Identify lost or damaged materials and either remove them from the system or tag them to prevent confusion after migration. Work with access services to create a plan for these resources.
- As you approach your migration date, make sure you have an accurate list of all your current loans. Once the library sends off the database, there will be a short period of system downtime when circulation transactions may need to be handled manually. Knowing which resources are still checked out and which resources have been returned during the system freeze will be important when you cut over to the new LMS.
- For more about item data, see chapter 5.

Patron and User Data

- Purge any expired patron records that have no outstanding fines or fees. This may significantly reduce the number of records to migrate.
- Evaluate any existing records that have fines or fees attached and clean them up where appropriate. For example, if your library has records with fines that are older than a certain date or less than a certain cost, consider purging them. Make sure you understand how existing fines will migrate to the new system.

- Examine your current patron groups. Determine which groups are still in use and which are obsolete. Delete any groups no longer used.
- Clean up any old loan rules that are no longer in use. If your library has been thinking about consolidating or making changes, now is a good time to undertake that project.
- Chapter 7 discusses the issues associated with migrating patron data.

Integrating with Other Systems

Providing a seamless user experience and efficient staff processes require LMSs to interoperate with other systems. Authenticating users, synchronizing fines and fees, and harvesting metadata all require communication with outside systems. Whether working in the back end of the LMS or searching the discovery layer, users expect a seamless experience; therefore, syntactic and semantic system interoperability are crucial. This is where a good relationship with your IT department and other campus departments comes into play. Keep in mind that for some of these services, your IT department and your vendor will be completing the bulk of the setup and configuration. Be prepared to play the role of the middleman and help facilitate communication where possible, especially if your IT department lives outside of the library.

External systems and data exchange may include but are not limited to:

- OCLC Connexion/SkyRiver bibliographic utility setup
- formatted file transfer
- programming to work with API
- proxy implementation
- authentication
- SFTP server setup
- networked printers

Make sure you provide your campus partners with enough lead time to work on the project and meet your deadline. Assign a team member to be a liaison who will help answer questions and provide assistance when it comes time to test the functionality.

A FEW WORDS TO THE WISE

- No matter how much and how well your team plans and prepares, not everything will migrate cleanly. Take advantage of the e-mail discussion list associated with your LMS to prepare yourself, your team, and your staff for potential cleanup projects.

- You will lose some data. If at all possible, maintain your legacy system for a period of time after you complete your migration.
- Not all the data from your previous system will map to your new system. If there is data from your legacy system that you must have in your new system, work with your vendor to determine whether there is a way to import the data. My library uses circulation history as a factor in collection building and retention decisions. We were disappointed to learn that a direct one-to-one mapping of circulation data from our old system to our new did not exist. We were, however, able to work with our vendor to come up with a solution that allowed us to import the circulation data into note fields in the item records. It may not be ideal, but it's something we can (and do) use.
- Your workflows will change. This is a great opportunity for your department to evaluate the hows and whys of existing workflows. "But we've always done it this way" no longer applies.
- If your library is moving from one vendor's system to another, system terminology may change.

Finally

- Document every step along the way. I cannot emphasize enough the importance of documentation!

CONCLUSION

Moving library data successfully from one online system to another is no small task. Just as technology and systems are far more advanced than at the advent of the first ILSs more than thirty years ago, the current LMSs are far more complex than their physical inventory control system predecessors. Gone are the days of transcribing descriptions and access points from printed catalog cards. Our systems have evolved far beyond the role of online repository, and they will continue to evolve to meet the increasingly sophisticated information needs of our consumers. Our expectations must evolve in tandem, and we must not be afraid of delving into the unknown as we move to new and better systems. Tapping into the skills of each member of the migration team is essential to the overall success of the project and preparing your library to take on the unfamiliar. From planning to extracting to implementing, a successful outcome rests on a strong team, good communication, and thorough preparation.

FORMATS AND DATA CLEANING

David Forero, Technology Director, Library at OHSU

T
ransferring data is more art than science, but understanding a few common issues will lead to more successful data transfers. This chapter discusses what you need to know before migrating data—particularly about available formats and how data is structured. After reading this chapter, you will understand how to use common tools to break complex problems into simpler components so you can perform sophisticated transformations such as reversing the order of data in a field.

UNDERSTANDING STANDARDS

The phrase "turtles all the way down" is often used to jokingly refer to the concept of infinite regression. The story usually goes something like this: some cultures believe that the world is on the back of a turtle. When a believer in this kind of system is asked what the turtle is standing on, the answer is "another turtle." The somewhat trite response is that "there are turtles all the way down."

Why am I talking about turtles? Defining a format almost always requires defining it in terms of other formats. For example, let us use one of the more complicated kinds of data: a video file. We can look at the file and think "This file has a specific format." It could be an MP4, Ogg Theora Vorbis, WebM, or one of many other possibly incomprehensible format names.

> **Defining what a format is almost always requires defining it in terms of other formats.**

Once we identify a format, we're done, right? Well, not really. Video formats are comprised of other formats. Taking MP4 as an example, this format turns out to be a container format for other formats to handle video, audio, and subtitles. Each of these sub-formats comes with its own panoply of specific format choices. Consider the simple example of subtitles. It's easier to understand than some of the other components because it is human readable. But this is where you can really start to see how far down the turtles go. The subtitle file might be in some published standard like Timed Text Markup Language, but there are more underlying formats. The most obvious is the human language. The content is in English, Spanish, Klingon, or some other written language. Then there is the text encoding of the file, for example UTF-8 or UTF-16.

If you are unfamiliar with these encodings you may recognize an earlier text encoding standard, ASCII (American Standard Code for Information Interchange). These text encodings map a set of characters that include the Latin alphabet to specific codes the computer can understand. For example, the letter "A" is 65 in ASCII or UTF-8, but the character "a" is 97 in both. As a side note, UTF-8 is an intentional expansion of ASCII in that its first 256 characters match ASCII.

However, this similarity causes problems because some systems store and display characters in a different format than that they use to export the data. Verifying your data should be done early and often. Do not assume data that was encoded as UTF-8 on import will export as UTF-8, because many systems modify content. You might end up getting ASCII and some characters may not be converted properly (see table 2.1).

> **Do not assume that data encoded as UTF-8 on import will export as UTF-8, because many systems modify content.**

TABLE 2.1

Example of UTF-8 text rendered as UTF-8 and ASCII

UTF-8 text treated as UTF-8	ᚹᛋᚻ·ᛒᛞᛞ·ᚹᚱᚠᚹᚾᚱ·ᚹᛁᚱᚠ·ᚷᛗᚻᚹᚻᛣᚾᚻ
UTF-8 text treated as ASCII	·öt·õá·öª·õ´·õí·õ¶·õ¶·õ´·öt·öt·õ©·öt·ö¢·öt·õ´·öt·ö¢·öt·õÅ·öt·ö™·õ´·ö ∑·õñ·öª·öπ·õ¶·õö·öº·ö¢·õó

This discussion of esoteric pyramids of formats and standards may seem mind-numbing. But the other nice thing about standards is you don't have to remember all the relationships and details—you can always look up a standard. And that is the point of remembering "turtles all the way down"—you just need to remember to look up the standards you are working with (see figure 2.1).

The first step in transferring data is identifying the turtles, that is, identifying the standards that were used to create the data. By extension, it will be necessary to examine the standards of where the data is going, and quite likely the standards and/or the transformations required to move between them. Although this can be complicated and tedious, it is not difficult. Rather, it mostly involves asking questions and looking up the answers in the standards.

FIGURE 2.1

The turtle model of standards

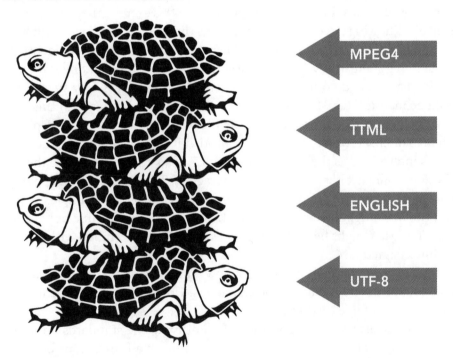

MAPPING THE TRANSFER

Data migration, conversion, and crosswalk are only some of the many ways we talk about taking data from one kind of organization to another. Again, the details are always different, but the process of planning can often be similar. Once all the standards have been identified, it is time to look at how the data map.

Let's leave the complicated world of video and talk about something with which everyone has experience, namely text. Because you are reading this book, you must already be familiar with many concepts around text. In this example, we'll download a text file from a Windows computer and put it on a Linux web server. Here is what we know about the text file:

> Language = English
> Encoding = UTF-8
> Origin = Windows

With a little research into UTF-8, we learn there is something interesting about how this standard is used. Different platforms use different characters to represent the end of a line of text. Unix uses LF (Line Feed) and Windows uses CRLF (Carriage Return and Line Feed). This can mean that once a file has been moved to the new location, it might be interpreted differently. Although technically Linux is not UNIX, for the purposes of this exercise they are indistinguishable. Knowing the difference about how the files are handled on different platforms helps you to look out for problems. Also, because you have identified the incoming standards, you can make sure there are corresponding standards identified at the end point of this transfer. In this case, it is very simple and would be identical (i.e., English and UTF-8). Why then bother with this kind of mapping? It is quite possible that the file would transfer and be displayed without a hitch. However, it is also possible that it could be rendered where the CR was interpreted as the equivalent of an LF. If so, then everywhere there is a CRLF it would act like two new line characters. This might not be apparent until the file is moved from the Linux system to a Mac, for example. At this point the Mac might be expecting only LF from a Linux machine but getting CRLF. The Mac might be replacing all LFs with CRs and end up with double new line characters

Table 2.2 gives an approximation of how different systems and applications would handle different end-of-line characters. However, each application can render the end of line very differently.

This emphasizes the importance of identifying the standards and then documenting them so that during the transfer (or in a future transfer) there are clearly defined steps that explain what happened to the file. In the above case, the people doing the second transfer could see there was no transformation of the Windows text files, so if there is a mixture of Linux and Windows files being transferred to the Mac they can identify the different files that need special transformation, either by documentation, or by developing a programmatic test for each file.

TABLE 2.2

An approximation of how different systems and applications would handle different end-of-line characters*

	ON MAC OS	ON DOS	ON LINUX
Carriage Return	First line Second line	Carriage Returned by CR	This is separated by CR^MCarriage Return
Carriage Return LineFeed	First line Second line	First line Second line	First line Second line
LineFeed	First line Second line	First line Second line	First line Second line

*Each application can render the end of line very differently.

DELIMITERS

I have been nonchalantly referring to files, assuming that we all understand what was meant. I imagine you have an image of a little tiny piece of paper with the corner neatly folded. This is the icon we are all most familiar with. But what is in the file? How are groups of logically similar information in a file distinguished in other groups of information? The answers to these questions are at the heart of how we manage the data.

Let's start by defining "file." That little icon represents a set of bits stored on computer, which have a beginning and an end. These bits need not be stored sequentially nor even on the same device. It is merely the list of what all those bits are that make a file a file. The values of those bits are what constitute the content of the file (and quite likely other properties or metadata of the file). Sometimes this sequence of bits is referred to as a bitstream. This term is useful in reminding us that a file is simply sequential bits. Often a particular file format will have component parts like a header (a beginning set of data that defines different aspects of the file) or an end-of-file component. This is especially useful when a file is being copied from one place to another. When a file is being processed in this way, being able to tell when the file begins and ends enables computer systems to deal with the file and keep it separated from other files. These aspects of files that tell us when sequences of data begin and end are one type of delimiter. "Delimiter" sounds very technical, but it is something we are all familiar with. The sentences you are reading are delimited with spaces and periods. We also commonly use commas and quotation marks to delimit specific ideas in a sentence. Delimiters in files act in much the same way, by separating certain ideas so they can be treated or used differently from other ideas.

When moving or transmitting files, things can go wrong. Often, when there are problems with a transfer, the cause may be that delimiters (like end-of-file components) are missing or malformed. Identifying this problem usually involves identifying content from two separate files that has commingled, and then tracing back the steps of transformation to locate where the problematic transformation occurred.

Record and Field Delimiters

Other kinds of delimiters that get far more attention are those within a file. There are enumerable kinds of delimiters. Computers often need delimiters to determine the beginning and end of logical pieces of data within a file. The comma is a very common delimiter. In the file format CSV (Comma Separated Values), you have a text file (encoded in something like ASCII or UTF-8) where discrete pieces of information are separated by the comma character. For example:

> Text for the first field,More text for the second field,Yet more test for
> a third field

The construction of CSV files uses commas to define fields (discrete units of meaning) and new lines to define records (groupings of fields). This is often referred to as a tabular file because it easily can be used as a table. The obvious problem is if the comma is part of the content. One example is when names are reordered. In most of Western culture, the name order is personal name first and then family name. That is why in these cultures (except Iceland), using the family name for sorting is standard. For that reason, listing the family name followed by a comma and then the rest of the name is common practice. This means that as a conceptual unit, the name contains a meaningful delimiter in the middle. When the file uses a comma as a delimiter, it is difficult for a computer to systematically distinguish between the commas that denote a reordering of the name and the commas that separate other pieces of information in the file.

Another example where commas are commonly used as part of the data is when writing a long numeral. Depending on where you live in the world, you might use commas to help you interpret written numbers. For example, in most of the English-speaking world, you might write a number like this:

> 12,345.67

which denotes twelve thousand three hundred forty-five and sixty-seven hundredths. However, if this were inside a CSV file it would be interpreted by the computer as two separate values of twelve and then as three hundred forty-five and sixty-seven hundredths. I can use another character, the double quote, to denote that the comma is content rather than a delimiter, which is being "escaped out" so that it is content:

12","345.67 **or** "12,345.67"

This brings us to the question of how a double quote is represented as content. The answer is, of course, double quotes. If I wanted to represent a single set of double quotes I would surround that double quote with double quotes, creating a string of three double quotes. It sounds confusing, and it can be. Understanding the delimiters in a file can help you when things go wrong. If fields are merged or separated in unexpected ways during a process, the first place to look is delimiters. Most formats (particularly text formats) have some sort of delimiter. And they all face similar problems with how to represent themselves as content.

> If fields are merged or separated in unexpected ways during a process, the first place to look is delimiters.

Markup Delimiters

Another kind of file with delimiters that are not necessarily tabular are object markup languages. HTML (Hyper Text Markup Language) is one of the more commonly recognizable formats. It is the format underlying the World Wide Web. In this format, files are also composed of text encoded characters (e.g., UTF-8) that are delimited with special characters. HTML can be considerably more complicated than CSV. Here is an example of a single line that ends in a new line:

```
<p>This is a sample</p>
```

The greater and lesser symbols are the delimiters and the kind of delimiter that is inside the delimiters. There are a great number of formats that use this structure. Again, the problem of representing the delimiter occurs. In this case, *less than* and *greater than* are represented as, respectively:

```
&lt;
&gt;
```

And once again this leads to the problem of how to represent the character that is used to denote that explicitness of the other characters. In this case the ampersand character (&) is represented as:

```
&amp;
```

This foray into delimiters illustrates not only the diversity of ways they appear in file formats, but also how in the end the same kinds of problems and patterns of solutions are used.

Before ending our discussion of the basics of formats, I would be remiss if I did not discuss XML (eXtensible Markup Language). Where HTML is a specific language for formatting data, XML is focused on organizing the information. This can take the form of labeling, placing data in a hierarchy, or describing the data with other data (i.e., metadata). XML often looks similar to HTML in that it places text delimiters around the content data (usually in this form <markup>data</markup>). A huge difference is that HTML has a very standard dictionary of terms and syntax that is widely used. XML is a much looser and simpler standard. There is no long dictionary of terms or syntax. The point of XML is that it is extensible. Users of the language can make up their own terms and syntax. But to do this they must use or create their own lists of terms and syntax. This is done using the mother language of both XML and HTML: SGML (Standard Generalized Markup Language). Because of this flexibility, XML is very popular. But at the same time, when people say the data is in XML, all they mean is that the data is text data in some sort of hierarchical markup structure. The definition of how that data is structured and the meaning of the markup delimiters and metadata are defined somewhere else, usually but not necessarily in a file called a schema. For example, I can use Dublin Core inside of XML. The file might look like this:

```
<?xml version="1.0" encoding="UTF-8"?>
<metadata
    xmlns:xsi="http://www.w3.0rg/2001/XMLSchema-instance"
    xmlns:dc="http://purl.org/dc/elements/1.1/">
    <dc:title>Winnie-the-Pooh</dc:title>
    <dc:creator>A.A. Milne</dc:creator>
    <dc:subject>Children's Fiction</dc:subject>
    <dc:date>1926</dc:date>
</metadata>
```

> **The biggest difference between XML and HTML is that in XML all terms must be defined, and in HTML many core terms are defined by the standard.**

Here the XML has tags around the data, such as dc:title. The definition of dc:title and how it should be used is defined by xmlns (XMLS namespace) values which point to the schemas used. Going back to our stack-of-turtles analogy, we have Dublin Core sitting on top of XML sitting on top of UTF-8. There is no reason more layers could not be embedded into this scenario. The critical point is that understanding the data and all the format dependencies will help you untangle problems when they occur. Discovering the assumptions and limits of the formats involved can be critical for easy migration.

> When people say that the data is in XML, all they mean is that the data is text data in some sort of hierarchical markup structure.

DATA CLEANING

Now that I have discussed how data are formatted and organized, let us look at the actual data to make sure our assumptions are true, and then correct the formats if they are not true. I am going to take a simple data set and explain how inconsistencies can systematically be addressed.

Often the terms "dirty data" or "clean data" are used to describe data in different stages of transformation. These are used to indicate if the content and delimiters of a file comply with whatever standards are being used. The following example shows some data in CSV format with an author's name, birth year, and year of death all separated by commas and new lines:

A. A. Milne,18 January 1882,31 January 1956
Agatha Christie,15 September 1890,12 January 1976
"Angelou, Maya", "April 4, 1928", "May 28, 2014"
Arthur Golden, 6 December 1956,

There are several different quote characters. So be careful—they may look similar but computers will treat them very differently:

NAME	REPRESENTATION	UNICODE VALUE
Quotation marks	"	U+0022
Apostrophe	'	U+0027
Grave accent	`	U+0060
Acute accent	´	U+00B4
Left single quotation mark	'	U+2018
Right single quotation mark	'	U+2019
Left double quotation mark	"	U+201C
Right double quotation mark	"	U+201D

This looks fine. There is nothing technically wrong with this file and it should be readable by any program capable of handling CSV. However, if I were transferring this data there are issues that might make this a dirty file. One record has five commas and the other records have two. This is not because there are extra fields in that record. It is obvious that the extra commas are trying to contain data within a field that contains commas used as content, not as delimiters. Often commas are used to denote a change of order in data. However, a computer program may not understand what is going on. This can cause difficulties, depending on what transformations are going to take place on this file. In a small file or in some applications there might not be any errors, but if the file consists of thousands of records, or if automated processes are manipulating the file, there could be errors. It is not necessary to have all the names in the same order; however, as you can see, the alphabetic sorting on this file may not be the most helpful order. The easiest way to fix this in a four-record sample is by manually correcting the difference, even if it would make all the records last name first. However, if this were a four-million record file, manual correction would not be practical. This is the kind of decision that needs to be made and documented to ensure that data is usable. Additionally, the date fields with ordering difference may or may not cause problems in different systems. Checking for consistency can help detect potential problems because often large and repetitive tasks are automated. Automation is fantastic as long as the instructions are exactly what are required in particular circumstances. The example above illustrates that, if a program is not told how to handle the delimited commas and is told to separate the first set of data delimited by a comma, or if there are missing fields, the program might crash the process or cause another error unless we also tell it to skip the missing field or how to handle delimited characters. Additionally, making systematic corrections when the data is not formatted consistently (or normalized) can be tricky.

SOLVING PROBLEMS AT A HIGH LEVEL

I've discussed a few common aspects of files that relate to the structure of content. I believe that an understanding of the underlying structure is critical to deal with the messiness that occurs in the real world. Inevitably, when transferring or transforming data, things will go wrong. Understanding what the structures are (or should be) will help avoid and even solve problems when moving data. I also believe that understanding how to fix the problems by hand can lead to the ability to take advantage of more powerful tools.

Correcting problems by hand can lead to the skills required to employ more powerful tools.

In this section, I will walk through ways to deal with a few problems using a spreadsheet application. I will use Google Sheets, but if your favorite tool is Microsoft Excel, the same techniques will work. There may be slight differences in the interfaces and formulas; however, they should be largely the same. More importantly, this section is not intended to be a tutorial in spreadsheet formulas. The formulas I will use may look complex and even intimidating, but the point is not for you to become experts and write these formulas. Instead, the purpose is for you to understand the techniques that are useful and warn you about common pitfalls.

Importing to a Spreadsheet

If we put those authors' data in a text file called "dirty.csv," the first thing we will do is examine our file by importing it into our spreadsheet. It is often possible to define how the import process is conducted. I will use the settings shown in figure 2.2 for this example.

FIGURE 2.2

Google Sheets import dialog

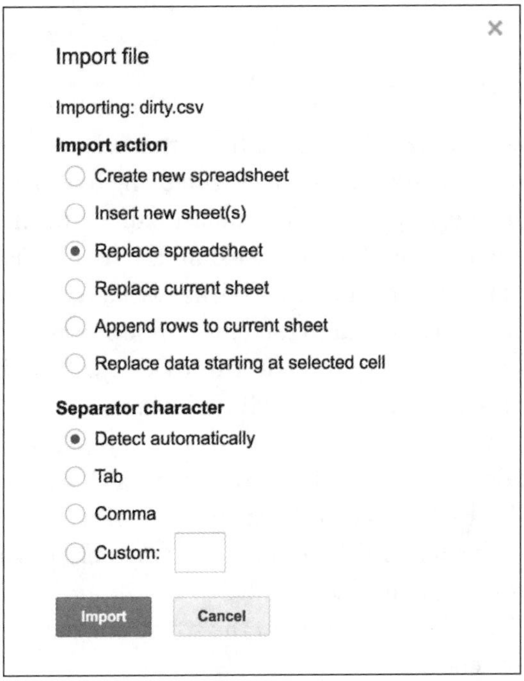

In this case, as shown in figure 2.2, we get a result with an obvious error.

FIGURE 2.3

Imported "dirty" data

fx	A. A. Milne		
	A	B	C
1	A. A. Milne	1/18/1882	1/31/1956
2	Agatha Christie	9/15/1890	1/12/1976
3	Angelou, Maya	4/4/1928	5/28/2014
4	Arthur Golden	12/6/1956	

As shown in figure 2.3, we have four records and three fields. This is the result I would expect. Note that sometimes different programs handle escaping characters differently. I have encountered many programs which, after parsing a file for import, came up with startling results. There are a couple of observations we can make now. The first is that three of the authors have first name first and one has last name first. The second observation is that the dates are formatted completely differently than they were in the file.

Reordering Names

Let's tackle the first "problem." It is quite likely that we would need to sort those names at some point. I could easily imagine needing to separate out the names entirely into first name, middle initial, and last name. But the process of doing either is fairly similar. I would prefer to list all the names last name first so as to easily sort the names. I am going to do this with a function (or formula). I'll start by getting the last name. But first let me define a term I will use frequently. A "string" is a sequence of characters. In this case, it will be the content of any cell. To get the last name I will use four functions:

LEN—Finds the number of characters in a string.
SUBSTITUTE—Replaces a character in a string.
RIGHT—Takes a defined number of characters from a string starting from the end of the string.
SEARCH—Finds the position in the string of a particular character sequence.

To do this I am going to use a little trick. Basically, we have two kinds of delimiters, one for within fields and one for between fields. They are currently the same character. I am going to substitute a character into the string temporarily, so that one delimiter is for between fields and another, different delimiter is for within fields. Having two different delimiters will make it easier to make systematic changes to the file. In this case I am using ß for the within-field delimiter and leave the comma as the between-field delimiter. This symbol is the German double S symbol. It is not used much anymore, is easy for me to type, and does not turn up in my work very often. You could use any character that does not appear in your file. So, if you are working with old German files, this would not be a good choice. In this case, we can easily determine that it does not cause a problem (figure 2.4).

```
=RIGHT(A1,LEN(A1)-SEARCH("ß",SUBSTITUTE(A1," ","ß",LEN(A1)-LEN(SUBSTITUTE(A1," ","")))))
```

FIGURE 2.4

Extracting last names

f_x	=RIGHT(A1,LEN(A1)-SEARCH("ß",SUBSTITUTE(A1," ","ß",LEN(A		
	A	B	C	D
1	A. A. Milne	1/18/1882	1/31/1956	Milne
2	Agatha Christie	9/15/1890	1/12/1976	Christie
3	Angelou, Maya	4/4/1928	5/28/2014	Maya
4	Arthur Golden	12/6/1956		Golden

Basically, we replace the spaces in the string with the ß as a placeholder. What is important is not the exact formula in this example, but being able to use another character to temporarily replace and then undo in a string. This sort of technique is very powerful. The key is not to make assumptions. For this formula to work, the following must be true:

- There are spaces in the string.
- There are no existing ß in the string.

We can improve the robustness of our formula by testing for those conditions by using three more functions (figure 2.4):

> AND—Combines two logical tests.
> IF—Tests to see if a condition is true and then resolves differently
>   dependent on that test.
> ISNUMBER—Tests to see if a value is a number.

```
=IF(AND(ISNUMBER(SEARCH(" ",A1)),ISNUMBER(SEARCH(CHAR(44),A1))),
"Leave alone," "Put last word first")
```

FIGURE 2.5

Testing need for reordering

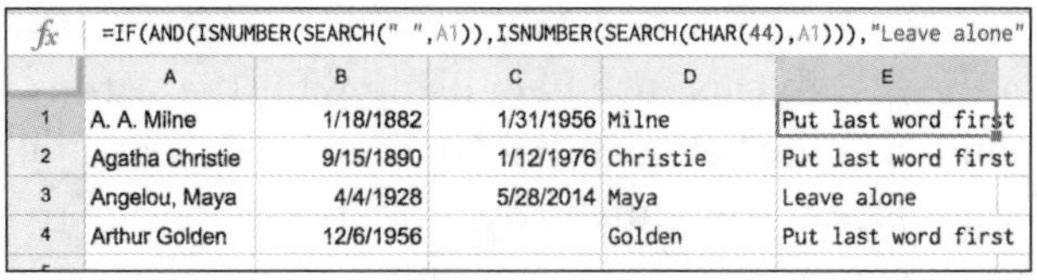

This formula tests the results for a SEARCH for those two characters in those cells and returns the status (figure 2.5). We can assume that any cell with spaces and commas needs to have the last word put in the front and all other cells should be left as is.

Using these techniques, I can make one massive formula to test the cell and manipulate the cell without worrying about my assumptions (figure 2.6).

```
=IF(AND(ISNUMBER(SEARCH("
",A1)),ISNUMBER(SEARCH(CHAR(44),A1))),A1,RIGHT(A1,LEN(A1)-
SEARCH("ß",SUBSTITUTE(A1," ","ß",LEN(A1)-LEN(SUBSTITUTE(A1,"
","")))))&CHAR(44)&" "&LEFT(A1,SEARCH("ß",SUBSTITUTE(A1,"
","ß",LEN(A1)-LEN(SUBSTITUTE(A1," ","")))-1))
```

FIGURE 2.6

Combining last name extraction with reordering need test

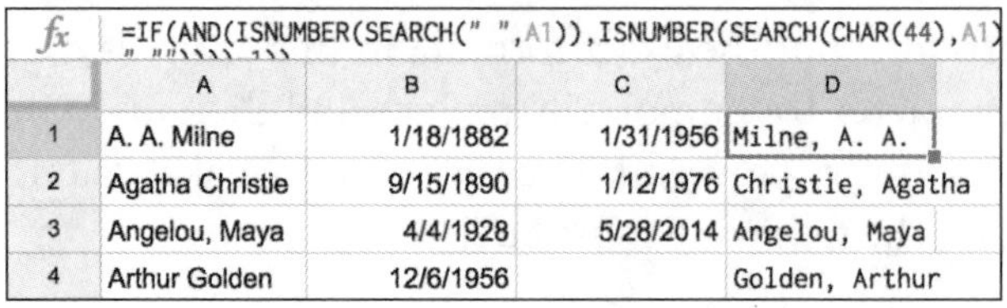

> Another assumption we might be making here concerns the type of white space between characters.

NAME	UNICODE VALUE
space	U+0020
no-break space	U+00A0
ogham space mark	U+1680
en quad	U+2000
em quad	U+2001
en space	U+2002

NAME	UNICODE VALUE
em space	U+2003
three-per-em space	U+2004
four-per-em space	U+2005
si10-per-em space	U+2006
figure space	U+2007
punctuation space	U+2008
thin space	U+2009
hair space	U+200A
zero width space	U+200B
narrow no-break space	U+202F
medium mathematical space	U+205F
ideographic space	U+3000

Cleaning up Dates

The names have all been successfully transformed and we know unexpected data will not freak out the formula. There is a critical point to note here. The cells with the formula display exactly what we want, however, that is not quite the same as the cells containing text that we want. So, exporting the data will likely "flatten" that data so that it is just the text and not the formula. Likewise, copying the whole column and doing a Paste Special as only values will also flatten the values. This is important because if the spreadsheet is imported elsewhere, it is possible that the formula will become the unexpected data in another system.

Let's now look at the date fields. Computers think of time a bit differently than the average person. We often think of them as a Venn diagram of a more and more specific labeling. For example, 1882 is the year and within that label is a month of January, and within that label is the 18th day. Computers think of time as a sequence of numbers starting from a specific point in time. These systems vary; for example, time zero might be the first day of January in the year 1900. Every day since then would be an additional 1, so the 30th of January 1900 is the value 30 and the first of January 1901 is 365. This makes it very easy for a computer to start doing math with dates. However, because we do not think of dates as sequential numbers, this can trip us up. When we export or transmit records, special attention should be paid to dates because they are the most likely to fall prey to being transformed in unexpected ways. This distinction between numbers and text happens with non-date fields as well, but dates provide a vivid example of the problems this can cause. In this case, the spreadsheet recognized both forms of the dates as valid and automatically converted them to a correct serialized number representing the date. We can use the format function to change the way the spreadsheet represents those values. The danger here is that spreadsheets have changed the representation of those initial field values. If assumptions are made about those values during a transformation, there may be some unexpected results. For example, we can combine two cells easily this way (figure 2.7):

    =A1&A2

FIGURE 2.7

Simple example of combining text cells

	A	B	C	D	E
fx	=A1&A2				
1	A. A. Milne	1/18/1882	1/31/1956	Milne, A. A.	A. A. MilneAgatha Christie
2	Agatha Christie	9/15/1890	1/12/1976	Christie, Agatha	
3	Angelou, Maya	4/4/1928	5/28/2014	Angelou, Maya	
4	Arthur Golden	12/6/1956		Golden, Arthur	
5					

However, if we combine the first two cells of the first record in the same way (figure 2.8):

    =A1&B1

FIGURE 2.8

Bad example of combining text and date cells

	A	B	C	D	E
fx	=A1&B1				
1	A. A. Milne	1/18/1882	1/31/1956	Milne, A. A.	A. A. Milne-6555
2	Agatha Christie	9/15/1890	1/12/1976	Christie, Agatha	
3	Angelou, Maya	4/4/1928	5/28/2014	Angelou, Maya	
4	Arthur Golden	12/6/1956		Golden, Arthur	

The right way to handle this would be something like (figure 2.9):

FIGURE 2.9

Combining text and date without losing human-readable date

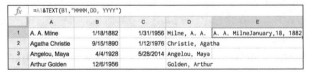

	A	B	C	D	E
fx	=A1&TEXT(B1,"MMMM,DD, YYYY")				
1	A. A. Milne	1/18/1882	1/31/1956	Milne, A. A.	A. A. MilneJanuary,18, 1882
2	Agatha Christie	9/15/1890	1/12/1976	Christie, Agatha	
3	Angelou, Maya	4/4/1928	5/28/2014	Angelou, Maya	
4	Arthur Golden	12/6/1956		Golden, Arthur	

    =A1&TEXT(B1,"MMMM,DD, YYYY")

Evaluating Spreadsheet Cleanup

The spreadsheets give us a visible way to track the data manipulations. With a little work, we can create some robust formulas to check, clean, and transform our data. Here is where I would insert a record scratching sound were this in audio. There are some very serious limitations with this kind of tool. First, there are general limits in spreadsheets. At the time of this writing, Excel can handle 1,000,000 rows and more than 16,000 columns, whereas Google sheets can only do 400,000 rows and 256 columns. That is fine for small data sets. But we frequently may have to deal with data sets larger than this. Also, we have seen there are problems these tools introduce by being "too smart." They can auto-format dates as well as URIs. Then there is the issue of automation. Though some spreadsheets offer automation scripts, they are very slow and require a great deal of processing power and memory. That said, spreadsheets are still great tools for some data sets. They are also great for breaking down and testing out a specific kind of transformation. But there are other ways of dealing with data that can build on the ideas and skills we have talked about already.

> When we export or transmit records, special attention should be paid to dates because they are the most likely to fall prey to being transformed in unexpected ways.

SOLVING PROBLEMS AT A LOW LEVEL

Now that you have had some experience with manipulating data and coping with common problems, let's look at how these kinds of techniques can be automated. The key to automation is to remove the human factor by making the computer do what we want by giving it explicit and precise instructions. The best way to do this is by using language. In the previous section, we used a graphical user interface (GUI) with a combination of keyboard entry and mouse clicks to convey to the computer what actions we wanted completed. Some tasks like splitting text by delimiters were accomplished exclusively using the GUI. However, more complicated tasks relied on formulas and functions, basically text. Even the formulas ended up becoming so long that understanding them becomes a daunting task. Automating turns out to be a slow and difficult to replicate process. For example, consider a directory filled with files, some of which were created on Windows and some on Linux. Let's suppose that we need to separate these files or even just do a slightly different operation to a single set of files. From a GUI, you would likely need to go file by file, examine them, then move them or at a minimum keep a list of what file is which kind. If new files were added, the process would need to be repeated. This does not scale well when thousands of files are added to the situation. What is needed is an explicit way to tell the computer what needs to be done, so that it can be repeated whenever needed. The best way to accomplish this is through language or via a Command Line Interface (CLI).

A CLI is a text-based interface. The user types a command composed of program names and various parameters, then the computer executes those commands. I am going to give you few example commands to interrogate the file and help change the file. The following section assumes you have access to the terminal program on any UNIX, Linux, or Mac OS X system. This can also be done on Windows with the addition of something like Cygwin (www.cygwin .com/) or on Windows 10 64-bit with Windows Subsystem for Linux installed.

Interrogating the File

Let's begin by determining some facts about our file. How long is it (how many records does it contain)? How many fields? Do all records have the same number of fields? What kind of new line characters are included? In the previous section I had to import the file to determine this kind of information. We also saw that not being aware of some aspects of the file can lead to bad imports.

I'll be using a program called AWK. The purpose of this exercise is not to make you a master of AWK, but instead to give you an understanding of how you can use simple tools to programmatically look and manipulate files.

To count the number of lines in our file I use this command where the filename is dirty.csv. This basically tells the computer to search for end-of-line characters in the file called dirty.csv and print out the total.

```
awk 'END {print NR}' dirty.csv
```

The output I receive is 5, which is surprising because I was expecting 4. This is because the file happens to contain an extra end of line after the 1956 characters. This is a great way to check if someone tells you he is giving you a million records but you get ten million or only a thousand; you can check the file and look for misperceptions on how the file is formatted. AWK can also remove those empty lines and we can create a new file called "clean.csv":

```
awk 'NF > 0' dirty.csv > clean.csv
```

Now let's check the number of commas we have per record. (Note that AWK suffers from the same commenting issues we have discussed above. In this example, the comma is being "escaped" out by a backslash):

```
awk -F\, '{print NF-1}' clean.csv
This returns:
2
2
5
2
```

Coping with Delimiters within Fields

As you can see, some delimiters are problematic. We can use the tactic from the previous section of replacing problematic characters. For example, this particular problem with escaped commas is not unusual. When I run into programs or processes that are not tolerant of escaped characters I often replace the problem characters with something else. There are two issues to be aware of here. The first is that this kind of operation can be expensive in terms of processing time and/or storage. The second is that whatever you use to replace the characters must not cause new problems. Let me address them in order. I tend to make these changes on copies of a file so if I make a mistake the original is intact, which doubles your storage usage. This tactic is fine for most files, but when dealing with very large files it may not be acceptable. As for the replacement characters, it is important that they don't already exist in the file (or are not likely to be in the file). Two ways I approach the replacement character problem are by using highly unusual characters or unique strings of characters. A highly unusual character might be something like ß (unless you are working in older German). A complicated unique string can also be useful, for example, COMMENTED-COMMA2016FORERO. I can assure you that this string will not appear in your file. This has the added benefit of being utterly transparent to anyone viewing the file, what has happened, and how to replace the original escaped commas. This command substitutes our special string of text for all the commas within double quotes and then creates a new file called "commas_replaced .csv."

```
awk -F'"' -v OFS='' '{ for (i=2; i<=NF; i+=2) gsub(",",
"COMMENTEDCOMMA2016FORERO", $i) } 1' clean.csv > commas_replaced.csv
```

The downside to this approach is that eventually you will need to change all those replaced commas back into commas because forgetting to do so will create a very confusing file. Alternatively, we could have chosen to replace the delimiter instead of the escaped comma. This might be an excellent choice if the system where this file will go can handle different delimiters. For example, some systems easily take tab-delimited files. Replacing all non-escaped commas with tabs, might make any further changes easier. However, there are three issues to consider when replacing the delimiter: 1) not all systems handle different delimiters well; 2) there may already be tabs (or whatever other delimiter you choose) in the file; and 3) tabs are nonprintable characters, which makes them hard to troubleshoot when things go wrong. Different situations may make replacing the delimiters the best choice.

Reordering Data within Fields

As before, we still have some inconsistencies in the file regarding the order of data in the fields. There are enumerable ways to deal with the inconsistencies, but I do not recommend making the changes manually. Systematic changes can often be reversed if necessary. but at minimum the systematic changes lead to better documentation. Changes with a written program or basic command-line tools are very easily recorded into documentation. As discussed above, breaking the problem into parts can often make the process easier. In this example, I can extract a single column from our file and then make changes on only that column, then merge the files back together. To extract the first column, I could use this command:

```
awk -F \, '{print $1}' commas_replaced.csv >
commas_replaced_column01.csv
```

I could do this for every column and manipulate each as needed. Because I do not intend this to be a deep tutorial on AWK, I won't go into the detail, but I will give an example of one possible transformation. I made a text file with the following content call LastNameFirst :

```
awk '
    /,/
    !/,/ {
    printf "\""
    printf $NF "COMMENTEDCOMMA2016FORERO "
    for (i = 1; i < NF; ++i) printf $i " "
    printf "\""
    printf "\n"
}
'
```

Then I ran the command:

```
./LastNameFirst < commas_replaced_column01.csv
```

I have glossed over some issues with programs files in a shell environment. In a UNIX/ Linux environment each file has permissions. This metadata about the file allows the system to determine who can do what with the file. When creating a file to run as a program (or an executable), the permissions on the file need to be set appropriately. Typically, the command **chmod FILENAME** o+x will allow you to execute the file: In this example, it would be **chmod o+x LastNameFirst**.

This resulted in this output:

```
"MilneCOMMENTEDCOMMA2016FORERO A. A. "
"ChristieCOMMENTEDCOMMA2016FORERO Agatha "
"MayaCOMMENTEDCOMMA2016FORERO AngelouCOMMENTEDCOMMA2016FORERO "
"GoldenCOMMENTEDCOMMA2016FORERO Arthur "
```

This isn't pretty, but the transformation has been made on only the records I wanted reversed. This process can be repeated for all columns (with the appropriate transformation scripts or commands).

I can then recombine all these columns into one file using a different command called "paste":

```
paste -d \, commas_replaced_column1.csv commas_replaced_column2.csv
commas_replaced_column3.csv > combined.csv
```

The last thing we need to do is replace all our commented commas with a command like:

```
awk '{ gsub(/COMMENTEDCOMMA2016FORERO/, ","); print }'< combined.csv>
ready_to_import.csv
```

Again, the purpose of these examples is not to make you black belts in AWK or Google Sheets. I am only illustrating that some challenges concerning how data is formatted can be broken down and addressed using common tools. (I use both tools frequently for everyday problems.) Each tool has strengths and weaknesses. Using a spreadsheet is expedient, familiar to many people, and often easy. But spreadsheets can work with only limited amounts of data and cannot always execute every transformation required. Using more powerful command-line tools or programming languages often means there are no real limits to the size of data nor the transformations that can be done. However, it takes longer to become adept with the tools. In developing these examples, I spent more time on the syntax of AWK than of the spreadsheet. However, you will find that when you do have a challenge with command-line and programming tools, there are active and friendly communities online who are eager to help. You will be able to post questions that will be answered quickly and often with multiple solutions.

REVIEW

My hope is that these examples show what you might do to test out a particular kind of transformation. There are many tools out there to help manipulate data formats. For example, both the Perl and Python languages have many libraries available for manipulating data formats. They were not selected for these examples, because despite their powerful functions, they vary greatly depending on their version, platform, and libraries installed. However, for automating in a production environment, these more powerful tools are likely to provide better performance and flexibility.

There are also many developed tools that can also be extremely helpful in formatting data. For example, Trifecta Wrangler, OpenRefine, and Karma are all tools that can help with these issues. (OpenRefine will be discussed in greater depth in chapter 3.)

In the end, the same concepts always apply. First you need to understand the nature of the data and how it is structured. You must know about variations in formatting. Then plan a systematic transformation that is well-documented. Note that these transformations often need to be broken into smaller tasks and transformations.

Understanding the assumptions of what the data is and how it is structured is critical for smooth data migrations. Interrogating the data to verify assumptions can help identify potential problems before they happen. When you find the discrepancies or errors, there are many tools at your disposal to correct these problems systematically. Even if you are not a programmer, simple tools can still help break down large problems into more manageable problems.

RESOURCES

Google Sheets: https://www.google.com/sheets/about/
Karma: http://usc-isi-i2.github.io/karma/
OpenRefine: http://openrefine.org/
Trifecta Wrangler: https://www.trifacta.com/products/wrangler/

THINKING
BEYOND EXCEL

Kate Hill, Electronic Resources and Distance Education Librarian,
University of North Carolina at Greensboro

M igrating data from one integrated library system (ILS) or electronic resource management (ERM) system to another is a complicated process that involves many stakeholders. Fortunately, there are software programs and simple computer scripting languages that can make the detailed work of cleaning and transforming data in preparation for migration easier. This chapter introduces some useful tools and skills that are not normally part of a librarian's standard arsenal of Excel and MarcEdit. In addition, it lays out the general thought processes and workflows for cleaning up and transforming data using a tool called OpenRefine. As well as discussing tools, this chapter touches on software-agnostic skills, such as the basics of using simple scripting languages that allow for repeatable, large-scale data transformations. The goal is not to make you an expert with a single tool, but instead to make you familiar with options and methods that can be used to improve and accelerate the migration process.

WHY LEARN A NEW TOOL?

Librarians tend to rely on a standard set of tools for working with technical services data, with special focus on Microsoft Excel. Although these tools often are essential for library tasks, they are not designed with large-scale data transformation in mind. Transforming and fixing data for something like an ILS migration regularly require working through hundreds of thousands of rows. Bringing in this quantity of data into Excel often causes it to crash. When it does successfully load a large file, Excel attempts to guess what data type a value should be, often transforming textual data into numbers or dates. This can introduce significant problems during migrations. For example, when system identifiers and patron/item barcodes are reformatted, record overlays stop working and relationships between items and people are lost, causing enormous damage to data and workflows. Finally, Excel lacks tools to assist the exploration and discovery of errors in data—an essential part of data transformation and migration. Fortunately, OpenRefine is well-suited for this purpose.

GETTING STARTED

The rest of this chapter describes using OpenRefine to assist with data migration. OpenRefine can be downloaded at http://openrefine.org/download and installed as a desktop application. Before ingesting the large data sets often involved in data migration, you will need to change some of the memory settings. This tool's default settings only allow for a small amount of memory to be used at one time, meaning that it usually can only handle roughly 100,000 rows before crashing. This amount can be adjusted through going into the OpenRefine file and finding the text file label "openrefine.14j or google-refine.14j." You need to find the line that says "max memory heap size" and adjust the number. Generally, a good rule is to not adjust this number to over half of your computer's available physical memory. Going beyond this amount will make your computer run very slowly (see figure 3.1).

FIGURE 3.1

OpenRefine

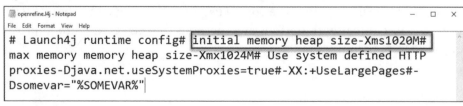

Once you have made the correct memory adjustments, you can load data. OpenRefine accepts most structured file types, including CSV, TSV, Excel, XML, and JSON. When working with library data, it's best to import CSV or TSV files, even if the data's native format is Excel. This is because text files are easier to process, and OpenRefine only gives you this option when importing CSV or TSV files. Bringing data into OpenRefine as dates or numbers can cause issues with fields such as call numbers that contain both numbers and non-numbers.

After loading a file, most of these tools allow you to preview what it will look when ingested. Use the file display options to make sure extraneous headers are removed and verify that all rows that are blank are kept blank. Recommended settings are highlighted in figure 3.2.

FIGURE 3.2

Recommended settings

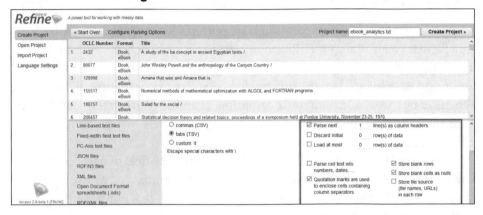

OpenRefine and similar tools allow for many types of structured data files, but do not recognize .mrc files. MARC files can still be brought into these tools using the free software program MarcEdit, which is discussed in detail in chapter 4. MarcEdit has a tool called "OpenRefine Data Transfer." This tool allows you to bring in a source .mrc file and transform it into a TSV file. It then automatically opens OpenRefine with a new preview of the file you just imported.

OpenRefine opens MARC records in a specific format (as shown in figure 3.3). All MARC files in OpenRefine have four columns. The first column indicates the record number and serves to group all the rows belonging to one MARC record together. The second column lists the MARC tag, the third column the two-digit indicator, and the fourth column includes all the actual field data, including subfield indicators.

FIGURE 3.3

OpenRefine opens MARC records in a specific format

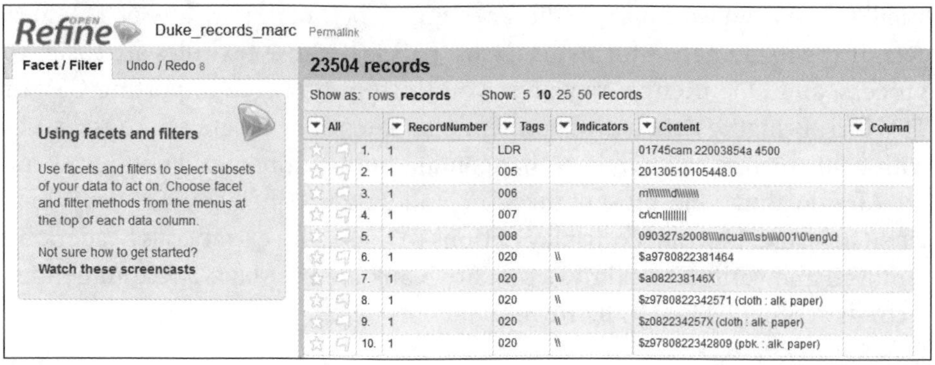

MODIFYING DATA STRUCTURES

One common task in data migration is mapping fields and data structures from one format to another. OpenRefine supports actions such as renaming fields, removing fields, adding new fields, joining together two separate fields, and splitting one field into two distinct fields to match a new structure. Before using OpenRefine to assist in data transformation, examine your current data's structure and map it onto the structure required by the new system, as detailed in chapter 12.

OpenRefine works on a column-level basis, with each field of data corresponding to one column. Each individual record is represented as a row (or multiple grouped rows in the case of MARC files). This means that most manipulation and exploration of data takes place via field. In OpenRefine, for example, most options can be accessed via an individual column's drop-down menu. There is one other drop-down menu, labeled "All," that does allow for multicolumn editing (figure 3.4). After loading a file, use the All drop-down menu to remove fields that are not needed in the final migration file. In OpenRefine, selecting "reorder/remove all fields" presents a nice drag and drop interface to quickly get rid of extraneous information. Using the individual column's dropdown, use the edit columns→rename column to rename any fields containing information that correlates one-to-one with a new field onto which you need to map.

While renaming, reordering, and removing columns can all be done easily within a tool like Excel (as discussed in chapter 2), the ability to join or split apart fields is where a tool like OpenRefine really shines. All you need to do is go to the desired column and select Edit Column→Split Column Into. As you can see in figure 3.5, this allows you to either select a delimiter (including just a space or multiple spaces) or field length on which to split. For example, if you have a holding that was written vol. 2, issue 6 (April 2006) that needs to be split into three fields containing volume, issue, and date respectively, all you need to do

FIGURE 3.4

The general layout of an OpenRefine screen, with drop-down menu highlighted

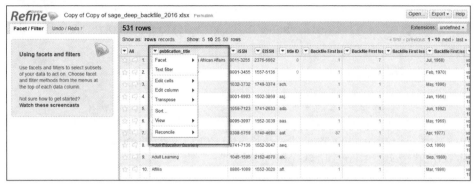

FIGURE 3.5

The splitting interface in OpenRefine

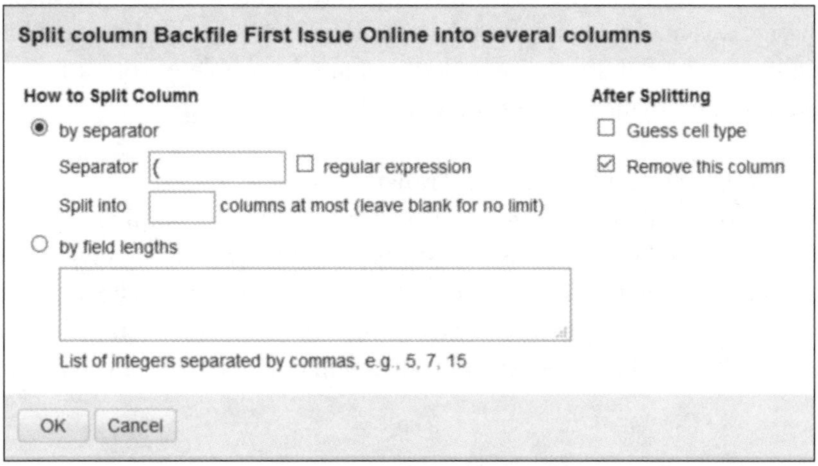

is first split on "(" to get two fields (v01.2, iss.6 and April 2006) and then split on the comma to end up with the three desired fields.

Joining columns together is also a technique that is useful, often in combination with splitting, to either add or remove information from the middle of a field. For example, if you want hyphens in your ISSNs but your old data does not contain them, first split the ISSN by field length to create two fields of four numbers each. Then you can rejoin the fields using what OpenRefine calls "expressions," which will be discussed in further detail later in this chapter. Whenever you want to transform columns or values, you can go to Edit Cells→Transform. To join cells, use the expression:

Cells["name of first column you want to join"].value +"any separator desired" + cells["name of second column you want to join"].value.

So for the ISSN example, you would write *Cells.[ISSN column one] + "-" + cells[ISSN column two].value*. This results in an ISSN with the hyphen correctly inserted.

▌ **Making mistakes is okay!**

One of the things that makes OpenRefine stand out is that it allows for mistakes. There are few ways OpenRefine does this. I hope these ideas will be picked up on by other tools soon!

1. **The Undo/Redo Panel.**
   On the left site of the OpenRefine interface there is a panel. One of the options that can be clicked on is called "Undo/Redo." Selecting this will show you all the steps that have changed the data. Each step can also be clicked, which will result in the data reverting to the state it was in just after that change was made. This means that if you have done something to a file and realize, even a few steps down, that it created a problem, you can get rid of it and not permanently mess up your file.

2. **The Preview Panel for All Data Transformations.**
   When you create your own data transformations (e.g., joining columns) or use any of the built-in transformations, there is a preview panel (as shown in figure 3.6) that shows you what the result of your transformation will be. This is helpful while you are learning how to use these transformations because it alerts you if something will or will not work before you commit it.

FINDING ERRORS IN YOUR DATA

Once the structure of the data is correct, you can use OpenRefine to find errors in the content. OpenRefine has many features designed specifically for exploring data. Having said that, it can be challenging to use with highly irregular data, which can include things like free text notes. But these tools work well for most of the data with which librarians deal.

If you don't know what issues to expect before loading a file into OpenRefine, it's best to pursue broad strategies for discovering anomalies. First examine columns where you expect repetition of content, which allows you to identify patterns. In OpenRefine, the main way to explore data patterns is through something called "faceting," which can be accessed from each column's drop-down menu. Faceting groups data by how many times it has been repeated in a column.

FIGURE 3.6

Preview panel

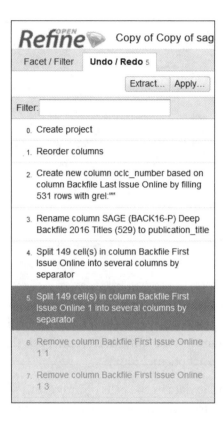

When a column is faceted, you can include as many options as you like. The data display then shows only the rows that include those values, as shown in figure 3.7. Facets can also be combined to build simple queries. For example, you could first facet on the tag field, which gives you a list of all the tags. You could choose to include the 245 field, which would change the display to only show you rows that had the tag value of 245. You could then choose to facet the indicator field. Because you had already selected to see only fields with the 245 tag, this new facet will only display indicator values that are found in rows with that tag. You could do this to check if there are any rows with a value of 00 that in fact should have non-displaying characters. Running these tag indicator combinations can be a powerful way to examine your MARC data.

On top of this simple faceting and some other built-in facets (e.g., checking for duplicate values or checking for blank values), if you are familiar with common error patterns in your data, you can create your own facets, by selecting Facet→Custom Facet. This requires a greater knowledge of your data, so it's usually best to explore data through the faceting process previously described first. Building custom facets requires the use of some concepts that these tools borrow from programming and scripting languages, which are useful to know

FIGURE 3.7

Faceting group data

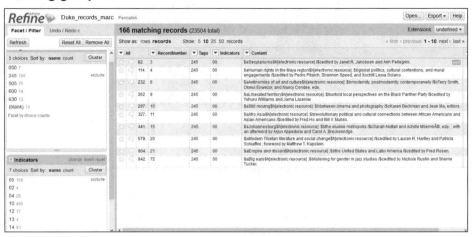

for any advanced data-transformation work. OpenRefine uses a vocabulary it called OREL, or the OpenRefine Expression Language. Although the other tools would use different signifiers for some of the concepts, the concepts remain the same. Some of these concepts include:

- You must refer to the data in the cells of interest in some way. In refine, the term "value" refers to every cell value in a particular column.
- Building on value, you can select specific columns or rows by adding their signifiers to value. Indicating specific columns usually only needs to be done if you are trying to refer to a column other than the one you initially selected. In OpenRefine, referring to a column is written cells["Name of the Column"]. value.
- Most of these tools have pre-written scripts that can be referred to by specific names. These scripts often require the input of a specific type of data. In most programming languages, including OpenRefine, these pre-written scripts are called "functions" and the types of data they require are called "arguments." Being familiar with the functions that are provided by any of these tools will help you create your own custom facets and transformations. In OpenRefine, they are written as value.name_of_function (). The arguments that the function requires are written between the parentheses.
- Functions can be chained together, and sometimes must follow another function to work properly.
- When writing expressions, if you want something to appear exactly as written, you need a "literal string." You indicate that something should be a literal string by placing it between two quotation marks.

Understanding how to create these functions and how they work is key to creating custom facets. Using MARC data as an example again, an example of something you can use a custom facet for is to check on the accuracy of fixed length fields, including the 020 fields and the LDR fields. The length function in OpenRefine gives you the length of the string. Writing value.length() as a custom facet indicates that you want this to look at the value in a cell and get its length. The empty parentheses mean you want to perform this function on every value in the column. Once you initiate this custom function, you will see that the column is automatically faceted around the number of characters in a string (as seen in figure 3.8). This lets you see if there are any values that do not match the standard length, and from there explore what might be causing these issues.

Content

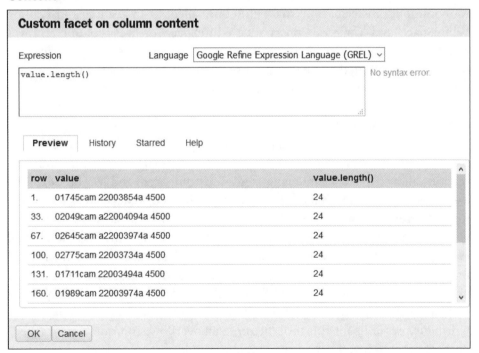

TRANSFORMING DATA

After fixing broad structures and finding errors, the final step in the process is to fix those errors. Fixing data is the most powerful and also the most complex part of using a tool like OpenRefine. Although data can be corrected one cell at a time, OpenRefine really shines in its ability to transform large amounts of data according to a set pattern, using both built-in and simple custom transformations. Neither of these options require the extensive scripting such processes usually would require. In addition, in OpenRefine, transformations only affect the rows that are currently displayed. This allows you to target very specific errors via faceting and then only fix the affected data, without having to worry about any scripts you create hurting your other data.

Developing common sets of transformations and applying them consistently are processes that can be useful for data migration. To develop your own set of transformations, it is important to pay close attention to the types and frequencies of errors that occur while working with your initial data sets. For example, using the common transformations in OpenRefine called "Trim Leading and Trailing WhiteSpace" and "Collapse Consecutive WhiteSpace" on every column removes all invisible and extraneous spaces in the data. Because these extra spaces are not readily apparent, they can often cause functions to fail quietly. They also can cause incorrect import of data back into your ILS. OpenRefine has other built-in transformations, such as the ability to transform text into dates and the ability to change text into all title case.

Built-in transformations and facets can help fix much of the data, but tools like this also allow many powerful custom transformations. Custom transformations allow the exact same language as custom facets and let you deal with a wide variety of issues that cannot be easily predicted. Like all areas that allow for custom expressions in OpenRefine, creating custom transformations is a forgiving process that allows you to see how your expression will affect data in real time before you perform the transformation. This lets you experiment with and improve your scripting skills without fear. If any of this is intimidating, the good news is that there is a great deal of both official documentation and unofficial help out there. StackOverflow, for example, has an entire channel dedicated to writing expressions for this tool (http://stackoverflow.com/questions/tagged/openrefine), and if you run into a problem, it is likely someone else has as well and has written about it here.

Because so many different expressions can be needed in data migration, it's not possible to list all the ones that might be useful here. However, the expressions listed below are particularly helpful, so that you can get an idea of how you might use them for your own data-migration process.

- Value + "literal string" or "literal string" + value
  - » This will add a prefix or suffix of exactly what you write between the quotes to every value in a column. So, for example, if you discover that some of the LDR fields in your MARC data are missing the last two 0s, you can write value + "00." This will add "00" to all the values currently displayed in OpenRefine.

- Value.replace("thing to find," "thing to replace") OR value.replace(/[regular expression for thing to find],[regular expression for thing to replace]/)
  - » This is a general find and replace, like you would find in Excel or Word. What is interesting here is that you can use regular expressions to find something that matches one pattern and then replace it with another pattern.
  - » For more information on regular expressions, see the section entitled "Global Editing Tools" in chapter 4.

- Value.match("literal string") OR value.match (/[regular expression]/)
  - » This is usually used as a custom facet, but it can also be used to first match text with a certain pattern and then perform additional actions to the matched text.

- Value.reinterpret(name of encoding)
  - » Often when bringing records in and out of systems, characters will be incorrectly loaded. This is especially true for non-Latin characters. This forces the values to go through a reinterpretation and hopefully fix any encoding errors.

- Value.substring(number from, optional number to)
  - » If you need to grab just part of a value for a subsequent transformation, add it to another column, or create a custom facet that looks for only that substring. You can use this to grab, for example, the first two letters from every value.

- Value.match(/(.*),(.*)/).reverse().join(" ")
  - » This expression uses regular expressions to find those strings that are any number of digits, followed by a column, followed by any number of digits. It then reverses the two blocks of digits around the comma and rejoins them together with a space. So, it takes a reverse order name (Hill, Kate) and transforms it into Kate Hill.

- Value.ForNonBlank(v,v,"") + cells["Other Column Name"].value.ForNon Blankc(v,v,"")
  - » This joins together the values in two cells as long as one of the cell values is not blank.

This list may give you some ideas about how you can bring together lots of functions in OpenRefine to create the kind of large-scale transformations required by your data. This will take some practice and lots of experimenting, but once you get the hang of it, you'll be better at working with data, as well as reading and understanding other forms of scripting and programming.

SAVING YOUR STEPS AND EXPORTING YOUR DATA

Using OpenRefine to transform data involves experimentation and sometimes takes longer than expected. But the benefit of spending time exploring data and constructing useful transformations is that the steps can often be saved as programs or macros that can then be run over other similar data sets. In Open-Refine, you can use the export function to select all the steps or only certain steps and convert them to JSON format (as seen in figure 3.9). These steps can then be copied into a text file and, when a file with a similar structure needs to be transformed, can be brought in through the Import button. The one thing to note is that this will only save steps that made permanent changes to the data.

FIGURE 3.9

Extract operation history

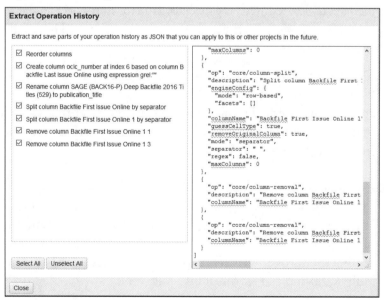

After you've done this, it's easy to convert the finished product back into many different formats, such as Excel, CSV, XML, or even JSON. To transform a tool back into MARC from OpenRefine, save the file as .csv and then use the same Open-Refine tool in MarcEdit to import the new .csv file back into a MarcEdit format

Data migration is a challenging process that requires a great deal of thought, experimentation, and coordination. Collections data has often been gathered and created with numerous different local practices and standards, and errors often spread throughout the data. Even if the data is relatively clean, it will need to be mapped and transformed to fit with new formats and standards required by new systems. Beyond the standard data tools of Excel and Access, additional tools, skills, and thought processes can make migration easier to handle. This chapter discussed tools and workflows likely to be useful during migration work, focusing especially on OpenRefine, currently the best-supported free data-transformation tool on the market. I also reviewed the use of simple scripting, a highly useful skill for textual manipulation that can be translated across numerous platforms. Although these skills and tools are helpful, the goal of this chapter is not that you become an expert in using these tools, but rather you understand a bit of what is possible in the current world of data transformation, and especially that the thought processes used to rearrange, explore, and transform data are out-lined. Armed with this introduction and the further resources listed following this chapter, you should be able to begin introducing these skills and tools into your own workflow processes for all types of data migration, whether the initial migration or the cleanup process after the beginning work is completed.

RESOURCES

Main OpenRefine Documentation

OpenRefine FAQ: 2016. https://github.com/OpenRefine/OpenRefine/wiki/FAQ
 This regularly updated guide provides answers to questions received frequently by the OpenRefine development community. It outlines troubleshooting techniques to try if OpenRefine is running slowly or not starting, basics on using GREL, and common areas of confusion, such as how to delete numerous rows at once.

OpenRefine Wiki. 2016. https://github.com/OpenRefine/OpenRefine/wiki/
 This is the main source of official documentation for OpenRefine and is regularly updated. It includes links to screencasts that introduce basic concepts, in-depth entries for constructing GREL expressions, descriptions of every function that can be used, and step-by-step guides for all available menu options.

General Tutorials

Verbough, Ruben, Mannens, Erik, Van de Walle, Rik, van Hooland, Seth, and De Wilde,
Max. (2016). Free Your Metadata. http://freeyourmetadata.org
A step-by-step guide to using OpenRefine not only for data cleanup, but for other
tasks such as creating linked data and developing controlled vocabularies. It provides
video tutorials and step-by-step instructions for you to follow, along with a sample
data set on which to practice. It goes into more depth on some common expressions
and processes like locating duplicates and grouping rows into records.

Heller, Margaret. 2013. A Librarian's Guide to OpenRefine. http://acrl.ala.org/
techconnect/post/a-librarians-guide-to-openrefine
One of the first posts to write about using OpenRefine for specifically library-related
tasks. It does a great job briefly summarizing the benefits of using OpenRefine over
spreadsheet tools like Excel. Written from a systems and institutional-repository
librarian's perspective, it discusses some ways to use OpenRefine with this type of
data. Processes include using OpenRefine to catch typos and transforming data
written in plain text into a column format.

Hirst, Tony. 2013. Using OpenRefine to Clean Multiple Documents in the Same Way.
http://schoolofdata.org/2013/07/26/using-openrefine-to-clean-multiple
-documents-in-the-same-way/
This blog post has a nice walk-through of the steps a data scientist used to clean
up spending data. Processes covered include how to change dates from one format
to another and how to remove commas from numeric values, and it includes good
illustrations on how to export steps from one data set and apply it to another data set.

Hirst, Tony. 2012. Chit Chat with New Datasets—Facets in OpenRefine (Was /Google
Refine/). https://blog.ouseful.info/2012/11/06/chit-chat-with-new-datasets
-facets-in-open-was-google-refine/
This blog post provides a thorough and heavily illustrated discussion of OpenRefine's
many types of facets and abilities, and what they can do. It goes into depth about
potentially useful types of facets, such as numeric, time line, and scatterplot, which
I was not able to review in this chapter.

Cheat Sheets and Specific Solutions

Falcone, Arcadia. 2013. Google Refine Cheat Sheet. http://arcadiafalcone.net/Google
RefineCheatSheets.pdf
   This two-page guide contains references to all the main components of Regular
   Expressions as they are used in OpenRefine as well as the most commonly used
   functions in OpenRefine. Functions are presented in a table, with each row describing
   how to write a particular function, and what it does, what kind of data it returns,
   what form of arguments it can take, and an example of it in use. I have printed this
   out and use it all the time.

Schmitt, Cassie. 2014. Clean Up: Dates and OpenRefine. https://icantiemyownshoes
   .wordpress.com/2014/04/24/clean-up-dates-and-openrefine/
   This blog post, written from an archival perspective, provides steps and formulas
   you can use to take messy textual dates, including those with months written out
   and entries with n.d. instead of a date, into a standard date format.

Hirst, Tony. 2013. A Simple OpenRefine Example: Tidying Cut'n'Paste Data from a
   Web Page. http://blog.ouseful.info/2013/05/01/a-simple-openrefine-example
   -tidying-cutnpaste-data-from-a-web-page/
   I find this blog post useful not necessarily for what it tells you *how* to do, but for
   the thought process it lays out for examining data structures and patterns. This is
   an incredibly useful skill to develop while working with OpenRefine or any type of
   data transformation and migration. In addition, it walks the reader through creating
   multiple columns out of data that comes in as a single column.

WORKING WITH MARC DATA

Terry Reese, Head of Digital Initiatives, The Ohio State University

A s organizations evaluate next-generation bibliographic management systems or consider schema migrations to new data models like BIB-FRAME, it is very likely that the organization will need to work with MARC data. Few standards used in the library community have been as durable, long-lasting, and resilient as the MARC format. Developed in the 1960s and made a formal standard in 1971,[1] the MARC format is still the lingua franca of the library community and the primary data model utilized within integrated library systems (ILSs). Despite its warts, MARC remains the principal format that libraries use to describe and share bibliographic metadata. Its longevity can be both a blessing and a curse. On the one hand, MARC is a well-understood data format shared widely within the library community. Despite the wide range of MARC flavors (UNIMARC, MARC 21, CHINMARC, FINMARC, etc.), the underlying data structure is based upon ISO 2709,[2] which enables the development of tools and utilities that can read a wide range of MARC-structured data.

Given MARC's long history within the library community, librarians, vendors, and library partners have developed well-established patterns and tools for working with MARC data. Likewise, a wide range of tools and workflows have been developed to support the migration of MARC data between systems. These resources represent a significant investment by the community, and though they are not sufficient to perform a wide-scale data migration, they provide a ready toolkit that can be repurposed and reused throughout the community.

The challenge of working with MARC data is that it is fragile. As a format, MARC was created to share data on tapes, and was designed as a directory/variable length data format. Likewise, given MARC's longevity, issues relating to character sets, and the need to support character sets beyond Latin-based languages, dramatically complicate the process of working with MARC data that include significant foreign language materials or come from user communities that utilize local character sets like Traditional Chinese Big-5 rather than more modern character encodings like UTF-8.

Additionally, MARC's longevity has resulted in a bibliographic melting pot, with data created utilizing different descriptive standards and punctuation rules. These variations in bibliographic description can significantly complicate a data migration, and result in large segments of bibliographic data being lost or otherwise rendered inaccessible when moved between bibliographic management systems.

This chapter takes a closer look at working with MARC data. It briefly examines available programming libraries and tools that exist within the library community, and then focuses on one specific tool, MarcEdit,[3] and how it can be leveraged to perform a wide range of metadata editing activities.

GETTING STARTED

It is important to note that there isn't a single best way to go about working with MARC data. Although this chapter will focus primarily on working with a utility known as MarcEdit, this is just one of many tools and programming libraries available to work with library data. As with any data migration, an organization needs to take stock of its staff's available expertise in order to better match the available tools and services with the organization's natural strengths. This means that though many of the concepts and strategies discussed in this chapter utilize MarcEdit, organizations should be able to take these general concepts and apply them to the specific tools or programming libraries that best suit their needs.

AVAILABLE TOOLS

As noted in the introduction to this chapter, MARC's longevity as a data format has led to the creation of a rich assortment of tools and programming resources available to libraries. At the same time, one of the most common critiques of MARC as a data model is its limited usage outside of the library community.

This is a fair criticism, especially when facing a data migration, because it limits the potential pool of programmers, metadata specialists, and data wranglers who can work with a library's information. Although MARC (as a structure) isn't overly complicated, the unfortunate mix of punctuation, relative positioning of data elements within the structure, and ambiguous descriptive guidelines create significant barriers for nonlibrary technical staff working with MARC data. It's precisely this mixture of structure, data, and context that renders MARC data so difficult to process, and causes nonlibrarian technical staff to run screaming from a project. Unfortunately, unless you have a background in library metadata creation, MARC simply won't make sense.

Fortunately, the availability of high-quality MARC processing tools and libraries has greatly benefited from the library community's investment in open source software development. In 1999, MARC editing tools were limited primarily to library catalogs, the Library of Congress's MARCBreakr/MARCMakr, and a set of Perl libraries known as MARC.pm. By no means were these the only tools available. There has always been a third-party vendor community that has created lightweight editing tools and resources tied to specific ILS systems, as well as local custom development that targets a specific organization. Over the intervening years, the library community has developed a wide range of MARC editing resources. Many of the resources that work with the MARC 21 format are tracked by the Library of Congress at www.loc.gov/marc/marctools.html, and ever more tools and programming libraries have found their home on code-sharing platforms like SourceForge and GitHub.

MarcEdit

MarcEdit is a software suite that provides metadata support and editing tools for a wide range of library and nonlibrary metadata formats. The project isn't open source (though many of the components that make up the tool can be found at https://github.com/reeset), but has been under continuous development since 1999, and supports a substantial and diverse community of nearly 20,000 active users[4] from all over the world. In 2015, MarcEdit international usage represented nearly 45 percent of the active user community.[5]

MarcEdit's success throughout the years has been its ability to support a wide range of national cataloging standards, by taking both a MARC-agnostic approach to library metadata, as well as being on the cutting edge for supporting emerging non-MARC metadata formats and character conversion tools. This approach is captured in the developer's core rules governing MarcEdit's development:

1. MarcEdit is a real-world metadata tool.
   The tool is designed to provide workflows for data problems facing libraries right now.

2. **MarcEdit is MARC-agnostic.**
   Too many metadata tools are Anglocentric. MarcEdit has been designed to work within the very heterogeneous metadata environment in which we find ourselves today, including:
   a. Support for MARC (not a particular flavor)
   b. Near universal character-set support (because the world is bigger than MARC-8 and UTF-8)
   c. Support for a wide range of library metadata standards beyond MARC

3. **MarcEdit is one part of the larger library metadata tooling environment.**
   MarcEdit has been designed to work with any workflow and integrate with a wide range of metadata systems and environments.

Following these guidelines, MarcEdit development has actively worked to integrate with leading metadata providers like OCLC as well as with ILS systems, and support metadata editing tools like OpenRefine. Likewise, it has resulted in the development of metadata bridges like the RDA Helper, as well as the inclusion of a research toolkit to support users interested in experimenting with linked data concepts or BIBFRAME.

WORKING WITH MARCEDIT

MarcEdit provides close to 200 different editing utilities—each one created to support a different part of the metadata editing process. Because this text is primarily focused on the migration of data, the remainder of this chapter will focus on those tools and utilities found in MarcEdit that are most commonly utilized when migrating data. The remainder of this chapter will be broken into five sections. Each section includes descriptions, examples, screenshots, and pro tips for working with the various utilities within the program. These sections are as follows:

1. Character conversions
   Very often, data migrations between systems require not only remapping and editing existing data, but also modifying the underlying character set data being utilized within the system. This is especially common within library ILS systems, which have traditionally supported MARC-8 character encodings, but are quickly transitioning to require UTF-8. Additionally, users working with the international community may receive MARC data in local character sets, which will need to be remapped and converted prior to loading within an organization's ILS system.

2. Data preparation

   MarcEdit includes a number of tools that can be used to split, join, validate, and extract specific records and records sets for editing. These tools allow users to extract subsets of records to simplify the editing process and enable data migrations to proceed incrementally.

3. Record editing

   MarcEdit's core functionality revolves around the editing of library metadata. This section will focus on the MarcEditor and the wide range of global editing functions that can be utilized to clean and edit large sets of records in batch.

4. Working with non-MARC data

   Libraries use a wide range of metadata types, and during a data migration, it may be necessary to ingest records from a wide range of systems using a variety of metadata formats. MarcEdit provides a number of tools for working directly with data-harvesting services like OAI-PMH[6] as well as non-MARC metadata schemas like Dublin Core, MODS, METS, EAD, MARCXML, and so on.

5. Merging record data

   Migrations often require doing reclamation work with resources like OCLC or local consortia. MarcEdit provides tools that enable data merging and deduplication.

6. Beyond the editor

   MarcEdit has a number of tools designed to support users interested in working outside of MarcEdit to perform advanced metadata manipulation. These include tools like MarcEdit's SQL Explorer, it's OpenRefine Integration, and Application Programming Interfaces (APIs) to support local utility development with MarcEdit's editing components.

Using these tools, organizations have all the necessary resources necessary to support a large-scale data migration, regardless of size or complexity. MarcEdit has no record or size limitations, and has been actively used to support metadata migrations of hundreds of millions of records and on file sizes of over a terabyte in size.

Character Conversions

One of MARC's least endearing legacies has been the perpetuation of the MARC-8[7] character encoding. The most vexing characteristic of MARC-8 is that it only exists within the library community. For all intents and purposes, MARC-8 is a made-up language. Although it enabled the library community to support multibyte languages through a single character encoding when few other options existed, it has now become an albatross that overly complicates library bibliographic data, and typically renders it inaccessible to anyone outside of the library profession. From a technical perspective, MARC-8 looks very similar to ISO 8859 or Windows-1252 encodings when dealing with Latin-based data, but utilizes an escape character-based structure when dealing with multibyte languages like CJK, Greek, Hebrew, or Arabic. These similarities to other character encodings cause problems for many data-processing tools because most tools utilize a heuristically process to guess character encoding, and the ambiguity of MARC-8 renders most nonlibrary-specific utilities unusable.

So why would one need to worry about character encodings as part of a migration of library data? Well, although MARC-8 is still predominately used in legacy library systems, newer ILS systems are requiring UTF-8 and phasing out support for MARC-8. If bibliographic data is made up largely of MARC-8 encoded data, this can be a significant issue—especially given the complicated nature of data conversion and the necessity to understand the different UTF-8 normalizations and how each normalization could potentially impact the indexing of one's content.

Character Normalizations

Character normalization is an important topic when thinking about character conversions and UTF-8 support. Although many will assume that putting the data into UTF-8 is all that is needed to ensure library data is displayed and indexed correctly by their local systems, the issue of normalization often makes this a much more difficult and nuanced discussion.

Currently there are presently four Unicode normalizations[8] (see table 4.1). For the purposes of library data, the two encodings of interest are the KD normalization and the C normalization. So what is the difference between the different normalization forms? It largely comes down to how characters are represented. In MARC-8, characters with diacritics are represented by multiple bytes. Let's consider the following example: an "e" with an acute (é). In MARC-8, this character is represented by the following multibyte sequence: 0xe2+0x65 (´+e). When converting this data to Unicode, the normalization used determines whether this character (é), is represented as a single character, or as a multibyte character representation. Currently, the Library of Congress requires data output in MARC 21 to utilize the KD normalization in order to retain round-tripability with MARC-8. Using the KD normalization, the character (é) would be output as 0x65+0xCC81 (e+´). Although the KD normalization may preserve round-tripability with the MARC-8 encoding, it complicates indexing for search. Because the diacritic isn't a part of the character that it modifies, most systems would index this value simply as "e," dropping the diacritic from the index. This may not be troublesome for most North American libraries, but it can be deeply problematic for international users. The appropriate normalization to use when indexing is a concern is the C normalization. In this case, this same value (é), when output as UTF-8 in the C normalization, becomes: 0xC3A9, or a single code point. As a single code point, this data can be properly indexed as a composed value, which in most cases may be the desired outcome.

TABLE 4.1

Normalization Forms

FORM	DESCRIPTION
Normalization Form D	Canonical Decomposition
Normalization Form C	Canonical Decomposition, followed by Canonical Composition
Normalization Form KD	Compatibility Decomposition
Normalization Form KC	Compatibility Decomposition, followed by Canonical Composition

MarcEdit provides several different tools to facilitate the transformation of data between different character encoding and Unicode normalizations. By default, MarcEdit's MARCEngine supports Unicode normalizations for the C and KD notations. Users define the specific normalization that they wish to use when executing character-encoding conversions via the MarcEdit Preferences. In MarcEdit, the Preferences are accessed by selecting MARC Preferences from the Tools menu or clicking on the Settings button (figure 4.1).

FIGURE 4.1

MarcEdit preferences

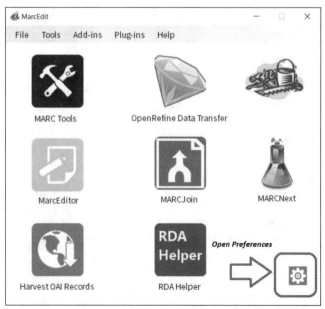

Once selected, MarcEdit's Preference window will be displayed. Navigate to MARCEngine, and set the Normalization to the desired output (figure 4.2). By default, the KD normalization will be selected. When finished, click on the OK button and return to the main window.

Once the normalization preferences are set, the user can utilize the character conversion tools in MarcEdit. MarcEdit provides shortcuts for doing character-encoding conversions as well as a stand-alone tool; this chapter will examine the stand-alone utility. From the main window, select the Tools/Character Conversion menu item (figure 4.3).

MARCEngine settings

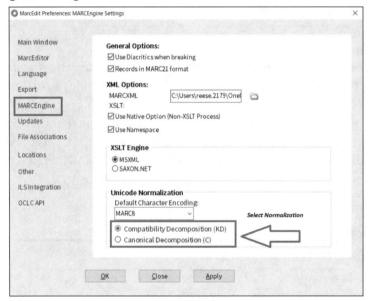

Finding the Character Conversion tool

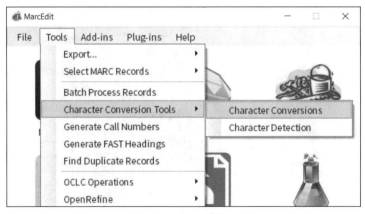

When selected, this will open the Character Conversion tool (figure 4.4). The Character Conversion tool requires users to identify the file to be processed, select an output file (which must be different from the input file), define the original encoding, and then set a final encoding. For users converting data from MARC-8 to UTF-8, the original encoding would be MARC-8 and the final encoding would be UTF-8.

FIGURE 4.4

Character conversion

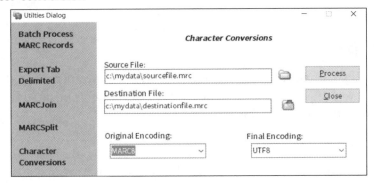

> ## 💡 PRO TIP
>
> MarcEdit's character conversion tool can be used to convert data from a wide range of character encodings. MarcEdit provides a predefined list of the most common character encodings as part of the application. However, it can convert data between any code page that the host operating system supports. To utilize a custom code page with MarcEdit, simply enter the code page number into the Original or Final Encoding Dropdown box. For a full list of code pages supported by Windows (and across all .NET instances), see https://msdn.microsoft.com/en-us/library/windows/desktop/dd317756(v=vs.85).aspx.

Depending on the size of the source file and the number of records to be processed, the character conversion process could take a significant amount of time to perform, but once the user has processed the data, the resulting MARC file will be encoded in UTF-8, with the resulting data in the specified Unicode normalization.

> ### 💡 PRO TIP
>
> Although MarcEdit has the ability to work with MARC data that is structurally invalid, this is not true when doing character-encoding conversions. If users are unsure if their MARC data is structurally valid, they may wish to run their data files through MarcEdit's MARCValidator, selecting the Identify Invalid Records option. This option will identify any records that have structural issues that may disrupt MarcEdit's ability to properly re-encode the data. For more information related to MARC validation, please see the following section on data preparation.

Data Preparation

Migrating library data, as part of an ILS migration or entrance into a data consortium, often requires working with a great deal of complicated data. Let's assume the following scenario:

> An ARL research library is migrating from its previous ILS system, to one of the many "next generation" library platforms. Data migration will be in MARC, and will require moving bibliographic, holdings, and financial data. In total, the institution will need to migrate approximately two million bibliographic records, and millions of other holdings and authority records. Starting with the bibliographic records, the organization needs to do significant data cleanup. However, when this data is exported from their existing system, the MARC file is over 3 GB in size.

In my experience, this type of scenario isn't atypical. Although the size of the database will vary, the problem with most data migrations is that pre-migration work will need to be done, likely on a subset of records that sometimes are not easy to identify and isolate within the legacy host system. As a result, organizations doing large migrations are faced with the difficult decision of whether to dispense with the necessary pre-migration work, or trying to do as much work as possible before embarking on a very large and unfriendly MARC data dump. Ideally, organizations doing large data migrations would be able to utilize tools that could slice up, and selectively export record groups for editing. These tools should be able to conduct data merges, validation, and potentially reassemble extracted records back into the larger whole for final processing. In many cases, organizations tend to outsource this work (unless they have dedicated development staff), which limits the amount of work done in-house. However, using MarcEdit and its suite of data-manipulation utilities, organizations may be able to handle more of this work in-house by leveraging local expertise.

Splitting up Files

In the scenario above, our imaginary institution has a 3 GB MARC file, and would like to break it into smaller parts to simplify processing. Although this is a common data-migration task, it's not limited to data migration. Libraries receive bibliographic data for eresources purchased from vendors each month. These files can be quite large, numbering upwards of 25,000 MARC records. In order to process this data, institutions often break these files into smaller chunks to better assess the quality of the records provided. And although all major operating systems provide command-line tools that can split a large file into specific lines or byte sizes, the binary structure of a MARC record and the need to preserve the leader/directory byte structure renders these types of tools unusable.

To support this use case, MarcEdit provides a tool called MARCSplit, which, as its title describes, splits MARC record files. The tool can be accessed from the application's main window, under the Tools menu (figure 4.5).

FIGURE 4.5

Opening the MARCSplit, MARCJoin, MARCValidator, and Extract Selected tools

FIGURE 4.6

MARCSplit utility

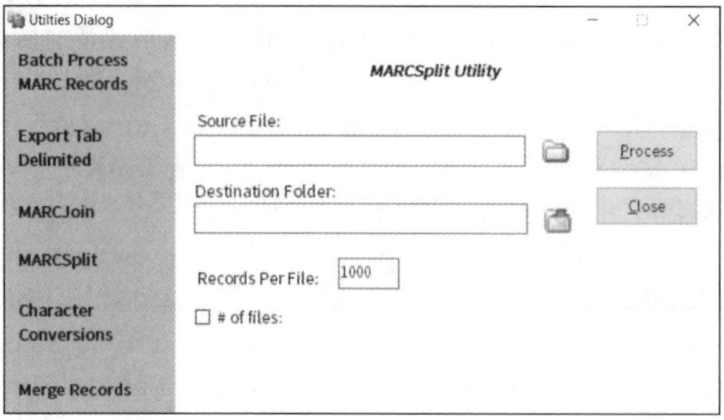

The MARCSplit utility (figure 4.6) provides several potential options for users who want to split large data files into smaller, more manageable data files. The tool has three specific modes. The first, and most common, splits a large data file into multiple parts based on the number of records desired in each corresponding data file. So, for example, if an individual has a MARC file of 10,000 records, and sets the MARCSplit Records per File setting to 100, the tool would create 100 data files, each with 100 MARC records.

The second mode allows individuals to simply shave off parts of a larger data file for further examination. For example, if an individual has a data file of one million records, rather than create hundreds or thousands of smaller MARC files, the individual might only want to shave off the first 10,000 records for examination. Users can check the # of files option in the MARCSplit tool (figure 4.7), and specify how many files should be generated by the split process. So, in the example, if we set the Records per file to 1,000, and asked to generate 10 files, MARCSplit would shave the first 10,000 records from the source file, generating 10 data files for review. MARCSplit will output the generated files into a new folder called "processed_files" located under the user-provided Destination Folder. The structure of the filenames generated by MARCSplit is msplit########.mrc. The file format is padded with zeros to enable files to sort numerically across all major operating systems. This allows users to avoid having to run data processing over an entire data file when only a subset of the file is necessary for evaluation.

The final data-processing mode is reserved for use cases when splitting a larger file into multiple files that contain just a single record per file. In those cases, MARCSplit will ask users if they would like to define the filename using information from a field/subfield combination. This way, users can output data tied to control numbers or any user-specified field.

FIGURE 4.7

MARCSplit: Limiting split to a specific number of processed files

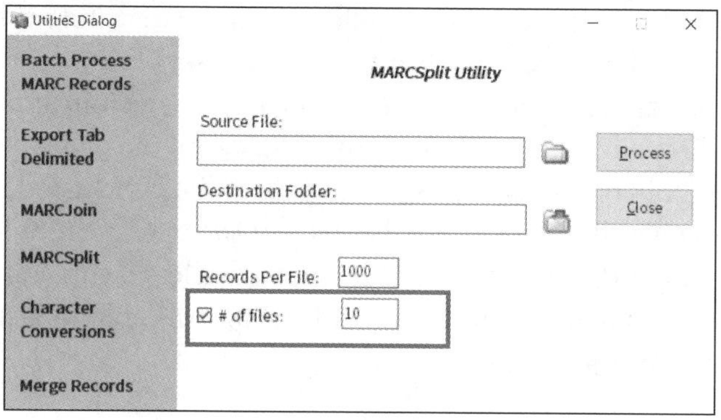

Joining Files

One of the natural outcomes of any large data migration is the generation of a large number of data files. These could be subsets of specific data, new data files, or the output from a previous process to split a larger file into smaller chunks. As the data processing comes to an end, it may be desirable to concatenating these data files back together into a more cohesive whole. MarcEdit includes a utility called MARCJoin that is designed for this type of operation.

MARCJoin is part of a suite of utilities that is located in the main application Tools menu. The tool has been designed to support a wide range of use cases. The tool allows you to

- Join selected MARC files to create a new data file.
- Join selected MARC files into an existing data file.
- Join all files of a specific type (as defined by file extension) in a folder to create a new data file.
- Join all files of a specific type (as defined by file extension) in a folder into an existing data file.
- Join all files of a specific type (as defined by file extension) in a parent and all subsequent subfolders to create a new data file.
- Join all files of a specific type (as defined by file extension) in a parent and all subsequent subfolders into an existing data file.

The MARCJoin tool determines the type of join and the files to join based on the parameters provided by the user. If a user selects an existing file as the Save File, the MARCJoin tool will ask if the file should be overwritten or if the change should be appended. This allows users to join data from multiple directories or multiple sources over an extended period of time, into a single "joined" file. Likewise, if a user checks the Join Individual Files option, MARCJoin will prompt the user to select the files to join. If the Join Individual Files option is unchecked, then the user is prompted to select the specific file type and parent folder that contains the files to join. Additionally, within this mode, users can select an option to process data only at the parent folder level, or navigate and join applicable data in all corresponding subfolders as well (figure 4.8). Given the wide range of joining options, MARCJoin provides access to a log file at the conclusion of the joining process that details all the files joined as part of the operation. When using the tool to join data at the parent folder or subfolder level, this log file provides crucial information detailing what data MarcEdit was able to locate and what data was successfully joined.

Extracting Selected Records

The Extract Selected Records tool in MarcEdit provides users with the ability to do much more granular extractions than with the simple MARCSplit tool. Rather than just breaking a large file up into a bunch of smaller files, the Extract Records tool provides users with the ability to extract data based on a wide range of search criteria.

 PRO TIP

A word about limitations: The Extract Selected Records tool utilizes a specialized listing element to display record information. This display element has a theoretical limit of approximately two billion items, although users will find themselves constrained by the amount of virtual memory available. If users find that they are running into limitations loading data, one method to overcome this obstacle is to split the records into three or four smaller files and then extract the subsets and join those records together.

This allows users to extract records that may be missing data, have data that need to be corrected, target specific subjects, call number ranges, and so on. The tool supports a wide range of search options, and has the ability to do searches via regular expressions and extract records based on multiple queries. Finally, the tool has a File mode that enables users to provide a file with multiple query statements, for example, thousands of ISBNs or record numbers for selection. Taken together, these tools provide a rich array of options that individuals can use to extract subsets of records for editing or evaluation.

The Extract Selected Records tool can be accessed from the main application's Tools menu (refer to figure 4.5). The Extract Selected Records tool (figure 4.9) provides a wide range of options—so many that users can sometimes become befuddled by the interface.

MARCJoin: Joining files by file type

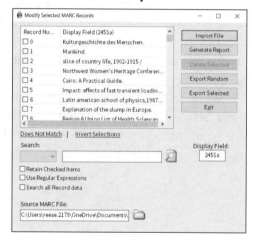

Extract Selected Records tool with sample data

Before looking at how an individual can use this tool, let's look at the options available and what they do.

Links

- **Does Not Match:** The Does Not Match link is a short cut to allow users of the application to select all the records in the file that does not have the defined display field within the record. This option is very useful when trying to isolate records that may be missing a field or field/subfield combination.
- **Invert Selections:** The Invert Selections link is a shortcut that allows users to invert the selected records. For example, if a user clicked on the Does Not Match link, all the records that did not have the specified display field

would be selected. That same user could click on the Invert Selections link and change the selected items from those records missing the display field to those records that have it in their records.

Buttons

- **Import File:** This button imports the data referenced in the Source MARC File into the tool. The tool selects the display field based on the information that the user enters into the Display Field textbox. A file must be imported into the utility before any other actions can be completed.
- **Generate Report:** This button will export a delimited list that includes the Record Number and Display Field data for the selected items.
- **Delete Selected:** This button is disabled. It is only enabled when using the Delete Selected Records tool. This tool isn't highlighted in this chapter, but it is functionally identical to the Extract Selected Records, except selected data is deleted, not extracted.
- **Export Random:** The Export Random button provides users with a mechanism to extract a random percentage of records from a file. This function is particularly useful when looking to spot-check records or record edits for quality. The user is prompted to define what percentage of the file to export for review.
- **Export Selected:** This button exports the selected items into a separate file. When selected, users have two options. The first exports only the data and leaves the exported records in the original source file. The second exports the records into a new file and deletes the exported records from the original source file.

Search Options

- **Search Options:** By default, users do not need to select anything from the Search dropdown box. Not selecting an option will limit searches made against the records *to the display field only*. If users want to utilize additional search options, they can select from the following search refinements:
  - » *Range*: Selects ranges of items. that.is, 1–6, 10–15, 20–455.
  - » *Field*: Using the following format: field number and optional subfield (i.e., 245$a), allows users to target a query to a specific field or field/subfield combination. This value does not have to be defined as the display field.
  - » *File*: Selects a file that contains search terms to query. Searches are run against the data in the display field, and support such use cases as querying for multiple control numbers, call numbers, or ISBNs.

» *Size*: Searches for records that are greater than or less than a specific size. This function comes in handy during data migrations when isolating temporary (brief) MARC records or an especially large (and possibly problematic) quantity of MARC data.

- **Search Qualifiers:** Select specific qualifiers when the user checks the appropriate check boxes:
  » *Retain Checked Items*: By default, each query will clear any selected items. If users want to perform multiple queries and retain the results from each subsequent search, this option should be selected.
  » *Use Regular Expressions*: MarcEdit will evaluate all queries entered into the search box as regular expressions. Regular expressions must follow the .NET regular expression language guidelines.
  » *Search All Record Data*: Searches across all record data (not just the data in the display field) for the specified query.

> **PRO TIP**
>
> As a C# application, MarcEdit utilizes C#'s regular expression language. Although the language is very similar to Perl 5's regular expression syntax, there are some very noticeable differences. Users interested in learning more about the .NET regular expression language should review https://msdn.microsoft.com/en-us/library/az24scfc(v=vs.110).aspx.

Examples

 QUESTION 1 How do I determine which records have two call numbers in the 090 field?

SOLUTION When working with the Extract Selected Records tool, MarcEdit utilizes an internal delimiter when the display field appears multiple times in a record. The delimiter "|end|," can be used as a convenient marker to identify records that have multiple versions of a display field. In the previous example, users would set the display field to 090$a and import the records. Then, utilizing the internal delimiter, they would search for the term "|end|" within the records. In the data used for this example, the screenshot (figure 4.10) shows the delimiter embedded within the selected record data.

FIGURE 4.10

Selecting records with multiple 090$a in a record

QUESTION 2 How do I target items that are coded as monographic computer files, or mm in the Leader at byte positions 6 and 7?

SOLUTION Although not applicable in every case, regular expressions offer the simplest method of querying against a field when an individual is only interested in evaluating specific data elements at a specific position. In this example, the user would set the display field to LDR to capture the data from the record leader. Although the MARC specification starts position counts at zero, .NET's regular expression language starts its count at 1, so when evaluating MARC positions 6 and 7, you'd use positions 7 and 8 within the regular expression. Because the user in this question is only interested in searching for data at a specific set of values, our regular expression will be quite simple, and written as ^.{6}mm.

Breaking down the expression, it should be easy to understand the pattern. The expression starts by using a caret (^), which tells the expression engine that evaluation will start at the beginning of the display field. The second value (.{6}) tells the regular expression engine that the next six characters can be ignored. In our case, we are only interested in evaluating the values that define the material type and form. The final two values (mm) represent the codes that would be used to identify the records, assuming the data is properly encoded. When combined, these elements would select the targeted data (figure 4.11).

FIGURE 4.11

Using regular expressions to evaluate data at an exact position

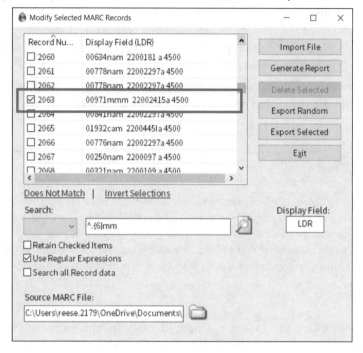

Data Validation

MARC can be incredibly fragile, in part due to its very rigid structure and the use of multiple character encodings found within records. MARC utilizes a leader/directory structure that has indicators and subfields along with a number of assumptions related to what makes a MARC record structurally valid. During data migrations, organizations will be working with many different metadata types, likely from many different sources—and it is not unusual for some of the data to become corrupted. Once that occurs, finding the individual MARC record within a file of 100,000 or more records can be incredibly difficult. What's more, because MARC is a block data structure, errors within MARC files tend to invalidate either the entire file or all records that follow a problem record in a file.

To simplify the process of data validation and enable individuals to quickly isolate problem records for later processing, MarcEdit includes a tool called the MARCValidator (figure 4.12).

The MARCValidator has three distinct functions:

1. Validate Records (Default)
2. Identify Invalid Records
3. Remove Invalid Records

Each of these functions perform a different type of validation on a set of MARC records. The first option, Validate Records (Default) (figure 4.13), provides a rules-based validation that determines if the fields, subfields, and indicators are utilized correctly. This validation function does not look at the structure of the records, but rather provides a report based on current MARC 21 rules for specific fields, subfields, and indicators. Users running this function can expect to receive a report upon completion that identifies individual records and potential errors in the record, according to the MARC 21 cataloging specifications.

 PRO TIP

The Validate Records (Default) option utilizes a delimited rules file for evaluation. This means that users can edit or replace the rules file, which opens up a wide range of validation opportunities. For example, when working with vendor files, users could create a custom rules file to ensure that specific data is always in a record. Users could also create rules files to identify records that are not RDA-compliant, or utilize pre-AACR2 encoding.

The second two validation options, Identify Invalid Records and Remove Invalid Records, specifically examine the structural validity of a MARC record (or records). These functions are designed to enable users to quickly identify which records may be structurally invalid, and also provides reports detailing the types of errors encountered and offers a method to remove the records and set them aside for processing at a later date.

When using these tools, MarcEdit will remove the structurally invalid records from the source file and move them to a separate data file in the same directory. This means that when the tool has completed its work, all the MARC records found within the original source file should be structurally valid and editable with any MARC editing software tools or programming libraries. The error file will contain the invalid MARC data as found in the original source file. Editing these data files may be more difficult, because some MARC editing tools require structurally correct data. Some tools, like MarcEdit and the MARC4J programming library, provide a pervasive mode that will enable a user to attempt to read structurally invalid data. Whether these tools can read the data will depend primarily on the severity and type of the structural errors.

Record Editing

Data cleanup workflows are the crux of any large data-migration process. No matter how clean or carefully curated one's metadata is, data migrations always

FIGURE 4.12

MARCValidator utility

FIGURE 4.13

Sample Validate Record report

```
Record #:  68
001 (if defined):  ocm36056764\
245 (if defined):  Creating a learning society :$binitiatives for education and
technology /$cAmy Korzick Garmer and Charles M. Firestone, rapporteurs.
Errors:
        0813-ind1:  Invalid data (\)  Indicator can only be 01.

Record #:  149
001 (if defined):  ocm02393225\
245 (if defined):  Living without gloves :$bmore letters of Simeon Stylites
[pseudonym].
Errors:
        0813-ind1:  Invalid data (\)  Indicator can only be 01.

Record #:  156
001 (if defined):  ocm25435513\
245 (if defined):  Freud :$bthe mind of the moralist /$cby Philip Rieff.
Errors:
        740-ind2:  Invalid data (1)  Indicator can only be b2.

Record #:  157
001 (if defined):  ocm01016316\
245 (if defined):  Philosophy and logical syntax,$cby Rudolf Carnap ...
Errors:
        0813-ind1:  Invalid data (\)  Indicator can only be 01.
```

require some data to be mixed, added, deleted, or modified. What's more, when a data migration involves multiple organizations or multiple data sources, the need to do large-scale data cleaning and editing prior to completing a migration increases. For any large data-editing project, multiple strategies are almost always in order. It's very rare that the entire data editing and cleanup process can be completed using a single set of tools or one set of scripts. As noted earlier in this chapter, a number of programming libraries exist to assist in these tasks. And as I'll note at the end of this chapter, MarcEdit provides an Application Programming Interface (API) for users who want to leverage MarcEdit's processing libraries directly via scripts or custom programs. But these options tend to require a great deal of programming knowledge and generally occur outside of an organization's cataloging department, where ideally the metadata expertise resides. It was partly for this reason that MarcEdit was developed. Although it has evolved and continues to do so, MarcEdit at its core has always been a tool designed to move batch metadata processing back into library cataloging departments. For organizations in the midst of a large data migration, these tools open the opportunity for catalogers with no programming knowledge, to handle complex data manipulations in batch, streamlining the data-migration process.

As noted, MarcEdit includes several tools and utilities designed to support a wide range of data editing tasks. However, the MarcEditor, a MARC-aware, batch metadata editor, sits at the core of the application. The MarcEditor (figure 4.14) provides users with a robust metadata editor that supports a wide range of global editing and reporting mechanisms.

FIGURE 4.14

MarcEdit's MarcEditor

PRO TIP

The MarcEditor has been designed to read large files using one of two data modes—as pages (with each page defaulting to one-hundred records per page) or in a preview mode. In the page mode, MarcEdit reads the entire file, counting the number of records and creating a map of the file in memory. This allows the tool to navigate extremely quickly between pages, but also includes a substantial penalty for very large files when it comes to re-indexing a file between global changes. This mode works best for file sizes up to ~200 MB. For larger file sets, MarcEdit includes a preview mode. This loads a small snippet of the file into the MarcEditor, but still supports all the global editing and reporting functionality. This mode has no file-loading penalties because the entire file is never read or indexed. As of this writing, the largest file set I've edited using the preview mode is ~4 TB.

The MarcEditor supports a wide range of different editing options, character encodings, and text orientations (figure 4.15).

FIGURE 4.15

MarcEdit's MarcEditor supporting right to left edit

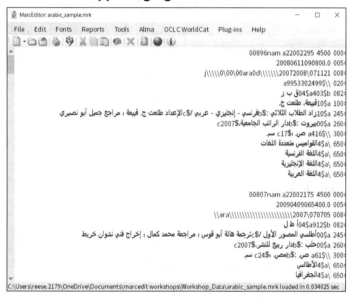

The tool has been designed to support MarcEdit's mnemonic-based language, a UTF-8 encoded language that when rendering MARC-8 data, replaces diacritics with mnemonic values. MarcEdit's mnemonic file structure (figure 4.16) utilizes the following data format:

- All fields begin with an "=" + tag (i.e., =100).
- Two blank spaces follow all "=" + tag combinations.
- Variable fields (fields >9) all must have indicators as defined in the leader.
- Comments begin with a "#"—this will be ignored when the record is compiled.
- All records must have a leader and directory field (LDR).
- Blank lines represent the end of a record.
- The "$" is a special character that represent field delimiters. The literal dollar sign is represented as a mnemonic {dollar}.
- "\" represents blank values in control fields and indicators.
- Full field format structure:
  » Equal sign + tag + two spaces + indicators + subfield data if applicable.

Global Editing Tools

MarcEdit's global editing tools rely heavily on the structure of the mnemonic file format to provide optimized editing processes as well as reliably read the data. If structural errors occur in the mnemonic file format during editing, MarcEdit's MARCValidator can be utilized to isolate and correct problems.

MarcEdit's MarcEditor has a wide range of editing tools and functions. For the purpose of this chapter, I'll limit the discussion to its eight principal global editing functions. Of those eight, I'll highlight the starred functions with comprehensive examples.

- * Global Replace
- * Add/Delete Fields
- * Build New Field
- Copy Field
- Edit Indicator Data
- Edit Field Data
- * Edit Subfield Data
- Swap Field Data

 PRO TIP

MarcEdit's MarcEditor can be automated utilizing a kind of lightweight macro recorder. MarcEdit's task manager and editor enables users to create tasks that can perform multiple data edits through a single keystroke. Although these may not be particularly useful for large data-migration projects, this functionality is vitally important for many organizations when handling the day-to-day work of loading vendor metadata. For more information, please see the following YouTube videos:

- https://www.youtube.com/watch?v=gmqTGfTubU4 for a summary of the Task Management tool

- https://www.youtube.com/watch?v=vOjGdkI_ft8 on chaining MarcEdit task together

FIGURE 4.16

MarcEdit's Mnemonic Text example

```
=LDR  01556cam  2200421 i 4500

=001  ocn945169933

=003  OCoLC

=005  20160804095616.0

=008  160317s2016\\\\maua\\\\\b\\\\001\0\eng\\

=010  \\$a  2016012601

=040  \\$aDLC$erda$beng$cDLC$dYDX$dOCLCF$dYDXCP$dOCLCO

=020  \\$a9781605354705$qhardcover

=020  \\$a1605354708$qhardcover

=035  \\$a(OCoLC)945169933

=042  \\$apcc

=050  00$aQL955$b.G48 2016

=082  00$a571.8$223

=100  1\$aGilbert, Scott F.,$d19410-$eauthor.

=245  10$aDevelopmental biology /$cScott F. Gilbert, Swarthmore
      College and the University of Helsinki, Michael J.F. Barresi,
      Smith College.

=250  \\$aEleventh edition.

=264  \1$aSunderland, Massachusetts :$bSinauer Associates, Inc.,
      Publishers,$c[2016]

=300  \\$axxiii, 810 pages, 100 variously numbered pages ;$c29 cm

=336  \\$atext$btxt$2rdacontent

=337  \\$aunmediated$bn$2rdamedia

=338  \\$avolume$bnc$2rdacarrier

=504  \\$aIncludes bibliographical references and index.

=650  \0$aEmbryology$vTextbooks.

=650  \0$aDevelopmental biology$vTextbooks.

=650  \7$aDevelopmental biology.$2fast$0(OCoLC)fst00891773

=650  \7$aEmbryology.$2fast$0(OCoLC)fst00908425

=655  \7$aTextbooks.$2fast$0(OCoLC)fst01423863
```

Global Replace

MarcEdit's global replacement tool (figure 4.17) provides users with an extremely flexible utility to perform a wide range of replacement functions. Like any normal text editor, the replace function can do regular in-string matching and replacements. These matches can be either case sensitive or insensitive, and can be used on a one-by-one basis, or as a single operation using Replace All. However, the replace function can do so much more. The replacement tool also supports .NET's regular expression language, allowing users to execute complex replacements based on regular expression criteria. This can be expanded by utilizing the Perform Find/Replace If . . . option. This option allows users to do a pre-search, using either an in-string or regular expression, to identify a subset of records prior to performing the find and replace. For example, if a user wanted to add the string "eb" to the end of the date in a call number, but only if the 020 identified that data as an ebook, the preprocessing function could be used to do this. By doing a regular expression search in the Perform Find/Replace If . . . , the user could isolate items with an ebook qualifier in the 020, and then perform a replacement on the 050/090 based on a set of regular expression criteria (figure 4.18).

Within the MarcEdit community, the replacement function serves as a type of Swiss Army Knife for data editing. When paired with regular expressions, the tool provides users the ability to modify any data in the record, using a wide range of criteria. Here are a couple of additional examples of how this tool can be used.

QUESTION How do I add a period to the end of a 500 field, but only when no other terminal punctuation exists on the field?

This is a common question that comes up on the MarcEdit e-mail list,[9] and can be easily accomplished using the replace function and a regular expression. The criteria would be as follows (figure 4.19):

> Find: (=500.*[^.-?])$
> Replace: $1.

OPTIONS Use Regular Expressions

EXPLANATION The Find textbox includes the specific search criteria. In this case, what is most important happens in the brackets. In a regular expression, brackets generally indicate a range of characters, like 0–9 or a–z. In this context, they represent the characters that are typically used for terminal punctuation in the 500 field. The ^ in the brackets indicates that the expression isn't looking for the characters in the range, but for items that don't have those characters. The $ at the end of the expression notes that this occurs at the end of the field. Iin total, the written expression says: match on any field that starts with =500.

Ignore all characters until the final character, and match only if the last character is not a ".," "-", or "?."

FIGURE 4.17

MarcEdit's Global Find/Replace function

FIGURE 4.18

Replacement example with pre-search option enabled

FIGURE 4.19

Replace Function example: Conditionally adding punctuation

QUESTION I have a 500 field with two subfields "a"s (i.e., =500 \\$aNote 1.$aNote 2). How can I split them into two fields?

Splitting fields tends to be necessary when moving data from an XML-based schema like Dublin Core into MARC. Using the above example, one would use the following criteria (figure 4.20):

> Find: (=500.{4})(\\$a[^$]*)(\\$a.*)
> Replace: $1$2\n$1$3

OPTIONS Use Regular Expressions

DESCRIPTION In this case, the expression needs to isolate the example 500 into three distinct data groupings. The first group should represent the field tag and the indicators. The second group, all the information in the first $a, and the third group, any remaining data. Because parentheses represent groups of characters, we use the parenthesis to designate the individual data groupings that we wish to create.

FIGURE 4.20

Replace Function example: Splitting data from one field to two fields

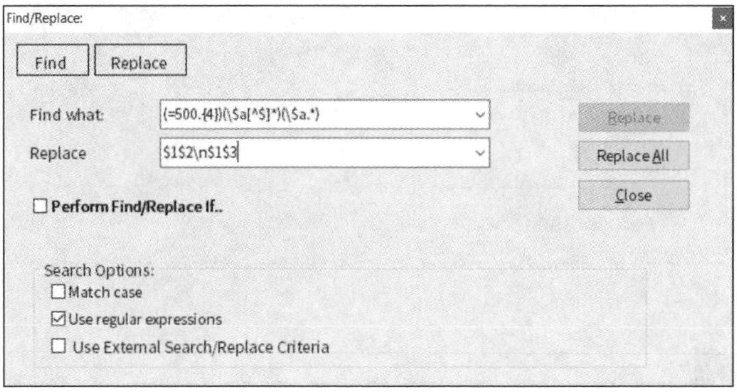

Add/Delete Field Data

MarcEdit's Add/Delete Field function enables users to globally add or remove a field. The function provides a wide range of conditional options that can support adding fields based on the presence of data, if it is not duplicate data, and deleting fields based on indicators, duplicate data, or data not matching a specific value. The tool breaks up its options (add versus delete options) based on position in the form (figure 4.21).

FIGURE 4.21

Add/Delete Global Editing function

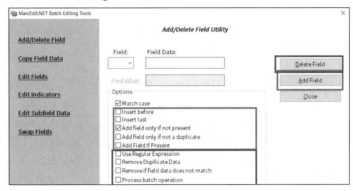

The tool has a wide range of available options that enable the tool to perform conditional adds and deletions. The options are:

- *Match Case*: Determines if any string matching will be case sensitive or in-sensitive. This option is applicable to both the Add and Delete function.
- *Insert Before*: Inserts new fields as the first field in a field group. That is, if inserting a 500 field, and there is a 500 field already in the record, the new field will be inserted before the existing field.
- *Insert Last*: Inserts new fields as the last field in a field group. That is, if inserting a 500 field, and there is a 500 field already in the record, the new field will be inserted after the existing field.
- *Add Field Only If Not Present*: Inserts the field only if the defined field is not present. In this case, the evaluation only occurs at the field group level. That is, if inserting a 500 field and selecting this option, the 500 field will only be inserted if no other 500 field is in the record.
- *Add Field Only If Not a Duplicate*: Inserts a field only if the defined field and its field data are not an exact duplicate of the field to be added. That is, if inserting a 500 field and selecting this option, the 500 field will only be inserted if no other 500 field and the field data is an exact match.
- *Add Field If Present*: Insert the field, but only if the defined secondary criteria are present in the record.
- *Use Regular Expressions*: This option only applies to the delete field function, and is used to evaluate fields for deletion.
- *Remove Duplicate Data*: Deletes fields that are either exact duplicates or, if field data criteria have been specified, duplicate the field criteria.
- *Remove If Field Data Does Not Match*: Delete all fields that do not match a specific set of field data.

- *Process Batch Operation*: A file containing search terms for deletion. This operation only applies to the delete field function.

With the above options in mind, here are a handful of common Add/Delete field examples from the MarcEdit e-mail list.

QUESTION How do I delete all the non-LCSH headings from a set of records?

This question occurs on the MarcEdit e-mail list often, and in various variations. In most cases, individuals are looking to remove specific headings like all MESH headings, or all FAST headings—but in some cases, the request is to remove all non-LCSH headings. What makes this example difficult is that depending on the scope of the deletion, this request may involve an evaluation of the field's indicators, or in the case of a specific data set, like FAST, just a specific subfield. For this example, let's look at both types of requests—one that deletes all non-LCSH headings and one that just target's FAST headings.

Delete criteria for all non-LCSH data (figure 4.22):

Field: 6xx
Field Data: ^=6.{5}[^0]

OPTIONS Use Regular Expressions

DESCRIPTION In the example above, the fields being targeted are all fields within the 6xx range. The tool seeks to evaluate the second indicator. In MARC 21, fields without a second indicator of zero would be indicative of non-Library of Congress subject data. Because the question above specifically asks about removing all non-LCSH data, we'll cast a wide net. In the example, the field box designates the fields that the regular expression will be run on. Users here can enter an exact field number, or use wild cards to designate groups of fields. By specifying 6xx, the tool has been configured to target all 600–699 fields for evaluation. The field data represents the regular expression that will be used to evaluate the data for deletion. We use a regular expression in this case, because we are specifically evaluating the second indicator, so we must evaluate a specific position within the field. There are many ways to do this. In this example, the expression denotes that we are looking at the 6xx series, and seeks to match any field that does not have a 0 in the second indicator. The expression could have also been written as: ^.{7}[^0]. This second expression doesn't explicitly name the fields being evaluated—so from a glance, it's less clear exactly what operation is being performed. But because this evaluation will only be run on the data designed by the field data designation, we can assume that this will evaluate only data in the 600–699 range.

However, if a user only wanted to target specific subject data for deletion, like FAST Subject fields, a regular expression would not be needed.

Delete Criteria for FAST Subjects (figure 4.23):

> Field: 6xx
> Field Data: $2fast

OPTIONS None

DESCRIPTION Unlike the first example, deleting a specific index generally requires just an evaluation of the data in a $2 field. As a result, a regular expression is not needed, and the field data can just include the very specific index data to be evaluated for deletion.

FIGURE 4.22

Delete Field example: Delete all non-LCSH fields in the 6xx range

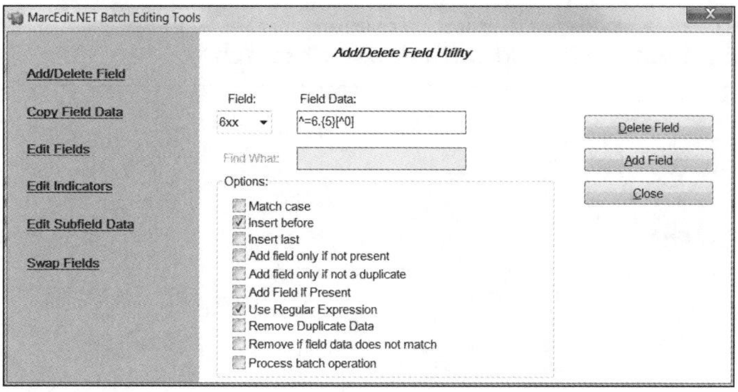

FIGURE 4.23

Delete Field example: Delete all FAST headings in the 6xx range

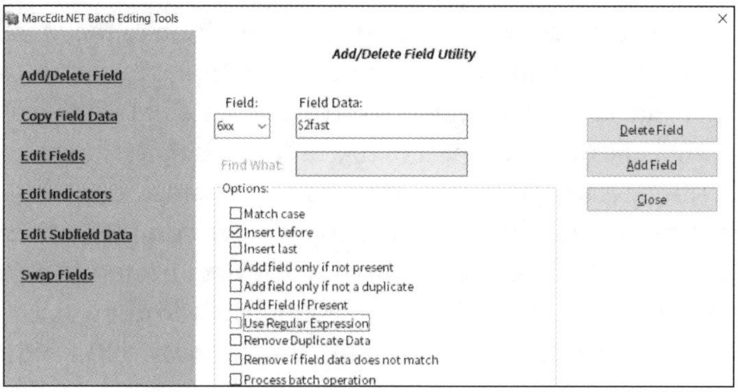

QUESTION   How do I delete an 856$u that doesn't include my proxy?

With the rise in availability of provider neutral MARC records, a number of organizations are now seeking to remove many of the 856 (URL) fields from records that don't directly pass through their organizations' proxies. To address this specific use case, the Remove if Field Data Does Not Match option was added. This option essentially allows users to evaluate a field for the presence of specific data, and if that data isn't present, delete the field. In the case of our example, users would query for their unique proxy domain. By using this option, any 856 that didn't include a reference to the organization's proxy would be deleted.

Delete if Does Not Match criteria (figure 4.24):

> Field: 856
> Field Data: my.proxy.edu

OPTIONS   Remove if field data does not match.

FIGURE 4.24

Delete Field: Remove if field data does not match

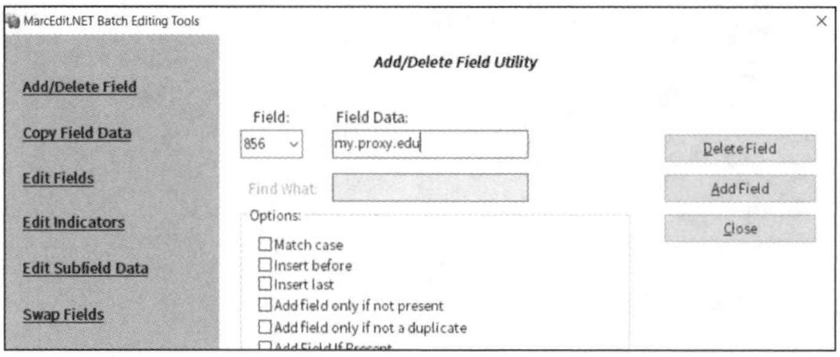

Build New Field

The Build New Field function is the most recent addition to the MarcEdit global editing toolkit. The function is also somewhat unique, in that it only creates new field data, and has been designed to create only a single field per execution. Additionally, the other unique aspect of this function is that it's based on patterns, that is, the utility has its own macro language and syntax.

The function was developed primarily to solve complex use cases where new field data needs to be created by extracting data from different parts of a record. A principal example of this can be seen when working with Innovative Interface's ILS software. Records loaded into the Innovative ILS require the use of a command-line string to design overlay, set item level call numbers, and so on. This information must be pulled from a variety of different fields or subfields. Prior to the inclusion of the Build New Field function, users would need to perform the creation of this field using multiple steps. Using the Build New Field tool, this can be accomplished in one operation.

The Build New Field tool works by using patterns. Users write out the entire MARC field that they wish to create, but use mnemonics to represent areas where data should be substituted from other fields or subfields. For example, if we were looking to put the data from the 001 in a new field, we would use the mnemonic {001} within the new field pattern. Likewise, if we wanted to extract the 090$a, we would use the mnemonic: {090$a} within the pattern.

💡 **PRO TIP**

In addition to mnemonics, the Build New Field tool also includes several data-manipulation functions. Using these functions, users can perform regular expression manipulations, extract substrings, and trim punctuation. These functions are documented at http://blog .reeset.net/archives/1853.

 How do I create a 949 field where both indicators are blank, and all data is in the $a, using the following format:

$aov={data from the 907$b};{data from the 001};{data from the 090}

This used to require multiple executions of MarcEdit's Swap Field function and then a final cleanup step to accomplish. However, using the Build New Field tool, this can be done by simply designating the pattern using the rules given above.

Build New Field Pattern (figure 4.25):

=949 \\$aov={907$b};{001};{090$a}

Copy Field Function

By default, MarcEdit's Copy Field function allows users to copy all the field and indicator data from one field to another. Copies result in the source data being deleted, unless otherwise indicated by the user. This function also includes a regular expression option that can be used to break up the copied field data, allowing for other some or parts of a field to be copied to a new location.

FIGURE 4.25

Build New Field example

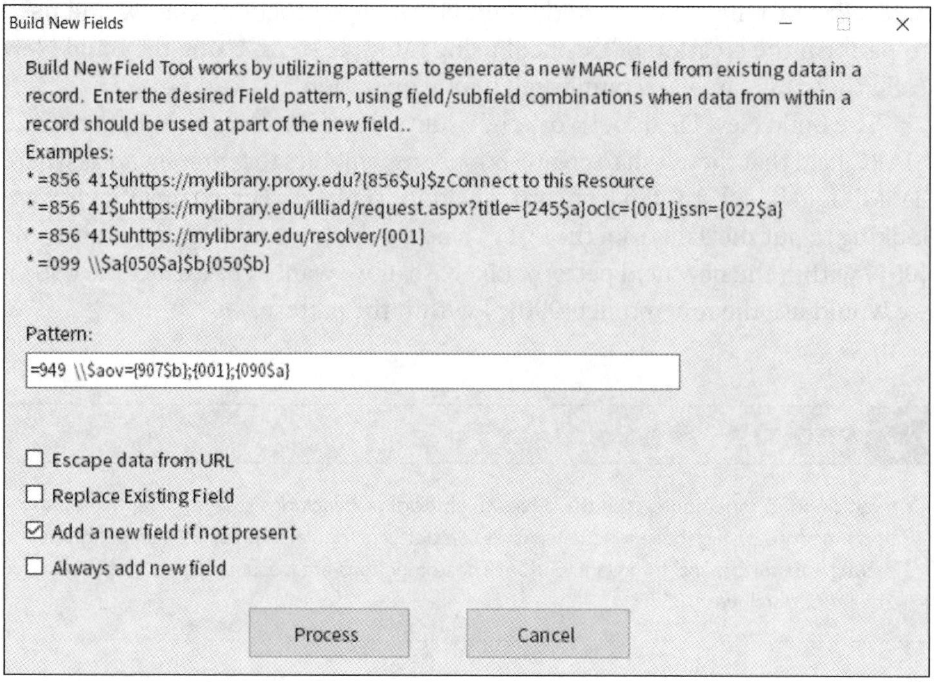

Build New Fields — ☐ ✕

Build New Field Tool works by utilizing patterns to generate a new MARC field from existing data in a record. Enter the desired Field pattern, using field/subfield combinations when data from within a record should be used at part of the new field..

Examples:
* =856 41$uhttps://mylibrary.proxy.edu?{856$u}$zConnect to this Resource
* =856 41$uhttps://mylibrary.edu/illiad/request.aspx?title={245$a}oclc={001}issn={022$a}
* =856 41$uhttps://mylibrary.edu/resolver/{001}
* =099 \\$a{050$a}$b{050$b}

Pattern:

=949 \\$aov={907$b};{001};{090$a}

☐ Escape data from URL
☐ Replace Existing Field
☑ Add a new field if not present
☐ Always add new field

Process   Cancel

Edit Indicators Function

MarcEdit's Edit Indicators tool enabled editing of just indicator values for specified fields. Users can utilize wild cards (*) to indicate when an indicator shouldn't be changed or for matching purposes.

Edit Field Data Function

The Edit Field Data function is a convenience function created to simplify certain types of field processing. When working with the Edit Field Data tool, the user can edit any data after the field subfield value. When using this field, indicator data is not accessible to the user and cannot be used as part of the find-and-replace process. If parsing indicator data is needed, users should utilize the general Replace function.

Edit Subfield Data Function

The Edit Field function supports the creation and deletion of subfields and subfield data. Prior to the creation of the RDA Helper, the Edit Subfield Data tool was the primary method used to generate general material designators (GMDs)

FIGURE 4.26

Edit Subfield Data function

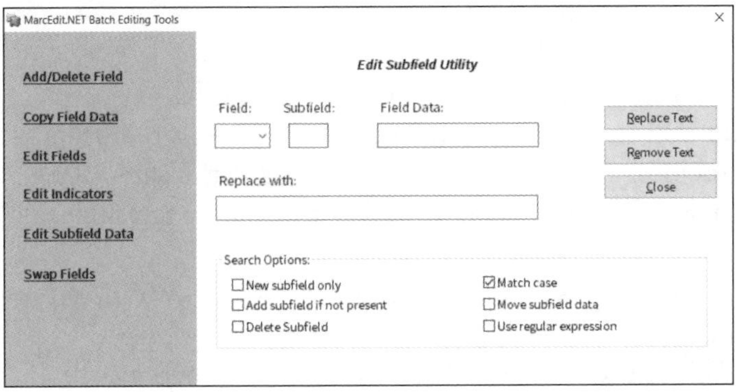

in MARC records. Although the RDA Helper has replaced that process, the Edit Subfield function continues to provide a method for user to edit, delete, or create new subfields (figure 4.26).

This tool is also a great illustration of how MarcEdit's design principles (MarcEdit is MARC-agnostic) can complicate editing tasks for MARC 21 users. In MARC 21, the placement of subfields within a field can have specific meaning. By default, MarcEdit places all new subfields at the end of the field. For users with ILS systems that don't assume display characteristics based on order or punctuation with the MARC record, this default behavior may have few, if any consequences. However, for most users, proper placement of subfield data is key to proper public display.

To support use cases where subfield positioning is important, MarcEdit includes a special conditional insertion syntax. MarcEdit recognizes the syntax and special processing instructions when brackets "[]" are present within the subfield textbox. Using the brackets, users define which subfields precede and which subfields follow the inserted data. For a real-world example, see below and figure 4.27.

FIGURE 4.27

Edit Subfield Data conditional insertion example

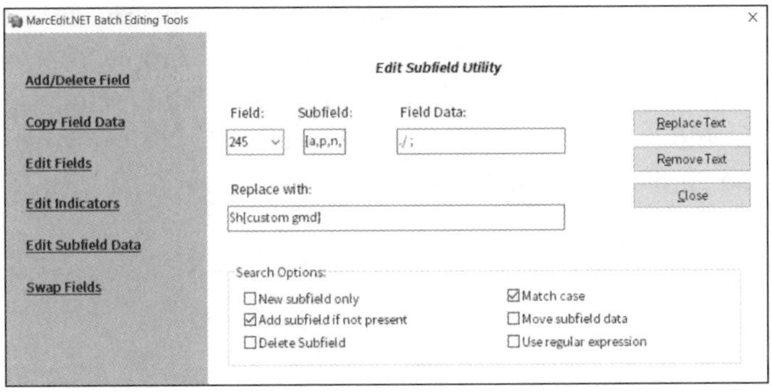

QUESTION I'd like to insert a custom (non-RDA) GMD into my records. However, I need this to come after the subfield a, p, and n; but before subfields b and c. How would I do that?

1. Field: Enter the field that you wish to modify.
2. Subfield: This is the biggest change. Subfields need to be bracketed so that the MarcEditor can apply the insertion rules to the data. Using the GMD as an example, the subfield data would be the following: [a,p,^c, ^b]. Breaking this down.
    » Brackets [ ]: This groups the arguments together. When using this function, data must always be bracketed.
    » ^: This tells the MarcEdit to insert the data before a specific field.
    » a,p: Tells the MarcEditor to do the following: insert subfield data before subfield p; if subfield p is not present, insert data before subfield a.
    » ^c, ^b: Tells the MarcEditor to insert subfield data before subfield b and subfield c.

3. Field Data: When in this mode, field data is used to note punctuation that should not be included when calculating field data.
4. Replace With: This is the subfield (or data) to insert.

QUESTION I need to update byte 6 in the LDR. How do I do that without writing a regular expression?

Because control fields don't have subfield codes, it might appear that this type of modification would require the use of a regular expression. However, the Edit Subfield function does provide a method to accommodate control field modification. When a value of less than ten is entered into the Field textbox, the subfield label automatically changes to reflect that edits will be done via position and length of data, not by subfield.

INSTRUCTIONS
1. Enter LDR in the Field textbox and tab to the subfield textbox.
2. When clicking on the subfields textbox, the label will automatically change to reflect the need for a numeric position beginning from zero. The format of this field is *position:length*. In the case of this example, this value would be 6:1. The Find Field and Replace Field boxes would include specific data to replace and the information that will replace it. If the change should be global, the Find box should be left blank.

See figure 4.28.

FIGURE 4.28

Edit Subfield Data editing control data example

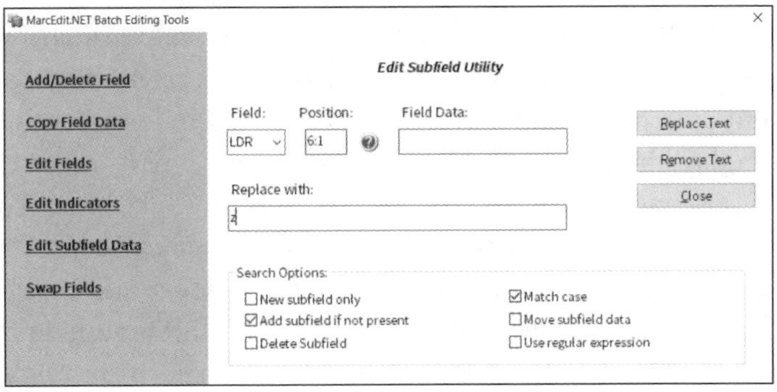

Swap Field Function

The Swap Field function is one of the oldest editing functions in MarcEdit. The tool has been designed to enable users to move data between fields and subfields. For example, if a user needs to add the 090$a to an existing 949 field and change the subfield code in the 949 to a $z, that would be possible. MarcEdit's Swap Field function exposes indicator data and field and subfield data, enabling users to build new fields from parts of other field data in the record.

PRO TIP

What is the difference between the Swap Field function and the Build New Field function? And when would I use each? This is a frequently asked question about these two tools—in part, because they can be used the same way in some cases. However, there are distinct differences between these two functions. First, the Build New Field function was designed to enable placing field data from multiple subfields within the same destination subfield. Likewise, the Build New Field tool utilizes patterns to outline the structure of the new field. The Swap Field function, on the other hand, just moves data between subfields within a record.

So when should we choose one over the other? Although these functions do overlap in many different use cases, the principal reason to utilize the Build New Field function is when field data must be output within the same subfield. Because the Swap Field function places "swapped" data into a new subfield, it is nearly impossible to merge data into an existing subfield using the Swap Field tool.

Working with Non-MARC Metadata

There was a time in the not too distance past when a migration of library data was exclusively a MARC records problem. Organizations were primarily concerned with moving record data between different ILS systems into consortia library systems—but always dealing with MARC records. However, those days have passed and today libraries store and maintain data in a wide range of tools and services. This also means that data migrations must now take into account library data stored in one of the many non-MARC, XML-based metadata formats used in libraries. This means that many data migrations will require a wide range of data transformations—moving data into and out of different metadata formats to normalize, organize, or merge data into various forms or systems.

As library metadata has diversified, so too have the types of metadata formats that can be utilized within MarcEdit. MarcEdit provides several specific tools to simplify metadata transformations between different library metadata formats, including providing templates to many well-known library metadata formats and providing a framework that enables metadata formats to be easily crosswalked between known formats without needing to do one-to-one data mapping between differing formats. Likewise, MarcEdit provides built-in tools, like the OAI Harvester, to simplify the processing and collection of metadata from disparate sources. This section will take a closer look at two specific areas in the MarcEdit application that support non-MARC metadata manipulation—the XML Functions/Framework and the OAI-PMH Harvester.

XML Functions/Framework

As library metadata standards are constantly evolving, so has MarcEdit. Although the tool may have primarily started as a MARC editing application to replace the Library of Congress's MARCBreakr/MARCMakr,[10] it has quickly evolved to support a wide range of XML processing. For most users, this integration is relatively seamless, showing up as available metadata functions within the MARC Tools utility (figure 4.29). The figure shows that outside of the first two options, all additional functions are built with MarcEdit's XML Framework—a set of tools and services that allow users to integrate eXtensible Stylesheet Language Templates (XSLT) or XQuery documents into the application to support metadata interoperability.

MarcEdit's XML Framework uses a very simple wheel-and-spoke model to support interoperability among metadata functions. The framework utilizes MARCXML as a control framework and supports the migration of data into and out of MARCXML. Utilizing a single control schema, MarcEdit can enable transformations between any registered XML format within needing to understand the one-to-one relationship between formats, simply because MARCXML acts

FIGURE 4.29

MARC Tools Window

as the communication layer between schemas. This means that as new metadata formats are added to the wheel, the user has the ability to crosswalk the new data format to any existing data formats.

So how does one register a new metadata schema into MarcEdit? The process is relatively straightforward. From the MARC Tools window (figure 4.29), users select the Tools menu and Edit XML Function list (figure 4.30). From this list, users can add, delete, or modify existing translations. Selecting Add opens a new dialog (figure 4.31) that guides the user through the process of defining an XML schema for use within MarcEdit.

Looking at figure 4.31, note a couple of specific elements:

1. *Function Alias*: This is the value that will appear in the XML Functions list in the MARC Tools window. This value should be descriptive and unique.
2. *XSLT Stylesheet Path*: Points to the XSLT path that provides the rules for translating data to and from MARCXML.
3. *Original and Final Format*: Essentially, MarcEdit fills many roles when moving data between XML formats and MARC. When starting from MARC, MarcEdit facilitates character-encoding conversions to UTF-8, as well as the binary data processing from MARC to MARCXML, before handing the process off to the XSLT processor to finish the translation. When ending in MARC, the

FIGURE 4.30

Finding MarcEdit's Edit Functions List option

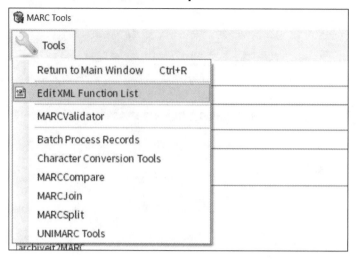

FIGURE 4.31

Adding a new XML Function to MarcEdit

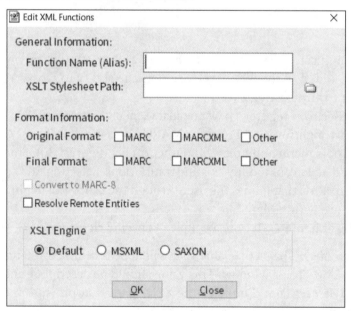

tool takes metadata the last mile, converting from XML into MARC's binary format. These options are important because they provide MarcEdit the information needed to understand how much facilitation will be necessary for the transformation between metadata formats.

4. *Resolve Remote Entities*: By default, MarcEdit doesn't resolve schema validation files (schemas or DTDs). The tool evaluates structural validity, but by default, assumes users have followed rules related to data validation per the metadata format's individual schema files. Users that wish to enforce schema validation can check this option—though it should be noted that because schemas are primarily web-based resources, users may be required to be online and maintain an active connection to complete the data transformation. When this option is checked, MarcEdit will not perform the data transformation until the remote entities have been resolved and validated.

5. *XSLT Engine*: MarcEdit supports two different XSLT engines—MSXML, the built-in XSLT engine provided by the .NET framework, and Saxon.NET; a .NET implementation of the popular Saxon engine. Both these engines provide fast and efficient data processing. The difference between the two engines has to do with data optimizations. The MSXML engine is optimized for use with XSLT 1.0 and XQuery 1.0. It has a smaller memory footprint and lower overhead, so for smaller data files (under 20 MB), it is significantly faster than the Saxon.NET engine. The Saxon.NET engine, on the other hand, supports XSLT 2.0 and 3.1 and XQuery 2+. It has a higher memory footprint and takes longer to initialize, but once started it is on par with the MSXML engine. For files over 20 MB, the difference between the two engines becomes negligible in most cases.

Once an XML function has been registered with MarcEdit, the transformation becomes available throughout the application (not just from the MARC Tools screen). This includes batch processing tools, harvesting tools, and so on—the application reuses the information provided by the user during the registration process to power a wide range of additional data-transformation functionality.

 PRO TIP

When MarcEdit is first installed, a handful of well-known XML transformations will be added to the MARC Tools window. However, these are just a small number of available XSLT style sheets provided with the application. Users can navigate to the XSLT Application folder and locate approximately forty different stylesheet templates that provide a wide range of data transformations and actions.

OAI-PMH Harvester

Built on top of MarcEdit's XML Framework, the OAI-PMH Harvester is a convenient tool that facilitates the capture and transformation of OAI-PMH data into MARC. The OAI-PMH Harvester can often be found on the main application window's menu, under Add-ins (figure 4.32). The OAI-PMH Harvester has two modes—one is a batch harvesting mode that is run via jobs, and one is a single-server harvesting mode.

FIGURE 4.32

Finding the OAI-PMH options

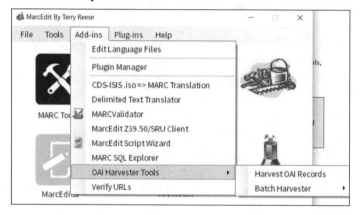

> ### 💡 PRO TIP
>
> MarcEdit's main window can be customized, so users can add links to their most commonly used applications to the main window. Users can customize this window to add shortcuts to the OAI-PMH client, as well as many other tools, by clicking on Preferences and selecting their desired application settings.

Batch Harvesting

MarcEdit can support batch OAI-PMH harvesting through the use of jobs. Users can create jobs by selecting from their list of configured OAI-PMH servers. This function was designed specifically for aggregators that regularly must harvest from multiple servers. Jobs can be run via the MarcEdit command line, and thus can be scheduled using Windows Scheduler, allowing these processes to be mostly automatic.

FIGURE 4.33

MarcEdit's OAI-PMH client

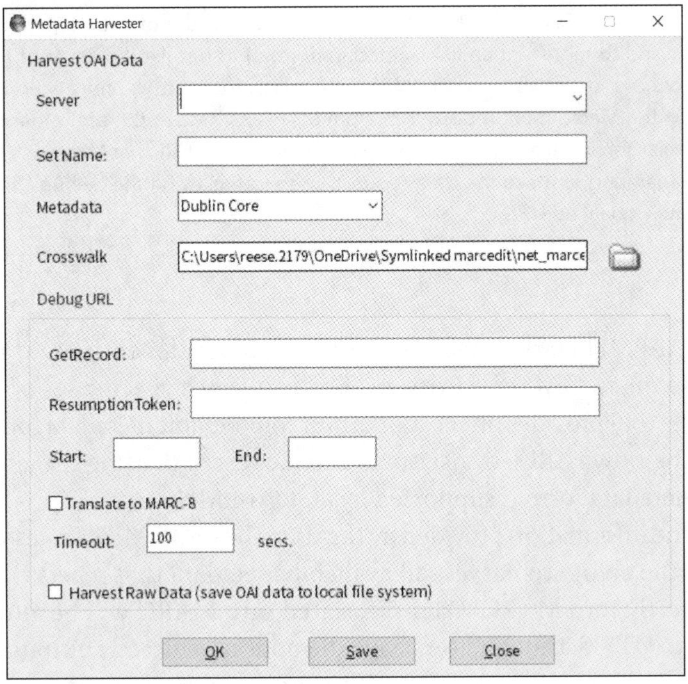

Single-Server Harvesting

MarcEdit's single-server harvesting mechanism is provided through MarcEdit's built-in OAI-PMH client (figure 4.33).

MarcEdit's OAI-PMH client provides users with a simple method for harvesting millions of records via OAI-PMH and translating the data directly to MARC. The client fully supports the OAI-PMH resumption token syntax, allowing the tool to harvest recursively from a server until all tokens have been processed.

By default, the tool provides support for the following OAI-PMH metadata formats:

- Dublin Core; metadata prefix: oai_dc—This is the default and baseline metadata support required for all OAI-PMH servers.
- OAI MARC; metadata prefix: oai_marc—At one point, this serialization of MARC data was popular in the OAI-PMH community. Today, this format is provided primarily for legacy server support.
- MARC 21 XML; metadata prefix: marc21—Provides support for MARCXML formatted data.

PRO TIP

When working with OAI-PMH, it is important to note that the metadata prefix identifier (the value used to represent an OAI metadata format), is not fixed outside of the oai_dc prefix. Therefore, users working with MARCXML data, for example, may need to change the value in the Metadata dropdown box from MARC 21 XML to the prefix identifier used by a particular service. If a user is interested in examining the URL that MarcEdit's OAI-PMH client is generating to make the data request, users can click on the Debug URL link and receive a fully qualified URL.

The OAI-PMH Harvester allows users to harvest an entire OAI repository, a specific set in an OAI repository, or data between a specific set of dates. And although the tool provides direct support for four default metadata formats, users can write their own XSLT translations and harvest data using the client for any available metadata format supported by an OAI-PMH server.

Using the information provided by the user, the OAI-PMH Harvester provides users with the ability to harvest all available metadata that meets the specified criteria directly into MARC. Data translated into MARC will be automatically converted to UTF-8, though users have the option to directly output the data in MARC-8 encoding as well. Additionally, users interested in obtaining copies of the raw XML metadata can forgo the data transformation, and utilize only the OAI-PMH Harvester to harvest the raw metadata and make it available to the user.

When harvesting, the tool will provide status outputs noting the number of records harvested and last resumption token processed. This information is also included on the final output screen, which is important information because many OAI-PMH servers have difficulty completing long-running processes. By having information on the last resumption token processed, users can restart a harvest using the last resumption token, restarting the process where it had stopped.

 PRO TIP

MarcEdit's OAI-PMH client has been used to harvest very large collections, including the entire HathiTrust corpus. However, the HathiTrust is a great example of a server that has trouble completing large requests. In most cases, large requests to this service eventually stop. However, using the last resumption token processed, users can restart the client and pick up where they left off by adding the last resumption token processed to the ResumptionToken textbox in the OAI-PMH Client.

PRO TIP

Harvesting errors sometimes happen. When the error occurs as part of the OAI-PMH harvest, the server will provide an error code and MarcEdit will display it as part of the final
harvest report. Sometimes errors are more subtle, as when a transformation error occurs
when converting data provided by the OAI-PMH server to MARC. This data will often show
up as blank data. Using a tool like Oxygen to test a raw harvested file against the provided
style sheet can quickly determine if the issue is related to the style sheet, the data being
provided by the server, or the communications with the client.

Merging Record Data

Data migrations are rarely simple or straightforward. As discussed in this chapter, data may come from a wide range of sources and systems—all needing to
be accommodated, translated, cleaned, and prepared for migration. One of the
more complicated aspects of working with data from multiple systems is the need
to merge or run deduplication routines across large sets of record data. Ideally,
this is the kind of processing that a new bibliographic management system
would support and facilitate, but this generally isn't the case. More often than
not, organizations are put in positions where they need to do large-scale data
merges between varying record sets to ensure that all necessary data is present
prior to doing record loading.

One common example that occurs regularly within the library community is
around reconciliation services like those offered by OCLC. Organizations with
bibliographic data that is missing OCLC control numbers, may send their data
to OCLC for evaluation. Once this process is run, however, organizations are
stuck trying to figure out how to get the numbers provided by OCLC into their
local bibliographic data. But this is just one example. Organizations may want
to merge access points, localized descriptions, call numbers, or need to merge
duplicate records into a single bibliographic record. There are a wide range of
use cases where data merging may occur, and these processes can be difficult if
no singular control number exists within a set of records.

MarcEdit provides a Merge Records tool (figure 4.34) that provides a wide
range of merging options for organizations needing to combine large sets of data.

MarcEdit's Merge records supports two very different data workflows. The
first involves merging of bibliographic record data from two separate files, while
the second workflow supports the merging and collapsing of duplicate record data
within a single large file. Both workflows are described and documented below.

FIGURE 4.34

MarcEdit Merge Records tool

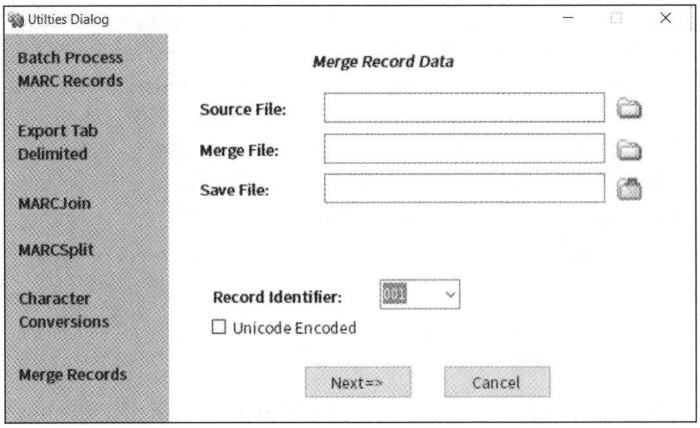

Merging Data from Multiple Data Files

MarcEdit's Merge Records tool supports the ability to extract user-defined data elements from one data file and merge the results into another. In the MarcEdit application, these files would be known as the Source File (the source bibliographic records), the Merge File (the file with the data to be captured and merged into the source records), and the Save File (the final merged output). MarcEdit's merge data process will not let users overwrite their existing source data—this was designed as a safeguard, so that if the merge process doesn't work exactly as expected, users can return to their original source and merge files and try again.

MarcEdit's merge process has a couple of different options. The first option is a well-defined merge data point. MarcEdit predefines some of these, including the 001, 020$a, and 035$a fields. These data points represent control numbers that generally can be utilized as good match points between bibliographic records. What's more, MarcEdit provides some additional data processing around the use of OCLC control numbers as match points. Given the ubiquity of OCLC data in libraries, the OCLC control number in the 001 field can often be the best match point. However, because OCLC bibliographic records can be merged and local systems can move this data into the 035$a field, MarcEdit provides special processing instructions when using the 001 as a match point. When using the 001 field, MarcEdit will evaluate the data, and if the data is determined to be an OCLC number, will also utilize the 019 (replaced or merged OCLC numbers) and the 035$a fields when evaluating record data for merging. By including multiple fields when doing OCLC control number matches, MarcEdit can ensure that legacy data can be successfully and efficiently merged with current bibliographic data—even though the current bibliographic data may have a different OCLC number due to a record merge or deletion.

In addition to MarcEdit's predefined merge fields, users can edit the merge criteria directly. If an organization wanted to use the title (MARC field 245$a) as the match point, a user could simply enter 245$a into the merge field and MarcEdit will treat the specified field data as a hybrid control number, normalizing the data (punctuation and letter casing) for data-matching purposes.

The final merge option is what is called MARC 21. This option is a heuristic algorithm that evaluates metadata from roughly twenty different metadata fields. The tool assigns a score to the various match points, creating a confidence level that is then used to determine a match. Users can modify the match points, select the items that are of most important, and remove data points that may cause conflicting results.

 PRO TIP

Modifying the MARC 21 merge options can sometimes be a tricky prospect. Think of the algorithm that runs the evaluation as a scale—each time an item is removed from one side of the scale, it must be rebalanced on the other side. There are cases when working with brief data, that removing too many options from the MARC 21 algorithm can result in an unbalanced equation causing false positives. Because of this, users should proceed with caution when removing large numbers of criteria from the MARC 21 merge option.

The final merge option relates to how data is evaluated by the merging algorithm. By default, MarcEdit's merging mechanism evaluates all record data in binary. By and large, this approach is both fast and accurate. However, when working primarily with multipart languages (e.g., Arabic, Hebrew, or most Asian languages), the process may not be ideal. Because the algorithm isn't doing exact matching, but rather like matching, multibyte data can be confusing and cause false merging. To solve this issue, users should note that the data is Unicode. By selecting this option, the tool shifts the matching mechanism from binary-based to character-based. Because all character-based matching is culture-sensitive, it supports exact and like matches when using multibyte languages, though it can be used for all merge operations. The trade-off with this approach is that data processing is slightly longer because data must now be evaluated as individual characters and not the component bytes that might make up a character.

Once the merge options are selected, the user defines the data to be merged. Selecting the next button opens the field selection options (figure 4.35).

MarcEdit's Merge Field selection allows users to select any field found within a record for merging. Additionally, users have the option to select additional processing prior to completing a field merge. For field data such as subjects, call numbers, or descriptions, users may wish to have MarcEdit evaluate the data for

FIGURE 4.35

Merge Record Field selection

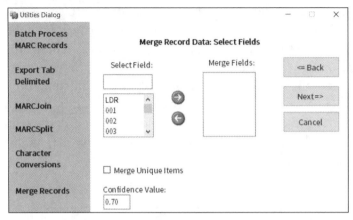

uniqueness prior to merging the data into a record. Users can check the Merge Unique Items option, which forces MarcEdit to evaluate both the source record and the merge record to determine that all data being merged into the source record are indeed unique. This can allow users merging data from multiple data sources to merge data-like subjects, and only merge the unique record data from the various disparate sources.

The final option available to users is the confidence value. MarcEdit's MARC 21 process generates a confidence score, and if that score falls below the confidence value, the record data will not be merged. There may be times when it is desirable to lower the confidence level to enable record merging; for example, a title like "12 Monkeys" versus "Twelve Monkeys." While MarcEdit's merge tool would identify a close match (due to the title being two words with one in common), the title would not merge because of the "12" versus "twelve." Users who are very familiar with their bibliographic data have the option to adjust the confidence value to enable matches to take place, despite these types of data normalization and entry differences.

 PRO TIP

Due to the nature of the matching algorithm, 70 percent tends to be the "sweet spot" when doing evaluation and eliminating false matches. However, if users notice significant numbers of false positives, this value can also be raised so that the program requires a more stringent set of matching criteria before merging record data.

Merging Duplicate Data in a Single File

The second use case MarcEdit's Merge Records tool supports is the ability to merge duplicate records into a single record. In this case, all options discussed above are the same (setting the merge field, selecting fields to merge, unique data options, Unicode evaluation options, etc.). The primary difference is found in the source, merge, and save files. When an individual has a large bibliographic data file with a number of duplicates that need to be merged, the user can set the source file and the merge file as the same file. When MarcEdit evaluates data for merge, the first operation that the application completes is an evaluation of the source file and the merge file. If these values are identical, the tool will assume that duplicate records exist in the source file, and that data in the duplicate records needs to be merged into a source record. By merging and collapsing the duplicate records, MarcEdit essentially deduplicates the file, while enabling the user to merge and keep unique data from multiple duplicate records in a single master record.

Beyond the Editor

MarcEdit provides a lot of tools and utilities to support a wide range of data-migration options—but what happens when you need to go beyond the stock tools? For organizations doing large-scale data migrations, this question will come up, and often. Although MarcEdit provides many of the resource organizations will need to migrate their records, the fact remains that sometimes data migrations can become very complex, leading organizations to look for a range of tools to handle specific data-processing tasks.

Fortunately, one of MarcEdit's strengths has always been its ability to integrate with other software and workflows. The tool provides several methods to move data into SQL tables, export for use in other third-party tools like OpenRefine, and expose a set of APIs that can be utilized by programmers to extend MarcEdit's built-in functionality to support custom data-migration needs. The remainder of this chapter will focus on these three potential use cases.

OpenRefine Integration

As noted in chapter 3, OpenRefine is a powerful text-processing tool that can be utilized to bring structure to very chaotic data. However, using OpenRefine when working with library data can involve a steep learning curve. This is primarily because OpenRefine doesn't understand MARC, and the processes used to move data into and out of OpenRefine are not well-suited for library data. Yet there are many data-processing tasks that simply work best within a tool like OpenRefine. In the past, users interested in working with OpenRefine would need to create their own import and export routines, which considerably limited the number of individuals that could work with these tools and added a very high barrier when working with library data. As a result, the use of OpenRefine has primarily been reserved for working with data that would be used outside of library systems or for reporting.

Enter MarcEdit. In early 2016, MarcEdit introduced a workflow for moving library data into and out of the OpenRefine application. This workflow ensures that data can be easily extracted, modified via OpenRefine, and then reassembled back into MARC. Additionally, MarcEdit's integration allows users to easily shift between multiple editing spaces. Users can edit data in the MarcEditor, then extract the results into OpenRefine, perform edits, and then re-import the data back into the MarcEditor for further work. This level of integration has opened new editing opportunities and potential workflows for metadata librarians.

Discussion of OpenRefine is out of the scope of this chapter (see chapter 3 for information on working with OpenRefine); understanding the integration process is not. In MarcEdit, OpenRefine integration can be a stand-alone tool or as a part of the MarcEditor. We'll look at the stand-alone tool. Users will find the stand-alone tool under the Tools menu in the main application window (figure 4.36).

MarcEdit's OpenRefine Import and Export tool supports two different Open-Refine Import/Export options: JSON and Tab Delimited format.

The Import and Export tool has been designed to be extremely simple (figure 4.37).

FIGURE 4.36

Finding MarcEdit's OpenRefine integration

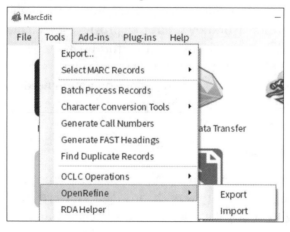

FIGURE 4.37

MarcEdit's OpenRefine Import/Export utility

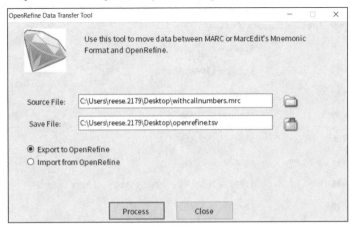

Users simply tell MarcEdit if they are doing an import or export process, and the format of the file that they wish to process or generate. And that's pretty much it. Once generated, users can follow the standard practices for importing data into and exporting data from OpenRefine.

QUESTION But how does MarcEdit retain relationships between records and files? And how are these relationships represented in OpenRefine?

To understand this process, let's look at some data. When a user runs a MARC record through MarcEdit's OpenRefine exporter, the following tab-delimited formatted file is generated (figure 4.38).

MarcEdit generates a report that breaks down the MARC record into four columns. The first column is RecordNumber. This value is how MarcEdit retains information about field/record relationships. This column should also be a cue for data wranglers who want to evaluate data between records or within records. The second value is Tags. This value represents the three-digit alphanumeric tag value found in the MARC record. Finally, the tool outputs two final columns: Indicators and Content. For the purposes of the delimited file, indicators are placed into a single column (because indicator values can range from 0–9 bytes) and the Field content is placed into the Content column.

QUESTION Does MarcEdit validate data when importing from OpenRefine?

The answer to this question is yes. When working with variable and control field data, MarcEdit knows the minimum requirements for data values that should

FIGURE 4.38

Sample MarcEdit OpenRefine output

```
RecordNumber TagsIndicators Content

1       LDR             01186nam  22003258a 4500

1       001             ssj{bsol}000566787

1       003             WaSeSS

1       005             20120915070148.0

1       006             m\\\\\\\d\\\\\\\

1       007             cr\cnu---auuuu

1       008             110912s2012\\\\nju\\\\\sb\\\\001\0\eng\d

1       010     \\      $a  2011032490

1       020     \\      $a9781119991519

1       035     \\      $a(WaSeSS)ssj0000566787

1       040     \\      $aDLC$cDLC$dWaSeSS

1       042     \\      $apcc

1       050     00      $aTK7882.I6$bL84 2012 ebook

1       082     00      $a621.39/87$223

1       100     1\      $aLueder, Ernst,$d19313-

1       245     10      $a3D displays$h[\lectronic resource] /$cErnst Lueder.
```

PRO TIP

The OpenRefine integration utility can be added as a shortcut (and icon) to the main window. Users that find themselves moving data between MarcEdit and OpenRefine often can open MarcEdit's preferences and select the OpenRefine Import/Export tool be added to their main screens.

PRO TIP

MarcEdit's OpenRefine Exporter provides support for OpenRefine's two primary import formats, JSON and Tab Delimited format. So, which one should you choose? That is a great question, and the answer really depends on your data. Although the JSON format is much cleaner and captures some relationship information found in the MARC data, it's also extremely memory-intensive to process. In working with OpenRefine, I've found a good rule of thumb: if the JSON output file is > 20 MB it's better to use the Tab Delimited options. Although OpenRefine can import very large JSON files, the import process requires that all data are loaded into memory for validation purposes. This results in significant virtual memory usage, which on larger file sets often cause OpenRefine to generate out of memory errors.

be in these fields. When importing data back from OpenRefine, MarcEdit will validate the data, actively correcting information when the data requirements are not met. At the same time, MarcEdit will not remove data that is technically invalid but has been assigned by the user. For example, according to the MARC specification control fields (fields 0–9) cannot have indicators. However, some ILS systems treat these values as variable length fields, so they contain subfields and indicators. MarcEdit will not remove the indicators or subfields from this data, even though this type of field usage is invalid. At the same time, if on import MarcEdit identifies a variable field missing the minimally required two indicators, it will autogenerate the missing content by creating undefined (blank) elements for the missing values.

MARC SQL Explorer

In addition to OpenRefine, sometimes users will want to export their MARC data into SQL data for further examination. To support this use case, MarcEdit includes a tool call the MARC SQL Explorer (figure 4.39).

The MARC SQL Explorer provides a built-in method for exporting data from MARC into SQL. The tool currently supports two SQL databases, SQLite (built in and provided by default in MarcEdit) and MySQL. When working with MySQL, the database can either be local on the user's machine, or a remote database.

FIGURE 4.39

MARC SQL Explorer

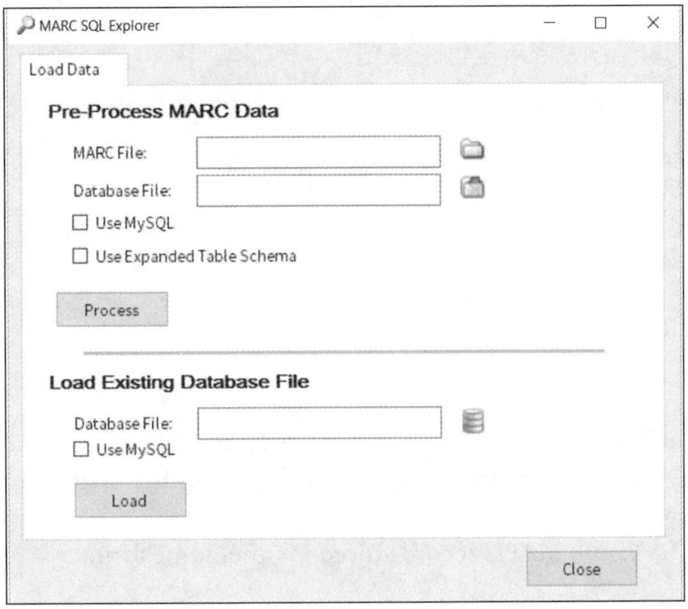

When exporting data into SQL, MarcEdit provides two table schemas. The first is a simple table schema that outputs data into two tables.

Basic Database Schema:
Table:
> MARC_DB

Schema:
- id INTEGER PRIMARY KEY: This is the unique database key for each record
- title TEXT: Pulled from the MARC record, title as identified in the MarcEdit Preferences
- marc TEXT: Full MARC record stored in mnemonic format

Description:
Table:
> MARC_FIELDS

Schema:
- cid INTEGER: Foreign key, links to the MARC_DB:id value
- fid as INTEGER: Primary key representing field in a record
- field TEXT: Field tag
- ind1 TEXT: Indicator 1 value if applicable
- ind2 TEXT: Indicator 2 value if applicable
- subfield TEXT: Subfield value if applicable
- field_data TEXT: Field data representing a control field or the specified subfield

Within the basic database schema, users can link the MARC_FIELDS and the MARC_DB tables together via the MARC_FIELDS:cid and the MARC_DB:id fields. These are the linking keys between the tables.

Extended Database Schema:
Table:
> MARC_DB

Schema:
- id INTEGER PRIMARY KEY: The unique database key for each record
- title TEXT: Pulled from the MARC record, title as identified in the MarcEdit Preferences
- marc TEXT: Full MARC record stored in mnemonic format

Table:
> T0x10-T9xx

Schema:

- cid INTEGER: Foreign key, links to the MARC_DB:id value
- fid as INTEGER: Primary key, representing field in a record
- field TEXT: Field tag
- ind1 TEXT: Indicator 1 value if applicable
- ind2 TEXT: Indicator 2 value if applicable
- subfield TEXT: Subfield value if applicable
- field_data TEXT: Field data representing a control field or the specified subfield

In the extended database schema, MarcEdit will generate eleven tables, with each field type grouped together. This enables users to do very complicated data analysis between field groupings using table joins or embedded SQL statements.

MarcEdit's SQL Explorer provides a simplified SQL client that supports the ability to query data and export the results either in MARC or various delimited file formats. At the same time, users can utilize their own SQL clients or utilities to work against the MarcEdit-generated database to perform whatever field edits or report generation for which they can write the SQL statements. Additionally, MarcEdit's MarcEditor can be connected directly to data files created by the SQL Explorer, allowing users to search for data via SQL or predefined indexes, import the data into the MarcEditor, and then save the data back to the database. This provides another level of integration between MarcEdit and various data-management tooling that can be used to help users seamlessly move between different metadata editing environments.

 PRO TIP

> Although MarcEdit's SQL Explorer was designed specifically to work with MarcEdit's SQL table schemas, users can point the client at any SQLite or MySQL database and connect to the database. What's more, if the database includes MARC data, MarcEdit can export that data for use within MarcEdit.

MarcEdit Application Programming Interfaces

When MarcEdit was first developed, it was just a set of programming libraries. The MarcEdit application, as most people know it, has evolved over a period of years to provide a graphical interface on top of the programming libraries. Because of this, users with programming experience can take advantage of MarcEdit's underlying data components to create their own new tools or workflows.

To help guide users through this process, MarcEdit provides a script generator and templating tool called the Script Wizard (figure 4.40).

MarcEdit Script Wizard

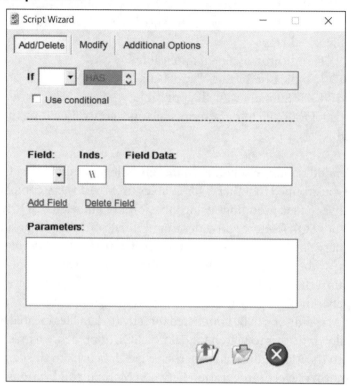

The Script Wizard provides a graphic interface that allows users to specify specific actions, which will be turned into code for the user. As a tool, the Script Wizard's functionality is lightweight and limited, but its primary purpose wasn't to be a script-writing tool, but a templating tool for users interested in interacting with MarcEdit's API. The tool has the capacity to generate script templates in both VBScript and Perl, and generates functions and stubs that can be used to interact with the various parts of the application. For example, here are two functions that demonstrate how to "break and make" MARC data, as generated by the Script Wizard.

VBSCRIPT

```vbscript
'========================================================
'FUNCTION/SUB: Marc_Break
'Description: Encapsulates the MarcBreaker functions
'========================================================
Function Marc_Break(source, dest)
Dim obj_MB
Dim lret
if fso.FileExists(source)=false then
msgbox "Local MarcFile Could not be located. Quitting"
wscript.quit
end if
Set obj_MB=CreateObject("MARCEngine5.MARC21")
lret=obj_MB.MarcFile(source, dest)
set obj_MB=Nothing
Marc_Break=lret
end Function
'========================================================
'FUNCTION/SUB: Marc_Make
'Description: Encapsulates the MarcMaker Functions
'========================================================
Function Marc_Make(source, dest)
Dim obj_MK
Set obj_MK=CreateObject("MARCEngine5.MARC21")
lret=obj_MK.MMaker(source, dest)
Set obj_MK=Nothing
Marc_Make=lret
end function
```

PERL

```perl
#=========================================================
#FUNCTION/SUB: Marc_Break
#Description: Encapsulates the MarcBreaker functions
#=========================================================
sub Marc_Break {
my $source = $_[0];
my $dest = $_[1];
my $obj_MB;
my $lret = 0;
if (-e $source) {
$obj_MB = Win32::OLE->new('MARCEngine5.MARC21')
or die "Cannot start Marc21 Object.\n";
$lret = $obj_MB->MarcFile($source, $dest);
return $lret;
} else {
die ("Local MARC file could not be located. Quitting.");
}
}
#=========================================================
#FUNCTION/SUB: Marc_Make
#Description: Encapsulates the MarcMaker Functions
#=========================================================
sub Marc_Make {
my $source = $_[0];
my $dest = $_[1];
my $obj_MK;
my $lret = 0;
if (-e $source) {
$obj_MK = Win32::OLE->new('MARCEngine5.MARC21')
or die "Cannot start Marc21 Object.\n";
$lret = $obj_MK->MMaker($source, $dest);
return $lret;
} else {
die ("Local MARC file could not be located. Quitting.");
}
}
```

MarcEdit's Script Wizard demonstrates how to interact with MarcEdit via its COM object interface. This interface has been documented and is available at http://marcedit.reeset.net/marcedit-com-api-documents.

CONCLUSION

MarcEdit is a powerful tool that allows you to read, analyze, clean, modify, and create MARC files as well as perform many other functions. It integrates with many library systems as well as other tools such as OpenRefine. Designed to work with very large files, it can read, write, and convert several formats and is an invaluable aid in migrations.

NOTES

1. *Wikipedia, The Free Encyclopedia,* s.v. "MARC Standard," https://en.wikipedia.org/wiki/ MARC_standards.
2. ISO-2709-2008; renewed and confirmed 2016. "Information and documentation—Format for information exchange," www.iso.org/iso/iso_catalogue/catalogue_tc/catalogue_detail .htm?csnumber=41319.
3. "MarcEdit," http://marcedit.reeset.net/.
4. "2015 MarcEdit Usage," http://blog.reeset.net/archives/1966.
5. Ibid.
6. "OAI-PMH," https://www.openarchives.org/pmh/. "Marc-8 Character Encoding," *MARC 21 Specifications for Record Structure, Character Sets, and Exchange Media,* http://loc.gov/marc/ specifications/speccharmarc8.html.
7. "Character Sets and Encoding Environment: Part 2: MARC 8 Encoding Environment," http://loc.gov/marc/specifications/speecharmarc8.html.
8. "Unicode Normalization Forms," www.unicode.org/reports/tr15/.
9. "MarcEdit Listserv," https://listserv.gmu.edu/cgi-bin/wa?A0=marcedit-l.
10. "About MarcEdit," http://marcedit.reeset.net/about-marcedit.

BIBLIOGRAPHIC AND ITEM DATA

Kelley McGrath, Metadata Management Librarian, University of Oregon

M igrating data to a new ILS is a massive undertaking during which you will inevitably encounter problems with bad data and data mapping. In this chapter I discuss common pitfalls to be aware of when preparing bibliographic and item data for migration and suggest methods for mitigating potential problems.

SYSTEM ARCHITECTURE

One of the most difficult, but most important, tasks for a successful migration is learning as much as you can about the structure of the system that you're migrating to and how its parts work together. Understanding its workflows and how they use different pieces of information, as well as what data points affect the discovery interface, is key for making migration-related decisions. These differences can be at a very fundamental level, such as the way different types of records are related to each other. In some systems, both holdings and item records are attached directly to bibliographic records, whereas in others items are attached to holdings records, which are then connected to bibliographic records (figure 5.1).

FIGURE 5.1

Bibliographic, holdings, and item records structure

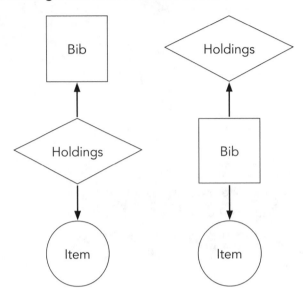

If you are migrating from a system where items are attached to bibliographic records to one where they are attached to holdings, there is a potential for problems connecting the migrated items to the correct holdings records. In addition, assumptions that work in your current system may not hold in the new one. For example, your current system may not require item records in situations where your new system does, such as when receiving new items on continuing resource records or for proper display to the public. It may be easier to add these records in your current system prior to migration. An additional benefit of making these kinds of adjustments pre-migration is that things will immediately function correctly in your new ILS.

One of the most difficult, but most important, tasks for a successful migration is learning all you can about the structure of the system that you're migrating to and how its parts work together.

It is also important to be cognizant of the structure of your current ILS. It is easy to assume that the way things work in your current ILS is just the way things work. However, your new system may have been constructed with a different underlying model. It is also important to be aware of this dynamic when communicating with your new vendor. Vendors are also prone to think their worldview is the only one. The staff supporting migrations don't necessarily have much knowledge about how their competitors' systems work. When migrating to a system from another vendor or to one structured differently than your current system, contact institutions that have made the same transition to find out what surprised them or those to which they had to adapt.

> **If you are migrating to a system built by a different vendor or that is structured differently than your current system, contact institutions that have made the same transition to find out what things surprised them or those to which they had to adapt.**

BIBLIOGRAPHIC DATA QUALITY

Moving data from one system to another exposes data-quality problems, such as missing, malformed, or incorrect data. For a smoother migration, identify, and if possible, remedy these problems pre-migration. At the most basic level, verify that your records are in structurally valid MARC. This can be done by exporting your records and using an external program, such as MarcEdit or MARC Report. Corrupt records can cause problems with both export from your current system and import into the new one.

MARC records can be structurally correct while still violating basic constraints of the format. Check for problems, such as:

- Records with more than one instance of non-repeatable fields, such as 100 or 245.
  - » 245 00 ‡ a Rashōmon
  - » 245 00 ‡ a 羅生門
  - » (the non-Roman title should have been in a linked 880 field and not a second 245)

- Records where explicit subfield markers have been entered in a field, such as 001 or 007, that should not have subfield markers in the underlying MARC record
  - » 007 ‡ a c ‡ b r ‡ d c
  - » (underlying MARC should have 007 cr\c with no subfielding)

- Records where nonstandard fill characters have been used
  - » =008 080326p20081951xx■083■g■■■■■■■■■■■vljpn■d

Look at the quality of coded data in fixed fields, which consist of characters that derive their meaning from their position in the string that makes up the field (see the 007 and 008 fields in the list above for examples of fixed fields). Many newer discovery interfaces use this information in facets, thereby exposing missing or badly coded data. This coded data may also be used in the migration process. For example, rather than mapping our existing item material types to item material types in the new system, our vendor generated material types based on the coded value for the record type (e.g., j for musical sound recordings) in the related MARC bibliographic records. In the past, fixed fields were often neglected, and many records retrospectively converted from catalog cards fail to code most of them. Your system may have internal non-MARC codes for things like format that are more obvious to people working in the system than the actual MARC coding. Even though these internal fields may be correct, it is the underlying MARC that will migrate. Check to see that these two values agree with each other and resolve discrepancies.

Be aware of diacritics and character-encoding issues. Know whether your records export in MARC-8, UTF-8, or some mixture as well as what kind of imports your new system accepts. Look for corrupt diacritics and be sure to verify that diacritics have transferred correctly during your test load. See chapters 2 and 4 for more help with character encodings.

Consider the option of sending your records to a vendor rather than undertaking bibliographic data cleanup in-house. As an alternative to having staff clean the data, consider having your vendor do it. Vendors have extensive experience with data cleanup and will have more sophisticated, comprehensive, and automated processes for identifying and correcting bad data than you will be able to develop on your own for a one-off project. If your local records will be loaded into your new system, rather than just matched against existing records, you may also want to think about combining RDA enhancement or authority control updating services with your data cleanup project. Vendors may also be able to address some deficiencies in fixed fields and update records to current standards (e.g., update the 008 form byte to use for online resources).

> Consider the option of sending your records to a vendor rather than
> undertaking bibliographic data cleanup in-house.

SYSTEM CONTROL NUMBERS

System control numbers play a critical role during migrations. Record numbers from bibliographic utilities play an important role in record sharing and are often used for record matching. The OCLC consortium and OCLC numbers play a unique role in library systems, and OCLC numbers have become an important identifier in many shared library systems and projects. Because these issues are so common, this chapter discusses OCLC numbers, but the issues are applicable to other kinds of control numbers.

If you are migrating to OCLC's WorldShare or to a shared consortial catalog where OCLC numbers are used as the primary match point, it is important to have accurate OCLC numbers in all your bibliographic records. Many things can go wrong with control numbers, including records with leading zeros stripped off, overlapping control numbers that are used for different purposes, as well as ones that are just plain wrong. Verify that your vendor uses a normalization process when matching control numbers or else make sure that all your control numbers are formatted the same way.

If you haven't looked before, you may be surprised by how many of your bibliographic records lack numbers corresponding to a bibliographic utility such as OCLC. If there are many records like this and you need OCLC numbers for your migration, the most efficient solution is to undertake a reclamation project by sending your bibliographic records to OCLC. In addition to synchronizing your holdings, a reclamation project can match your numberless records with existing OCLC records and add new records to WorldCat when a match is not found. You will then receive a copy of your records with the new numbers added that you can load into your local system. OCLC will perform reclamation for a library once for free, but after that there is a fee. If your records already have OCLC numbers and you only want to check the accuracy of your holdings, you could try the method described by Johnston (2015) (http://journal.code4lib .org/articles/10328). You may have brief records that include unverified OCLC numbers that you do not wish to use for matching purposes. Consider removing these numbers before export.

Export your ILS's internal record identifier and the field in your records that contains the OCLC number to an external file. Use this file to identify problems with records with more than one valid OCLC number (e.g., a record with two 001 or two 035$a fields, each containing a different OCLC number). For example, you might have a single record that includes both of these 035 fields:

035 $a(OCoLC)681501143
035 $a(OCoLC)756452689 $z 904378234

The only way to resolve these is to manually review the records to determine the correct number. Information in chapters 2 and 3 may help you identify and fix these problems.

Use this same file to find instances where more than one record has been assigned the same OCLC number. These also need to be examined individually and compared with the master record to determine the correct course of action. Do the records need to be merged or should one of the OCLC numbers be changed? This can be complicated if a library has locally edited master records for different editions.

ILS SYSTEM CONTROL NUMBER	OCLC NUMBER
1	681501143
1	756452689
2	681501143

The table shows that record 1 has two different OCLC numbers and that the same OCLC number is associated with both record 1 and record 2.

In addition to obvious duplicates, there are many cases where OCLC has merged records that the institution downloaded separately when they were two different records. These are more difficult to identify. If you are an OCLC member, it can be done by using WorldShare Collection Manager to create a local collection with all your holdings by searching for records that are held by your OCLC symbols. You can use the li command for this (li:oru). Request a download of these records and use a program like MarcEdit to extract all the 035 $a and $z fields from these files. Split out all the 035$z numbers and pair each one with the $a number from the same record. Make a list with all the $a/$z pairs as well as a $a/$a pair for each record. Export all the valid OCLC numbers (001 or 035$a, but not 035$z) from your ILS. Normalize all the OCLC numbers by removing "(OCoLC)," "ocm," and "ocn" and deleting any leading zeros. Match the OCLC numbers from your ILS against the second number in the giant list of pairs of 035 fields that you downloaded from WorldCat. If any 035$a from the downloaded file matches more than one OCLC number from your local file, you have two separate records that have been merged into one in WorldCat. You may wish to verify that the merge is correct and either merge your own records or change the OCLC number on one of them.

WORLDCAT 035$A	WORLDCAT 035$Z
1000	3000
2000	

035 $a and az exported from WorldCat.

WORLDCAT 035$A	WORLDCAT 035$A/035$Z
1000	1000
1000	3000
2000	2000

WorldCat 035$a numbers associated with each 035$a and 035$z from the same record.

BIBNO IN ILS	OCLCNO IN ILS	WORLDCAT 035$A/035$Z	WORLDCAT 035$A
Bib001	1000	1000	1000
Bib002	2000	2000	2000
Bib003	3000	3000	1000

Bib001 and Bib003 have different OCLC numbers in the local ILS, but because they link to the same 035$a in the WorldCat record, the two records were merged in OCLC sometime after they were downloaded to the local ILS.

If a system number that is being used for matching is in the 001 field and your new system takes the corresponding 003 field into account when matching, verify that the 003 field is present and correctly formatted. For OCLC numbers, this value is OCoLC. Any other system numbers (e.g., YBP numbers or MARCIVE shipping list numbers) that are used as match points for loading records should migrate such that they can still be used in the new system.

> You may have other system numbers that are used as match points for loading records, such as YBP numbers or MARCIVE shipping list numbers. Make sure these migrate in such a way that they can still be used as match points in your new system.

LOCAL DATA AND LOCAL EDITS

It is important to determine what will happen to any local data during migration or in your new system. For example, a local field that can be used to trigger reminders for actions in one ILS may do nothing in another.

One challenge facing institutions migrating to a shared catalog where their original records will be matched to a master record and will not be retained is the potential loss of many years of local data enhancements. There are several scenarios where this becomes a problem.

Local Record Has a Bibliographic Utility Number That Describes a Different Resource

Especially in the early days, many catalogers used OCLC master records as a base for a description of a different edition in the same manner they used to modify purchased catalog cards. Catalogers would download a near-match from Connexion and modify it locally to describe the item that they actually had. In the worst-case scenario, they downloaded any record on the same record format to modify locally. This means that the local record is now linked to an inappropriate

OCLC record. As well, in some cases there may be two records with the same OCLC number in the catalog that do not describe the same thing because one or both have been locally edited. There is no easy way to identify these.

Local Edits to Enhance or Correct Master Records

Even when using a matching record, libraries have often corrected errors in records or added additional information, such as contents notes, only in their own local catalog records. In the past, it was not possible for many institutions to make these changes in the OCLC master record, and even now, when OCLC has significantly expanded the types of users who can edit the master record, some institutions continue to make only local edits. It is not easy to identify these. You may also have information in your local bibliographic record, such as tables of contents that cannot be added to the master record for licensing reasons. This type of data must be handled using the methods described below for true local data.

Institution-Specific Local Data

A third category is truly local data. If you are migrating to a system that uses a master record approach, the system should provide some way to record local data. You should be able to migrate your existing local data to these new local fields if you can identify and mark it in some way. The challenge is identifying it. Data that really is only locally applicable include the names of special collections or information describing characteristics of the item that only apply to the library's copy. It also includes things like local headings for theses and advisor's names, which are not allowed in WorldCat master records. In the past, it may not have been considered important to identify this local information in your local catalog by using 590 notes rather than 500, or by using subfield 5 with your institution's MARC organization code. In some cases, local practices have been documented, making the related local fields easier to identify. You may be able to use information about the local collection to come up with likely keywords that can be used to find local data. You may also wish to export notes and headings fields from the records in collections that are likely to contain local notes and analyze them externally. For example, notes for review can be selected using keywords that often represent local information, such as "copy," "sign*," "donat*" or the name of a library. Looking at the initial list of local notes will likely suggest additional keywords to search. This review can also be accomplished with direct searches in the ILS, but an external list prevents redundant review. Another strategy is to export the bibliographic records for the items you hold from WorldCat (using the technique described in the earlier section on system control numbers) and compare the number of headings or notes in the current master record with the number in your local records. Focus on those record sets that are likely to contain local or value-added data. In cases where your local record has more headings or notes, there is additional information in your local record that should either be marked as true local data or added to the master record. OCLC's batch loading process may be able to add some data, such as contents notes and summaries, to master records that do not already contain those fields. Chapters 3 and 4 include information that will help with analyzing your data and marking local information. However, all methods for retrospectively identifying and retaining local data are labor-intensive and unlikely to be complete.

Whether you are migrating to a system that uses a master record rather than your local data or not, you may also find that you have some nonstandard practices or uses of fields that improved indexing, display, or functionality in your old system, but that cause problems or don't work in your new system.

ONLINE RESOURCES

You may need to identify all your records for online resources separately so that the URLs will migrate properly. Now is a good time to verify that all your online records include links and that those links work. In some cases, the new system includes a knowledge base of information about online resources, such as Alma's Community Zone. Consider whether it will be easier to re-create your online holdings using the new vendor's system or to try to convert your existing data. If you are currently managing some records in a stand-alone ERM, there may be some duplication between records in your ILS and in your ERM. If you are migrating to a system with an integrated ERM, you will want to identify duplicate records and remove the extra copies from the data being migrated.

In the past, it was common to combine print and electronic holdings on a single record. It is now more common to use separate records for maintenance purposes. You should investigate the effects of your existing practice in the new system. Does your new system require separate records for accurate faceting and limiting in the discovery interface? If the new system relies on information in the bibliographic record to distinguish print and e-resources, the single record approach will provide incorrect information about one or the other format. In this case, you may wish to split the records before your migration. Separate print and electronic records can be easier to maintain over time, but the single-record approach may result in a more user-friendly display. It is also possible that your new discovery interface will merge the print and electronic records for display even if you have separate records on the back end. See chapter 9 for more information about migrating electronic resources.

OTHER CLEANUP

Think about whether you have records in your current catalog that it would be better not to move to your new ILS, such as brief records for equipment, reserves, or other records created for circulation purposes, and delete them if necessary. Look for anomalous situations where record statuses are out of sync or related records are missing. It is a good idea to:

- Identify brief records and consider upgrading or deleting them.
- Check for unsuppressed bibliographic records that have no associated holdings and should be suppressed or deleted.
- Check for suppressed bibliographic records that do contain items and should display to the public.
- Look for bibliographic records with no holdings or other associated records. If you cannot figure out what they're for, you may want to delete these.

It is often easier to do cleanup in your existing system where you are familiar with the search options and tools for batch editing. In addition, once your new system goes live, you will be very busy developing and implementing new workflows and are unlikely to have time to focus on data cleanup. Take advantage of any error-checking reports offered by your current vendor or export your records and examine them with an external program. If you have a small collection and database maintenance has been neglected, taking an inventory to identify items to remove may be helpful

ITEM RECORDS

MARC bibliographic and holdings records use a standard format and, in theory, should be able to migrate losslessly, although some systems store holdings records in nonstandard ways that don't support the export of accurate MARC. Systems also vary in the degree to which they respect some parts of the MARC standard, for example, constraints on the length of records and number of allowable fields. However, where there is no standard format, such as for item records, data loss is almost inevitable. There are often similar fields that are defined differently from system to system. Fields may be present in one system but not in another. There may also be data that you can't export from your old system (assuming you want to). Although you would expect any ILS to be able to do a complete data dump of the library's information, unfortunately this is not possible in all systems. This is especially a problem for item records or non-MARC fields associated with bibliographic records.

Make sure that you know what information you can export and what you can import into your new system. One library found that an item record field in its old ILS that it used for managing an off-site storage facility would not be imported into its new system. Staff had to find a work-around so that the 100,000 items in the storage facility would not need to be re-inventoried.

Find out what fields the item record in your new system contains and determine how to map your existing data to values that will produce the functionality you need in the new system. Migration presents a good opportunity to rethink and possibly simplify your circulation policies, location codes, and material types. Find out how the fields in the item records function in your new system. Ask questions, such as:

- Is there a hard-coded list of values or does each library create its own?
- What processes use a given field?
- Where and when does each field display?

For example, in our former system, material type influenced circulation policy, whereas in our new one it is only used for display and statistics.

There are several reasons why it might be difficult for you to migrate data in item records that you'd like to keep. There may be no corresponding field in the new system. Alternatively, there may be a field that exists in both systems, but can't be mapped for some reason. For example, the field could be free text in your old system, but the new system uses a controlled vocabulary. Sometimes data that has no equivalent in the new system, such as loan history, can be mapped to note fields where it can still be searched or used for statistics. In some cases, your only option may be to export and store this data in a separate file.

Some item record fields have lists of controlled terms associated with them. Common examples include status, location, and material type. The available values for the equivalent fields in your new ILS may be different. You may also wish to change the list of values that you use for a field if that field functions differently in your new system or because you have rethought your workflows. In these cases, you will need to map your existing values to new values that will work in the ILS to which you are migrating. Whether mapping or migrating codes as-is, be sure that they conform to the new system's requirements in terms of length and presence or absence of non-alphanumeric characters and spaces.

If an item record field is supposed to be limited to a controlled list of values, search for null values in your current system and, if they are allowed by your system incorrect values that are not on the list of valid terms. This will prevent erroneous or unusable data from migrating.

Fields that affect loan policies vary from system to system. In some systems, a variety of fields may combine to determine the conditions under which an item circulates. In others, circulation may be dependent on a single variable such as a location code or a lending policy. Systems may also have ways to override the default value, which should be taken into account. Systems also mark statuses and processes differently.

Export data from various item record fields and look for outliers that might represent miscoded data, such as barcodes in volume fields. If your item records include "variable" fields that are repeatable (such as v for volume), check to see if any of these are repeated in an item where they shouldn't be.

Export a list of all your barcodes and identify any duplicates for cleanup. You can also use this list to identify incorrectly formatted barcodes, barcodes with the wrong number of characters, or barcodes that begin with the wrong characters. Chapters 2 and 3 address this kind of cleanup.

You may have many items in a temporary status, such as in-process or at the bindery, which should have been removed from that status long ago but were somehow missed. Resolve as many of these as possible prior to migration. You may have lost or withdrawn items that are being kept for historical reasons. Now is a good time to export these to external files if they must be kept and then delete them from your database rather than migrating them. If your new system requires items be attached to bibliographic or holdings records for some functions, identify records that lack the items, and add them.

BOUNDWITH RECORDS

In the past, it was common for libraries to bind a group of pamphlets or other separate publications into a single volume that is circulated as a unit. However, to provide access to the contents, bibliographic records were created for each of the individual publications. These individual bibliographic records must somehow be linked to the single barcode and item record information for the bound volume. These record groupings are commonly known as "boundwith records" and can be tricky to migrate. Systems handle boundwith records differently. Some systems link a single item record to multiple bibliographic records, but others link items to many holdings records or chain item records together (figure 5.2).

If your catalog includes boundwith records, find out early on how your new system handles these and how the vendor plans to migrate them. Test the completeness and functionality of migrated boundwith records thoroughly. Check whether the export process is associating the correct call number with boundwith items. We often only had call numbers in the individual bibliographic records for each part of the boundwith, so we had to add a call number to the item record that represented the range of volumes present in the boundwith. Otherwise the export process would just pick up the call number from the first bibliographic record and interpret it as the call number for the whole resource.

FIGURE 5.2

Bibliographic records for boundwith resources can be linked by shared holdings or item records on linked item records

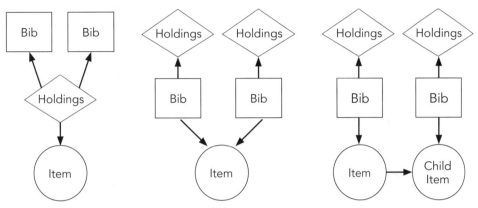

CALL NUMBERS

It is extremely important to migrate call numbers correctly or you'll never find anything again. Different systems handle call numbers in different ways. Call numbers associated with an item may be stored only in item records, in bibliographic records with an item-level override, or in holdings records with an item-level override (figure 5.3).

FIGURE 5.3

Call numbers stored only in items, in bibliographic records with an item-level override and in holdings with an item-level override

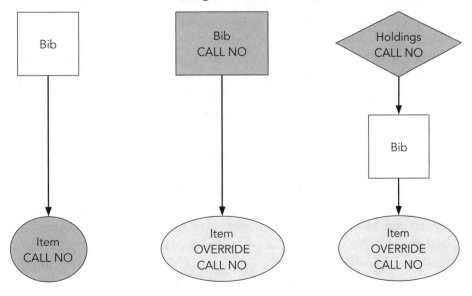

Item and holdings call numbers that are linked directly to bibliographic records may need to be linked to each other*

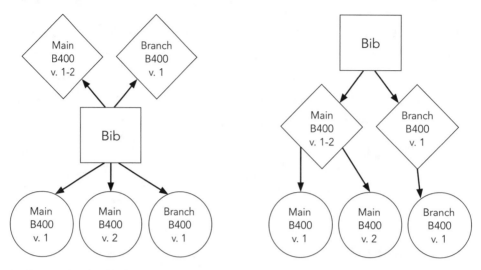

*As shown on the right of the diagram.

When migrating from one model to another, there is a potential for mismatches. Migrating from a system where holdings and items are linked to the bibliographic record independently to one where items are linked to the bibliographic record via the holdings record can cause problems. A MARC holdings record is designed to record a summary of the specific volumes held by a library, along with their associated location and call number. Generally, a separate record is made for each location and call number. Libraries where the call number is stored in the item or the bibliographic record may only create holdings records for serials or serials and multivolume monographs.

I will describe some examples of challenges my experience migrating from a system where the item call number was associated directly with a bibliographic record to one where the call number is always associated with a holdings record. When there is not a holdings record related to a bib, the migration process automatically created a brief holdings record using the item location and call number. However, if both items and holdings related to a bibliographic record exist in the old system, the items should be associated with the correct holdings record (figure 5.4).

During our migration, in most cases the item records were matched to a holdings record based on location. We sent the vendor a call number associated with each item as well as the call number in the holdings record. Because these existed independently of each other, in some cases the two call numbers didn't match. Sometimes the vendor put the non-matching call number in the alternative call number field in the item. Unfortunately, the vendor's matching process did not normalize the call numbers before comparing them, so we ended up with tens of thousands of unnecessary alternative call numbers in item records because of differences in spacing or in the use of periods. It is very important to make sure that your vendor is normalizing any values, such as call numbers or system numbers, that are used for matching. If your new vendor will not properly normalize such data, try to normalize as much as possible yourself. Normalization will take data that has been input in different formats and put them into a standard format. Although a human can easily see that the call numbers in the first column in the table below are all meant to be the same number, the literal-minded computer will look at them character-by-character and see three different strings. Removing all the spaces and periods before the comparison creates strings that even a computer can match, as shown in the second column. See chapter 2 for help on normalizing data.

CALL NUMBER ENTERED IN ILS	NORMALIZED CALL NUMBER
Z678.93.I57 B6	Z67893I57B6
Z678.93 .I57 .B6	Z67893I57B6
Z678.93.I57B6	Z67893I57B6

In other cases, we ended up with two holdings records: the migrated holdings record with no items attached and a system-created holdings record with a different call number and the migrated items attached. Although we already had call numbers in our holdings records, some libraries migrating to a system that is looking for call numbers in holdings records have had to use a script to add them.

In a system where there is no direct link between holdings and item records, it is possible to list the volumes in multiple locations, such as general stacks and current periodicals, in a single holdings record. However, when the holdings record is the link between a bibliographic record and its items, then each holdings record can contain only one call number and one location. If you are migrating from the first scenario to the second, you will want to split your holdings records pre-migration.

Locations in holdings and items can also get out of sync if one is updated and the other isn't. Look for holdings records with no items in the same location. Check for items where you expect a matching holdings record in the same location, but one doesn't exist.

In our previous system, call numbers were often stored in the bibliographic record. The field being used to generate the call number for the associated items was marked as such with a non-MARC tag that wouldn't export. Our new vendor initially suggested associating each location with a specific call number type and taking the call number for the associated items from the MARC field in the bibliographic record for that call number type. In many cases, this would have resulted in an item being assigned a different call number than what was on the piece. This would have been disastrous. However, as you are migrating your call numbers, verify that they are being mapped in a way that item records remain associated with their correct call numbers.

We ended up exporting all our call numbers as part of the item record. However, our old ILS could not output the subfielding that delineated the class and Cutter numbers in our call numbers nor could it export the tag that identified the type of call number (i.e., LC or Dewey). We therefore lost all our subfielding. To assign a call number type in our new system, we had to associate each of our locations with a specific call number type and clean up the exceptions post-migration. This is an example of data that exist in the current system and have an equivalent in the new system, but cannot be migrated because of the export limitations of the current system. Make sure you understand how information about call number types (e.g., LC or Dewey) is being migrated.

Our volume designation information was stored in a single item record field in the form "v. 2, pt. 1." However, our new system expects each part designation to be entered separately, which prevents an easy mapping. If your volume designation cannot be separated from your call number information, but your new system expects them to be separate, this is also a problem. These are examples of a mismatch in data format between two systems, which is always a problem when moving from a less granular system to a more granular system.

We used "input stamps" at the beginning of call numbers in our old ILS to indicate information like oversize. These displayed, but were not indexed and did not affect call number sorting. Because our call numbers were migrating as un-subfielded strings, these input stamps would have become part of the actual call number in our new system. We moved this text to the end of the call number pre-migration and slated it for post-migration cleanup.

Finally, check to see if you have records with empty call number fields and identify the appropriate call number where possible. Identify improperly constructed call numbers or call numbers associated with the wrong call number type and fix them.

These are some examples of the many things that can go wrong with call number migration. Be sure to ask:

- Is the link between items and their call numbers being properly maintained during the migration process?
- How is call number type being associated with call numbers?
- Do you have subfielding between the classification and shelflisting parts of call numbers and, if so, can you migrate this information? Will this affect shelflisting in your new system?
- If you have call number prefixes, do you know how these will migrate? How will they be indexed in your new ILS and in your discovery system?
- Are call numbers being properly normalized if they are being used for matching purposes, such as matching item and holdings records?

- If item call numbers are being linked to existing holdings records during migration, what information is being used to make the connection—location alone or both location and call number?
- Do you have call numbers in holdings records if your vendor requires them?
- Do you have holdings records that contain multiple locations or multiple call numbers? Will this be a problem?
- Do you have discrepancies between the call number or location in the holdings record and the call number or location in the associated item records?
- Do you have records with empty call numbers?
- Do you have records with improperly constructed call numbers?
- Do you have records with call numbers that are associated with the wrong call number type?
- How is volume information structured and how is it mapping to the new system?

GENERAL ERROR CHECKING

Run as many reports as you can in your current system. These can be used both as tools for identifying problems to fix and as resources to refer to when trouble-shooting your migrated data later.

Counting is important when determining the completeness of migrated data. Count the number of records of any given type exported, as well as the number that show up in your new ILS. Counting is especially important for mapped data. Count the number of items where a given field, such as location, contain a certain code in your old system before you migrate. If possible, reconcile this with the number of items that appear in your new system. If you are mapping data from more than one code to a single code, match the total number of items with the original codes to the total number of items with the new code.

> Counting is an important tool for checking the completeness of migrated data.

EXPORTING DATA AND AFTER

If you have a large quantity of bibliographic or item records, the size of the exported files can become unwieldy or may exceed the limits of your ILS export function. Consider how to split up your records to make smaller files. Can you use record numbers, date ranges, locations, or some other method? Can you be sure that you aren't missing some records? For example, if you group records by location, are there some records that don't have locations?

It is a good idea to keep a backup of your exported data at the point of migration. Although large files can be cumbersome, exported MARC records can be
viewed and searched with tools such as MarcEdit. Item data and non-MARC
data associated with bibliographic records can be exported in tabular form for
use with database or spreadsheet software. If something goes wrong, you will
have a record of the state of your data at the point of migration to which you
can refer. If it is financially feasible or if your old ILS is locally hosted, you may
wish to maintain access to it for some time post-migration for problem solving.

When importing data, your new system must have some way to associate
item and holdings records with bibliographic records. There are two main strategies for doing this. Item and holdings record information can be exported in
8xx and 9xx fields in your MARC records. This can potentially make individual
records containing many items very long. In fact, it may be impossible to generate a valid MARC record when large numbers of items are involved because of
the MARC format's limit of 99,999 bytes. You may need to distribute the items
across multiple copies of the bibliographic record and recombine them later.
Alternatively, item records can be exported in a delimited text format, such as
CSV, with an identifier that links them to the appropriate bibliographic record.
Holdings records can also be exported separately with an identifier, such as the
OCLC number or ILS system number, for the corresponding bibliographic record.

If you are able to run a trial import, check as many different types of data
and functions as possible. Keep a list of data-migration problems that can't be
resolved and will need to be cleaned up post-migration.

RESOURCES

Tools for analyzing and editing MARC records:
- MarcEdit. http://marcedit.reeset.net/.
- Marc Report/Marc Global. www.marcofquality.com/soft/softindex.html.
- The Library of Congress. MARC Specialized Tools. https://www.loc.gov/
  marc/marctools.html.

Vendors for record cleanup:
- Backstage Library Works. www.bslw.com/.
- Library Technologies, Inc. (LTI). www.authoritycontrol.com/.
- MARCIVE. www.authoritycontrol.com/.

OCLC holdings reconciliation:
- OCLC Reclamation Project. www.oclc.org/support/help/batchload/Content/
  004_Filling_out_form/003g_Select_one_time_project_type/Reclamation
  _Project.htm.
- Johnston, Sarah. "Homegrown WorldCat Reclamation: Utilizing OCLC's
  WorldCat Metadata API to Reconcile Your Library's Holdings." *Code{4}Lib
  Journal* 27, 2015. http://journal.code4lib.org/articles/10328.

ACQUISITIONS

Siôn Romaine, Acquisitions Librarian, University of Washington

Pity the acquisitions librarian facing a migration. Like Auntie Em, she is at one moment on the porch, contentedly knitting as she watches her staff peck out orders and squawk over damaged text blocks. The next moment, Uncle Henry is sprinting over from Circulation yelling, "Migration!" and oh dear, oh dear, over the porch rail goes the knitting as Auntie Em rushes out to gather her staff and shepherd her orders to safety. There is just enough time to ensure the firm orders are accounted for, the invoices paid and tucked away, and the subscriptions tidied up before she scurries down to the tornado shelter. But good gracious, where is Dorothy the mono series? How could she have forgotten about the mono series?

Acquisitions staff dread the prospect of migrating to a new system, and with good reason. The lack of international standards for acquisitions data generally makes it difficult to migrate orders, invoices, and other acquisitions records, particularly if the institution's ILS is from a different vendor. A lack of local standards may compound the problem. In a department where the day-to-day routine typically involves processing new orders and inventory as quickly as possible, there is little free time to prepare for migration or learning a new system. During the migration period, new orders will still need to be keyed, new inventory will continue to arrive and need to be received, and new invoices will need to be paid. Proper preparation is therefore critical to avoid headaches and heartache down the road.

DECIDE WHAT TO MIGRATE . . . OR NOT

Determine Your Institutional Requirements

Begin by determining, at the 30,000-foot level, what records or subset of acquisitions records you *must* migrate. Most institutions do not migrate regularly, and many institutions do not remove or purge acquisitions-related records unless forced to do so. However challenging a migration may be, remember that this is also a once-in-a-generation opportunity to start fresh! Migrating only what you absolutely need will make post-migration cleanup easier and your new database less cluttered.

Consider:

- What does your institution require you to retain? Many public institutions may be governed by records retention schedules that require records to be retained for at least six years or longer. Determine whether your order records and any associated invoice records are subject to your institution's records-retention schedule. Some institutions may retain paper or online copies of invoices outside the ILS; if so, confirm that your accounting office has the copies it needs to meet any records retention schedules. If you were to be audited by your parent institution after you went live, could you retrieve the information required by the auditors?

- Do you have an operational need to retain closed or cancelled order records? Occasionally, a closed or cancelled order record for an online purchase may contain information required to prove to a publisher that access or content was paid for, or include notes indicating who initiated (or cancelled) the order and why. Does it make sense to migrate all closed order records or could you migrate only a subset?

- If you are required, or wish to retain the records—but do not wish to migrate them to the new system—are you able to extract them from your existing system and store them on a local server for future reference? If so, will you need authorization or technical support from your IT department?

- How long will you have some form of access to your legacy ILS? If your legacy ILS is locally hosted and you can keep it running indefinitely or for a certain number of months in a view-only mode, you may opt to create some or all records from scratch in your new ILS. Be wary, though, of running parallel systems. Creating records from scratch in your new system may not be more efficient than migrating existing records with messy data. Staff may take longer to adjust to using the new system if the legacy system remains available to use as a crutch.

Note: It's also entirely possible that either your old or new ILS vendor will not support migrating acquisitions data and that all records will need to be created afresh after going live in the new system. In this situation, you should work with your institution to determine whether your acquisitions data will need to be migrated from your existing ILS to another system to meet records retention requirements.

Determine What Records Should Be Migrated

Most acquisitions departments will have four main record types to consider migrating: order records, vendor records, fund records, and invoice records. For some acquisitions departments, license records may also be a consideration if license records are stored in the existing ILS and licensing falls under the jurisdiction of the acquisitions department. For a more in-depth discussion about license records, see the chapter on ERM.

Of all the record types to be migrated, order records may be the most difficult. Unlike bibliographic or holdings records, there are no standards for how data or fields are constructed in an order record; even if two ILSs are owned by the same vendor, migrating the order records can be problematic. For this reason, many institutions—particularly smaller institutions with fewer orders—may opt not to migrate acquisitions data at all.

Once you have determined your institutional requirements (i.e., what you must migrate), consider:

- What *order records* can be deleted or archived? In your existing ILS, is it possible to separate only those records that will meet your institutional requirements for retention? For example, is it able to migrate only active or open orders (whether for monographs or serials and continuing resources)? Can you migrate only active orders plus the last six years of closed or cancelled orders and then delete or archive anything else?
- Are there fields or data in your existing order records that do not need to be migrated? For continuing resources, where the same order record is often reused year after year, there may be information or notes in the order record that are no longer relevant and that do not need to be migrated.
- What *vendor records* can be deleted? If the vendor record hasn't been used in many years, there's a good chance the vendor information may be out of date and will need to be re-entered or updated in the new system anyway. If you decide to delete a vendor record, what are the implications for any associated order records? Will any information required for auditing purposes be lost?

- Are there obsolete *funds* that can be deleted? If you decide to delete an obsolete fund, what are the implications for any associated order records? Will any information required for auditing purposes be lost?
- Typically, *invoices* are not migrated to new systems; payment data from invoices in the old ILS may migrate to the new ILS as a note or other field in a migrated order record. However, it may be possible, if the invoice data in the old ILS exists and can be extracted in a standardized format, to export the invoice information to the new ILS.
- Do you have paper or online copies of invoices stored outside the old ILS that will satisfy most needs, including any institutional records retention requirements?
- If you decide to migrate invoices, what operational need will be served by migrating old invoice information? What extra setup may be required in the new ILS? Will you need to set up additional fiscal years to accommodate old invoices?
- Is there a risk that attempting to migrate the invoice data to the new system will only result in greater confusion? Will migrating historical payment information to a field in the order record suffice?

Note: If you opt not to migrate certain acquisitions data, be sure to document what you migrated and what you left behind. If you migrate data out of your old ILS to somewhere else (e.g., a text file placed on a shared drive), be sure to clearly document where that information was placed and what is contained in the file. Also document whether the information is to be kept permanently, or if it can be deleted at some date in the future.

UNDERSTAND THE SYSTEM ARCHITECTURE AND MAP THE DATA

It's critically important that anyone planning to migrate acquisitions data has a solid understanding of how acquisitions data are built and structured in both the old and new systems. Understanding the underlying architecture of both systems will enable you to correctly map data, build new workflows, and have a sense of what might go wrong during the migration process. If you are a visual learner, consider mapping out diagrams of record structures in both systems so you can better visualize where data must flow from one system to the other during the migration process.

As you review the system architecture, consider how acquisitions records are built and linked to other record types and how the architecture will affect how data is mapped from one system to another.

Order Records

Depending on the ILS, order records may exist in a stand-alone index, or be hard- or soft-linked to other records types; for example, bibliographic records, holdings records, item records, ERM records (including license records), vendor records, invoice records, funds, and possibly, in the case of on-order items, patron records. Many of these other record types may be beyond the overall purview or responsibility of the acquisitions department. In planning your migration, consider:

- To what are your order records hard-linked in your existing ILS? Are they hard-linked to bibliographic records (i.e., an order record cannot exist unless it is first attached to a bibliographic record) or do they exist in their own silo? How will these hard links be preserved upon migration?
- Are order records hard-linked to multiple record types (i.e., are some linked to bibliographic records and others linked to ERM records)? How will the new vendor handle migrating order records linked to multiple record types?
- Are your order records soft-linked to other acquisitions records (e.g., vendors, funds, and invoices?) What about other record types (e.g., holdings records or item records)? How will those soft links be preserved upon migration? Is any coordination required with other departments to ensure that these links are preserved through the migration process?
- If you order the same title for multiple locations and use separate order records for each location, what will preserve the soft-link between the order record and the holdings or item record so that upon migration each order is linked to the correct location?
- How are order record numbers generated or formatted in your existing system versus your new ILS? (Will the new ILS accommodate order record numbers from your existing system?)
- Will you be able to migrate all fields in your existing order records or just a subset? To where will these fields migrate in the new order record? If you must select a subset of fields to migrate, how will you prioritize which fields are most important?
- How are EDI orders transmitted to the ILS? Which library department will take responsibility for setting up the EDI loader and working with the vendor to ensure it works?

Special considerations for consortia:

- If you are migrating from a single institution ILS to a shared ILS, will your order record numbers duplicate or overlap with another institution's? If so, can the ILS vendor append a prefix or suffix to one institution's order numbers as part of the migration process (e.g., PO#1233-main and PO#1233-law)? If not, how will the orders be distinguished in the new system?

- If you are migrating from a single institution ILS to a shared ILS, will identical bibliographic records be merged? If so, how will order records attached to each bibliographic record migrate?

Vendor Records

In most systems, there is some kind of soft link between order and vendor records; ideally, this soft link will be retained as part of the migration process, so that staff do not need to edit or update migrated order records with vendor information in the new ILS.

- How are vendor accounts structured in your existing system?
- Are sub-accounts or nested accounts supported? How will they migrate?
- If the new system requires or supports a different structure, will new codes be required or can existing codes be reused? If new codes are required, will existing order records need to be updated with the new vendor code prior to migration or can order records be mapped to new codes as part of the migration process?
- To what record types are vendor records linked? Only orders and invoices? Or are there links to holdings or ERM records that must also be considered?

Special considerations for consortia:

- If you are migrating from a single institution ILS to a shared ILS, will your vendor record codes duplicate or overlap with another acquisitions unit's or institution's vendor record codes? Can you share vendor records? If so, how will order records from each institution be mapped to the new shared vendor record in the new system? Who will be responsible for maintaining the shared vendor record in the new ILS? Remember that sharing a vendor does not mean that your institutional account information, vendor contacts, or payment/remit-to addresses will necessarily be the same as everyone else's in the consortia. If you opt for using a shared vendor record, confirm what fields can be configured locally, and whether sharing a vendor record will be problematic when paying invoices.

Funds

If both funds and active order records are to be migrated, then the soft link between the two must be maintained or re-created after migration.

- How are your funds structured in your existing system? Are sub-funds or parent funds used or supported? How will fund hierarchies migrate?

- If the new system requires or supports a different structure, will new fund codes be required or can existing codes be reused? If new codes are required or desired, will existing order records need to be updated with the new fund code prior to migration or can order records be mapped to new codes as part of the migration process?
- How will funds encumber upon migrating to the new system? Will migrated active order records be encumbered automatically upon migration?
- How will fund balances and allocations migrate to the new system?
- How will links to funds be retained in both active and closed orders? Will orders need to be relinked to funds post-migration? For split-funded orders (e.g., 50 percent paid on Fund A, 50 percent paid on Fund B), will the fund-split be preserved on migration or need to be rekeyed post-migration? How and where will the fund-split information be preserved or migrated to the new order record so the funds and fund-split percentages are not lost?
- Will migrating fund information have any effect on how payment is mapped to your parent institution's accounting system?

Special considerations for consortia:

- If you are migrating from a single institution ILS to a shared ILS, will your fund codes duplicate or overlap with another acquisitions department's or institution's fund codes?

Invoices

Although many institutions opt not to migrate invoice data, an institution that operates the ILS as a shadow system will need to map invoice and payment information to its parent institution's accounting system. Consider:

- How is invoice and payment information in the old ILS presently mapped to the parent institution's accounting system? How will that change with the new ILS?
- Which department will take responsibility for mapping and testing invoice data between the library and the parent institution? The acquisitions department? The library IT department? Who will act as a liaison between the library and the parent institution's central accounting office?
- How are EDI invoices transmitted to the ILS? Which library department will take responsibility for setting up the EDI loader and working with the vendor to ensure it works?

License Records

Regardless of what department is responsible, if online license records are to be migrated, there is a good possibility that there will be a link to order or payment records. Consider whether it is possible to retain these links or if they must be re-created post-migration. Will cleanup need to be coordinated with a department outside acquisitions?

Authorizations and Permissions

How authorizations and permissions are assigned in two different systems will vary greatly. Review how authorizations and permissions are assigned in the old and new ILS and determine any workflow implications there may be. For example:

- Who can view, create, edit, and/or delete a bibliographic record? What about holdings, item or other inventory records?
- Who can view, create, edit, close, cancel, and/or delete an order record?
- Who can view, create, edit, and/or delete a vendor record?
- Who can view, create, edit, and/or delete a fund?
- Who can view, create, or edit an invoice?
- Who can view, create, edit, and/or delete a license record?
- Who can load records, EDI orders, or EDI invoices? Set up a DDA?
- What authorizations will each of your staff need in the new system to do her daily work? If it is not possible to authorize your staff for a certain task, who will do the work? (For example, only a professional librarian can be given authorization to load records because the authorization to load records is tied to other ILS authorizations that cannot be given to lower-level staff.) Will workflows, duties, or staff classifications need to be changed to accommodate the ILS's authorizations?

KNOW YOUR DATA . . . AND CLEAN IT UP

One of the most important things you can do prior to any migration is to determine what's in your records. (In fact, even if you choose not to migrate any acquisitions data, it's still a good idea to get a sense of what you're leaving behind.) Knowing what's in your records will give you a better sense of how the data will migrate and what you and the vendor's migration support team will need to watch. As suggested above, start by reviewing the architecture of the new and old systems and begin to map out where fields will migrate.

Mapping Your Data to the New System

Take a selection of records that you intend to migrate and review each field and subfield, with the goal of determining to where that data will migrate in your new system. (Depending on where you are in the migration process, you may not be able to determine exactly where the information will go.) For example, can you answer where the following fields will migrate?

Order Record

- Acquisition method (e.g., purchase versus gift)
- Acquisitions unit responsible for creating the order
- Claiming history
- Discount
- Expected date of receipt or expected claim date
- Format or material type
- Fund
    » *Will link to order record be preserved on migration?*

- Location for which it's been ordered
    » *If order is linked to holdings or item records, will links be preserved on migration?*

- Note fields
    » Local or internal note
    » Receiving or processing note
    » Vendor note
    » Uploaded attachments

- Number of items ordered
- Order record modification history
- Order record number or key
- Order record type (e.g., one-time versus continuing)
- Payment or invoice information
- Price (estimated or list)
- Selector
- Status (e.g., open order versus closed order)
- Vendor or supplier
    » *Will link to order record be preserved on migration?*

- Vendor status reports
- Vendor title or reference number

Additionally, for continuing or subscription orders, consider
- Receiving history
- Prediction pattern
- Subscription period or renewal date
- Print + online order information; to which bibliographic record will a print + online order record be attached?

Clean Your Data (Before and After)

Most likely, you will need to clean up acquisitions data before and after migration. But keep in mind that cleaning up data in a system you know and are familiar with is generally easier than cleaning up data in a new system, regardless of the batch update functionality promised in the new system. Where possible, try to clean up as much as you can beforehand. Remember, too, that once you go live in the new system, you will still need to do some cleanup in addition to testing and rebuilding workflows.

A lack of local standards in your existing order records will make migrating data difficult. If your institution is already committed to migrating, you may not have enough time to develop new standards for the old system and then clean the data up prior to migration. Clean up what you can and consider developing standards for the new system prior to migration or as quickly as possible after migration so that you have a clean database to work with moving forward. Using the checklist under "Mapping Your Data to the New System" above, what standards do you presently have for inputting information into these fields? What new standards will you need to create in your new system?

REVIEW AND DOCUMENT EXISTING WORKFLOWS AND BUILD NEW ONES

By reviewing and documenting your existing workflows, you'll have a better sense of what you'll need to rebuild after migration. Reviewing existing workflows will allow you to determine if there are processing procedures that can be eliminated or streamlined; remember, the fewer exceptions that you have in your workflows, the easier it will be to rebuild them once you go live. Because most acquisitions units are production-based—materials come in, materials go out—workflows should be set up to be as efficient as possible. A migration, however unwelcome, can be an excellent opportunity (and justification) for eliminating "boutique" processing practices that may have been created years ago to satisfy a particular department, but which from an efficiency standpoint can no longer be justified post-migration.

Additionally, if existing workflows are documented, you'll have something you can refer to the vendor's migration support team in case you need to explain why you need something in the new system configured a certain way. And workflows that are documented can help with testing workflows in the new system.

Workflow Checklist

1. Ordering
   How does a selector or patron transmit an order to the acquisitions department?

   Create a monograph order.
   - » How are EDI orders created and loaded (approval or firm orders)?
   - » How are print and online orders distinguished? How do you distinguish between formats (e.g., print versus DVD)?
   - » Are streaming media orders considered one-time or subscription orders?

   Create a subscription order.
   - » How are subscriptions and standing orders distinguished?
   - » How are print + online subscriptions handled?
   - » How are combination, membership, and package orders handled?

   Create a rush, course reserves, or patron purchase request order.

   Create an order for a DDA program.

   Edit an order.

   Close or cancel an order.

   Delete an order.

   Audit trail and authorizations to determine who can create, edit, or close an order.

   How do on-order records display in Discovery?

2. Receiving and Check-in
   Receive a monographic or one-time order.

   Receive a shelf-ready order.

   Receive a rush, course reserve or patron purchase request order.

   Receive or check in a serial or continuing order
   - » How are prediction patterns and claim delays established?
   - » Are monographic series received or processed differently than periodicals?

3. **Claiming**

   Claim a monograph.

   Claim a serial.

   How are EDI claims processed?

4. **Invoicing**

   Create an invoice.

   How are EDI invoices loaded?

   Approve an invoice.

   Send an invoice to the parent institution.

   Close an invoice.

   How are sales tax and service charges handled? If sales tax and service charges are disbursed from a separate fund than collections, how are they handled?

   Audit trail to determine who can create, approve, pay, and close an invoice.

5. **Relinking and Transferring Orders**

   Move an order record to a different bibliographic record.

6. **Record Loading and EDI**

   Set up an import loader for invoices.

   Set up an import loader for firm orders.

   Set up an import loader for approvals.

   Set up an import loader for shelf-ready materials.

7. **Rapid Cataloging**

   Quick-catalog an item (if your acquisitions unit uses some form of copy or expedited cataloging).

8. **Funds and Fiscal Rollover**

   Create a new fund.

   Allocate money to a fund.

   Close a fund.

   Roll over a fiscal period.

9. Reports and Statistics

What statistics are you required to report out? (For example, statistics for accreditation or for your library's membership in an organization like the Association of Research Libraries.)

What statistics do you keep to track workload?

10. Audit Trails

What workflows are in place to support audit trails?

In a dream world of unicorns and rainbows, you will have a set of perfect new workflows ready to go on the new system's Day 1. However, attempting to build a workflow in a system to which you have yet to migrate is not only difficult but may also be undesirable; realistically, it will take some time doing daily work in the new system before the most efficient workflow can be determined. It is not unrealistic to expect that the acquisitions unit at a medium-sized institution may take six months to rebuild all workflows after migration; for large institutions, it may take 12 to 24 months to rebuild all workflows, depending on the complexity of the migration.

Note: Be sure to document any acquisitions configuration settings you make in your new system, both prior to go-live and post-migration. Knowing how you configured your acquisitions module, and at what point in time, can greatly help with troubleshooting during and after migration.

COMMUNICATE

Good communication can be half the battle to survive an acquisitions migration. If you are the point person for acquisitions, remember that not only should you push for good communication from those coordinating your migration, but you should also make an extra effort to communicate what is going on to your coworkers. Because the complexities of acquisitions workflows may not be well understood outside of technical services (or perhaps even outside of the acquisitions department), you may need to be prepared to act as an advocate for acquisitions, explaining why more time is needed for testing or why a certain configuration change is required.

Vendors

Depending on the complexity of your migration, you may need to delay ordering, receiving approval materials, or paying invoices. Keep your vendors and suppliers informed of your migration plans and let them know if you anticipate any possible delays with your workflows due to migration. Will you need extra time to pay invoices? Will you need to hold incoming shipments? Who will your vendor contact be for setting up and testing EDI ordering or invoicing?

Information Technology Staff

In many institutions, the library's or parent institution's Informational Technology (IT) department plays a central role in the ILS migration. Acquisitions staff may rely on the IT department to configure settings in the new ILS and/or build bridges to external systems. Ensure that you have a good communication channel with your IT department so that you know who will be responsible for:

- Configuring acquisitions-related settings in the new ILS
- Testing and loading incoming EDI files
- Testing and loading incoming files of bibliographic records (e.g., approval records and/or WorldCat Partners records)
- Building and testing any bridges needed between the ILS and the parent institution's central accounting system so that invoices can be paid as quickly as possible post-migration

Central Accounting

If you operate your ILS as a shadow payment system, and actual invoice payment is processed by your parent institution's central accounting department, be sure to notify central accounting that you will be moving to a new ILS, and that you (or the IT department) will need to work with someone to test-load invoice files. If responsibility for sending invoice data to the central accounting department is handled by another library department (i.e., there is an acquisitions department and a library accounting department), be sure to keep in touch with that department so that you are up-to-date on testing invoice loads; as necessary, keep your vendors informed of any developments.

Library Staff outside Acquisitions

Communication with library staff can be just as important as with nonlibrary staff. Consider whether selectors, reference librarians, course reserves staff, circulation staff, ILL staff, or catalogers will need to be informed about:

- adjusted order deadlines to accommodate an early fiscal close
- delayed processing during the technical freeze-migration cutover period
- handling rush and/or reserve ordering and receiving during the technical freeze/migration cutover period
- backlogs that may develop because of migration

It's quite probable that processing backlogs will develop because of migration. Will you need to request temporary staffing to clear the backlog? How will you keep library administration informed of the acquisitions department's progress in clearing any backlogs post-migration?

Library Staff inside Acquisitions

Finally, do not forget to communicate with your own staff! If you are representing acquisitions on the migration team, remember that you will be involved on a daily basis and therefore develop a sense of how the new system will work before anyone else in your department. As you begin to prepare for migration, consider how you will ensure your staff are kept up-to-date in what is happening. What is your plan to train your staff? How will they become familiar with the new vocabulary and architecture of the system?

RESOURCES

Many ILS vendors have some type of user group; these user groups will manage or support e-mail lists to which institutions that use the products may subscribe. There is tremendous value in subscribing to these e-mail lists, either as a lurker who merely reads the posts or as a more active participant who uses the list to ask questions. If you do not understand something about your migration process and cannot get a satisfactory answer from the vendor, consider posting to the user group list or searching the list archives. Do not worry that your question may be stupid; migrating acquisitions data is always difficult and you generally only get one shot at getting it right.

Chapter 3 of Wilkinson, Lewis, and Lubas's *The Complete Guide to Acquisitions Management* (2015), provides some helpful information on what to look for in a new acquisitions system.

RELATED ISSUES DISCUSSED IN OTHER CHAPTERS

Other chapters of this book that may be of interest to staff managing acquisitions data include:

- Chapter 5, "Bibliographic and Item Data"
- Chapter 8, "Serials"
- Chapter 9, "Electronic Resources Management"
- Chapter 11, "Migrating to Shared Systems"

REFERENCE

Wilkinson, F. C., L. K. Lewis, and R. L. Lubas. 2015. *The Complete Guide to Acquisitions Management.* Santa Barbara, CA: Libraries Unlimited.

PATRON DATA
AND AUTHENTICATION

Nathan Mealey, Manager of Library Technologies, Portland State University

MIGRATING USER DATA: OVERVIEW

Migrating user data is a key component of your transition to a new integrated library system (ILS). Successfully migrated user data ensures that any loans that are active at the time of your transition will be correctly reflected in your new system, any historical loan information that your library might want to retain will appear correctly post-transition, and ongoing synchronizations between your campus data systems and the new ILS will be easier to set up and maintain.

Thankfully, the process of migrating user data from your old to new system is fairly straightforward. The process of transitioning your user data from one system to another is comprised of a series of discrete steps in which you identify what data you have now, what data you need in your new system, and how to get there. Simple—though perhaps deceptively so.

STEP 1 HOW DOES YOUR NEW SYSTEM STORE AND USE PATRON DATA?

This step is without a doubt the most critical in the whole process of migrating your user data to your new system. Developing a thorough understanding of what user data the new system will store and how it will use that data is key for the migration process to go smoothly. Even if the new system stores data in a way that is similar to your existing system, it is likely that the data will be used differently for processes such as circulation, billing, notices, and authentication. Knowing how both aspects of user data work in your new system will enable you to map data effectively as you move forward.

Determining What User Data Fields to Plan

At this stage, it's useful to break user data down into two groups: core user data (name, address, etc.) and supplementary data (notes, notification preferences, proxy-for info, etc.). All systems will support core data (though perhaps in different ways). But how supplemental data is handled varies greatly from system to system.

Core Data

Core data is comprised of the following fields:

- name
- user group (e.g., faculty, student, etc.)
- physical address(es)
- e-mail address(es)
- phone number(s)
- barcode
- expiration date

Depending on when your current system was installed, the way your new system will accommodate this core data may be very different. For example, many older systems were developed at a time when database and memory usage were at a premium, and so the number of physical addresses, or e-mail addresses, or the length of certain fields may have been very limited. In contrast, applications written today are typically much more dynamic and less space-constrained, and so can accommodate data more flexibly.

For core data, this type of distinction is likely the biggest difference between your current and new systems. But knowing how this could play out down the road is important. For instance, if your new system allows for a given user to have many e-mail addresses, it also most likely requires that you indicate which is the preferred address (e.g., so the system knows which to use for notices). You may not yet know whether your users will have multiple e-mail addresses, but it's good to know what the possible implications might be.

One area where this type of decision is likely to play out concerns university staff, who may have both a campus and a home address. In this case, you will want to determine a consistent approach to indicate by default which of these two addresses is preferred. In addition, the decision you make will likely have ramifications in terms of offering campus and home delivery of items, sending printed notices, and so on.

Supplementary Data

Once you move beyond the core data elements, the range of supplementary data elements is unpredictable. Each system has a different selection, which may not translate directly from one system to the other.

Supplementary data can include some or all of the following:

- university ID (or sometimes called primary ID)
- notes
- fines
- statistical categories
- blocks
- proxy-for
- pin number
- home library
- password

This list is not exhaustive, because each system includes a unique selection of supplementary data fields. Nonetheless, the idea here is that there are fields that may be present in your new system and which you have not had to work with or consider before. Identifying these and understanding how the new system uses them will give you a clearer picture of the overall data structure for user records in the new system, and perhaps some insight into how this data structure drives other functionalities as well.

Identifying How the New System Uses Patron Data

Once you've developed an understanding of what data your new system will store, you should next look at how the system uses that data. As mentioned in the previous section, you may have developed insight about this when looking at supplementary data fields. For instance, if the new system stores proxy-for info, then you can explore how this functionality is used as part of the circulation process. However, how the system uses other data points may not be clear at first glance. For both core and supplementary data fields, it will take some investigation into other aspects of the system to determine how they will be used to support different system processes.

Fields to focus on include:

- *User group*: This field will likely be used for setting up loan rules, but may also be employed for setting up rules for the delivery options patrons see in your discovery interface (e.g., which users will see the local holds option), or possibly even which patrons can see or access specific databases.
- *University ID*: This field, which can go by different names, can be used in a variety of ways by your new system. However, the most critical involves authentication for your discovery system, where this field is likely the match point used when a patron signs in.
- *Home library*: This field is typically used to indicate where the bulk of the services offered to a given patron should be located (e.g., hold pickup options). But there are other ways that this field can be used, such as limiting whether patrons can request something from a library other than their home library.

In the case of any supplementary data that your new system will include, evaluating how that field is used by the system to support other processes is a very useful step to take at this early stage of the process. Doing so will potentially head off any surprises that could otherwise appear farther along in the process.

STEP 2 HOW DOES YOUR NEW SYSTEM STORE DATA RELATIVE TO YOUR CURRENT SYSTEM?

Now that you know what data your new system will store, and how that data will be used, it's time to look at the data that you have now and determine how it compares. At this stage of the process, the goal is to understand how the structure of your current patron data differs from that of patron data in the new system. Understanding this will enable you to plot an effective migration strategy for your data.

What Data Do You Already Have?

The first step is to catalog the data stored by your current system. Using the previous discussion of core and supplementary data fields as a guide, list all the patron data fields that you use now. Start with the core fields, because you can rely on those being present in the new system, and then move on to the supplementary fields.

As you do this, note whether any current fields are used in ways that are unique to the system. For example, your current system may use brief codes for indicating what user group a patron is a member of, or what her home library is. These codes may not indicate their meaning in an obvious fashion (for example, in at least one older system, only single alphabetical codes could be used for some fields) or could hold only a limited number of values (in the example of the single alphabetical code, the system limited the number of possible values to the twenty-six letters of the alphabet). Or the system may store users' passwords in an encrypted format that you may not be able to export.

After you've run through all the data points that your current system stores, you can begin comparing them to the patron data in your new system.

Comparing Patron Data between Your Old and New Systems

The simplest approach for doing this is to build a table or spreadsheet where you directly align a data point in your current system with the same (or similar) data point in the new system. In one column, list all the data points from your current system that you plan to migrate, and then use the second column to indicate the matching data point in your new system.

When doing this, leave out any fields that are part of the new system but are not included in your current system. Down the road, you'll need to make decisions about these fields, but for now, focus on the data you currently have and how they compare with your new system.

The comparison table that you build might look something like this (though with many more fields):

CURRENT SYSTEM	NEW SYSTEM
Name	First name, last name, middle initial (separate fields)
Univ ID	Primary identifier
PCODE1	User group
Exp Date	Expiration Date
MBlock	(no parallel field)
Home Library	Campus
. . .	. . .

Once this table is completed, you will have matched up all your existing fields with the matching fields in your new system. You should begin to see your data-migration strategy taking shape. You will be able to clearly see all those places where the data line up cleanly, where some data massaging may need to take place, and where your new system doesn't have a matching field.

This base-level understanding of how the data matches up between the two systems will pay dividends as you begin to build out on your migration strategy in the next step.

STEP 3   IDENTIFYING AND UNDERSTANDING THE TOOLS THAT YOU'LL USE TO MIGRATE YOUR DATA

The next step is to comprehend the migration process as laid out by your new vendor and the tools it will provide you to facilitate the migration. Every vendor will have a different approach to this, and will provide varying degrees of support. But for the most part, you can anticipate extracting and preparing the data yourself. Therefore it is very important that you thoroughly understand your vendor's expectations.

Does Your New Vendor Provide System-Specific Migration Tools?

Many vendors will provide migration tools that are oriented towards data coming from a specific system. For example, if you currently use Innovative Interface's Sierra and are migrating to Ex Libris' Alma system, Ex Libris will provide tools to facilitate migrating data between these systems.

This may not always be the case. For instance, if you're migrating to or from an open source ILS, system-specific data-migration tools may not exist for the open source system.

But for larger, vendor-supported ILSs, migration tools are typically provided. Examples include:

1. A mapping form that specifies how specific fields in your current system will map to the new system. This will be similar to the table that you created earlier, and should indicate, for instance, that the field labeled "UNIV ID" in your current system maps to the field "Primary ID" in the new system.
2. A mapping form that indicates what field names the vendor is expecting from your current system, and whether the actual field names differ in any way. This type of form would, for example, indicate that the vendor is expecting a field labeled "UNIV ID" and may give a definition for which data it expects to find in this field. If this field is named something different in your current system, such as "UNIQUE ID," you would indicate that here.

Because the naming of any given field in two separate systems is almost certain not to match, and the implementation of any system is likely to be unique, these forms are vital to ensure that when you hand over data to the vendor to import into the new system, everything goes smoothly and the data loads as expected.

Does Your Vendor Expect a Specific Format for the Data?

Vendors principally want to deal with data in a consistent format, because it makes the migration process easier for them to anticipate and manage, and to provide guidance. But the required format will vary by vendor.

In general, the format will likely come down to one of a few options:

- Microsoft Excel spreadsheet
- CSV (comma-separated values) file
- other delimited file (e.g., tab-delimited)
- XML (Extensible Markup Language)

There can be significant differences among these formats, and the way your current system extracts data will work better with some formats than others. For example, depending on how your current system separates multi-value fields, working with CSV or tab-delimited formats can be challenging. The same can be said about extracting your current data to a spreadsheet, where Excel will often try to "interpret" data in a newly opened spreadsheet, which can lead to issues with the data after the file has been opened. This is often the case with numeric barcodes, which Excel often converts to scientific notation.

If you're exporting to XML, be aware that this can be a significant undertaking. If your current system does not export directly to XML, then you'll have to reformat the exported data to the XML format needed by your vendor. Even if your current system does export to XML, it is highly unlikely that the XML format of the exported data will match the format required to import the data into your new system. In this case, you'll also need to reformat the XML to comply with your new vendor's expectations.

Finally, your vendor may offer multiple format options for your patron data. If this is the case, the optimal approach will be to weigh the pros and cons of each option relative to some of the following questions:

- Does my current system export data in one or more of the data formats the new vendor will work with?
- Will the format of the extracted data or the methods for extracting the data from my current system work better with one format versus another? For example, if your current system can export as CSV or tab-delimited, but does not surround multi-value fields with quotes, then tab-delimited would probably be the better option.

- Do I have the skill set(s) in-house to extract and prepare the data appropriately for each of the format options? If not, then you'll need to focus on the format option that you do have the skill set(s) with which to work.

In this case, your new vendor will be able to provide you with some guidance regarding the different options available to you. But it will ultimately be up to you to determine the optimal path forward.

STEP 4 DEVELOPING AND TESTING YOUR DATA-MIGRATION STRATEGY

With all the preparatory steps behind you, you're ready to map out and begin executing your data-migration strategy. All the information about what data your new system will store, how that relates to your current data, the tools your vendor will provide you, and in which format the vendor expects your data has laid the groundwork for what your data-migration strategy will look like. At this point, it's only a matter of putting all the pieces together.

The optimal approach is to start with what the finished, ready-to-load into your new system, data needs to look like. Visualizing the data you will hand over to your vendor (what fields the data will contain, what those fields will be named, etc.) and what format that data will be in (CSV, XML, Excel spreadsheet, etc.) will enable you to work backwards to determine the steps necessary to arrive at that finished data set.

Will You Need to Do Any Data Transformation, and Can You?

At this step in the process, you should identify whether you will need to do any transformation of the data that you export from your current system. You may need to add fields that you don't already have (more on this below) or convert the exported data to XML. If either of these is necessary, it's important to determine whether you have the skill set among your library staff to do this work. If not, then you'll need to figure out how it will be accomplished.

If your exported data includes multi-value fields, such as barcodes, these can be problematic. Older systems often supported one or more barcodes per patron, which may not be true in your new system. If that's the case, you'll need to determine how to select a preferred barcode from the multiple values that are exported from your existing system.

There are a few options you can explore for this:

- Some vendors will help you with this work, though an additional fee is almost certainly going to be included.

- Your campus IT staff may collaborate with you to perform this work. This is advantageous both because you may already need their help to gain access to additional, current data to add to your exported data set, and because including campus IT staff in the loop on your migration will help to prepare them for any support you may need down the road.
- You can hire a programmer on a temporary basis to assist with this work. If you foresee needing programming support at other points during the migration, this may be a sound approach. But the downside is that once the temporary programmer leaves, she will take a lot of knowledge that may be important in the future.

Are There Any Gaps in Your Exported Data?

Next, identify whether there are any gaps between the data that you will export from your current system and the final data set that you need to hand over to your new vendor. If there are any, you'll need to determine how you are going to add them to the data set before moving forward.

For example, your new system may require that every patron record contains an entirely unique identifier, such as university ID number, or campus username. But, if until now you have relied on barcodes to look up patrons, it's possible that your current system does not store a reliably unique identifier for every patron. Thus, in this instance you would need to figure out how to add a unique identifier into every exported patron record, and what that identifier would be.

This is not an unlikely scenario. Many older systems used combinations of fields such as last name and barcode to authenticate patrons to the online catalog, and thus did not need to store campus usernames or university ID numbers. In contrast, contemporary systems that have a discovery layer built on top of them that is often designed to use campus authentication systems. Such a configuration will almost invariably require that a field such as the campus username be present in the patron record *for those patrons who will be using campus authentication,* so that when a patron signs in to the discovery system using that field, it can then be used to locate the patron in the ILS. This may impact a great number of your patron records, and so it can be important to prepare for this problem.

There are many strategies for doing this. For something such as campus username, at minimum you will likely need to use the following steps:

1. Get a list of the campus usernames for all active campus users. Your campus IT staff should be able to help with this.
2. Identify a match point between the information you get back from your campus IT staff and the data exported from your current system. For instance,

you may not have had campus username in your previous system, but may have had each user's campus ID number.

If there is no match point between the patron records in your current system and those you receive from your campus IT staff, it will be difficult (and perhaps impossible) to do this process programmatically.

3. Develop and run a process using your favorite programming language that can compare the two files of users and copy the campus username into the appropriate record in your exported data.

Every programming language supports some sort of text manipulation that will enable you to do this.

Will You Need to Convert the Format of Your Data?

The most likely scenario where you will need to do additional data transformation is if you need to provide your new vendor with the data in XML format. In this case, you will need to convert your data from the format in which it was exported from your current system into the XML format needed from your vendor.

This can be a challenging process, and will require some programming (using one of the options discussed above). Note that you will need to do more than simply convert your data from its current format (e.g., CSV) to XML. You need to convert it to the XML format as required by your vendor.

There are many resources on how best to do this using the tools and programming languages with which you are most comfortable. Each programming language includes one or more libraries for manipulating XML (e.g., Ruby, Python, PHP), and can be used to do this work.

If you don't have the skill set among your library staff to do this work, then the same considerations as discussed above will apply.

Conducting a Test Load of Your Patron Data

Once you've prepared your data for migration, most vendors will offer the opportunity to do a test load of the data. This is a critical step, and it's best to consider what you will be looking for when evaluating whether the test data loaded properly or not.

Examples of things that to look for include:

- Did each data field migrate to the correct field in the new system?
- Did the data values migrate to each field correctly, or did some elements of the data—such as special characters—migrate incorrectly?
- Did data for both campus and community patrons (if you included the latter) migrate correctly?

- Is any data missing that should have migrated?
- Are you able to search for and find patrons in the new system based on the migrated data?

This is just a sampling you must be prepared to look for once your test data is loaded. This is a very critical step in the overall migration process. You are likely to get only one opportunity to do a test load of your data, and so you will want to check the migrated data as thoroughly as possible to identify any errors or issues that will need to be corrected before you conduct your final data load.

STEP 5   MIGRATING YOUR DATA AND POST-MIGRATION TESTING

Depending on how your test data migration went, the run-up to your final data load could be relatively straightforward, or you could be working diligently to clean up errors and resolve issues. In either case, the remaining steps in preparing for your final data load are ostensibly the same.

1. If you've identified any problems with your test data load, you'll need to first resolve these before producing your final data export. Because most vendors provide reasonably clear guidance on transitioning your data from one system to another, if you've followed these carefully (and worked through the steps outlined above), the issues that you discovered with your test load are most likely the result of necessary data transformation that was not done. To resolve these, you'll need to diagnose what the issue is and then work with whomever did the previous data transformation to apply a fix. The optimal approach would be to run some test data transformations and double-check their results by reviewing the modified data. Knowing what went wrong with the test data load should give you the information that you need to eyeball the newly transformed data and be relatively certain that it will load properly.

2. Once step 1 is complete, or if it was not necessary, you can then move on to a final export of patron data from your current system. Your new vendor will likely lay out a migration and time line for the data load, and should be able to provide recommendations on when to do the final export. With most ILS transitions, you'll have a cutover period where you stop making changes in your current system while data is loaded to your new system. The final export will coincide with this time line.

3. After the vendor loads your final data export, use the test questions and any others that arose during your review of the test data load to thoroughly review the newly loaded patron data. Most vendors will give a very brief window following the data load during which customers need to approve the migrated data. Be prepared to jump into the system and use your test questions to review the data.

Based on the results of your review, you'll end up compiling a list of any issues that need to be resolved or data that must be fine-tuned. Unless something has gone significantly awry with your data migration, most of the items on your list should be ones that can be dealt with through the regular patron loads that you'll be doing once you go live.

STEP 6   MOVING FROM DATA MIGRATION TO DATA MAINTENANCE

Once you've migrated your patron data, signed off on it with your vendor, and begun to use your new system for day-to-day workflows, it's time to turn your attention to ongoing maintenance of your patron data. Looking forward, you'll need to load new and updated patron data to your system on a regular basis. Although this process is similar to the one that you followed for your initial data migration, it is typically different in a few important ways.

Developing Your Regular Patron Load

The key ways in which your ongoing patron load process will differ from your initial data migration include:

1. Some vendors require ongoing loads of patron data to be treated differently than the initial migration. Whereas you may have submitted a CSV file for your data migration, you may need to submit XML files for ongoing data loads.
2. Ongoing patron data loads require that incoming records for patrons already in the system be able to match against a unique identifier.
3. The process should be scheduled and automated if possible.

You'll need to account for each of these as you begin developing your approach for ongoing data loads. These are all topics that you may have already dealt with to an extent while negotiating your initial data migration.

If you do need to format your ongoing data loads differently than you did for your migration, refer to Step 4 above for some guidance on how to do this. The significant difference relative to the steps you followed for your migration is that in this case you are not needing to transform data that has been exported from your previous system. Instead, the data will need to be exported from whatever campus system stores information about campus users.

This is a case where you will need to collaborate with your campus IT staff. One approach is to share with them all the relevant documentation from your vendor on how the regular patron data needs to be formatted, how it is loaded into the system, and any sample patron load files that are available to you. The vendor may have sample files, or you may be able to generate them from your new system. If neither is true, members of the customer community are often willing to share sample files.

Ensuring that there is a match point between the regular incoming data and the patron data already in the system should be straightforward. If the data point (e.g., university ID) already exists in your new system, you'll already need to include it in the incoming data. But there can be a couple of wrinkles:

- *Case sensitivity*. If you are using campus username (e.g., "johndoe") as the match point, be sure that case sensitivity will not be a problem. You'll need to know how the system will respond if the incoming data is in all caps and the data in the system is not. If the two data points won't match due to case sensitivity, then this needs to be accounted for when preparing the incoming data.
- *Usernames can change*. We often think that campus usernames are a reliable match point, but in reality are not. There are certainly cases where patrons' campus usernames will change, typically because of a change in their real names. If this happens, then the system would fail to find a match and would create a new record, which is likely not the outcome you wanted.

Finally, the ongoing patron data loads should ideally be scheduled and automated. The schedule that makes the most sense will vary by institution. But daily patron loads are ideal to ensure that your system always has the most up-to-date database of patrons possible. If you automate your patron loads, keep in mind that there are several steps you may want to automate:

- the extraction of data from its host system
- transforming the data into a format appropriate for your new system and the actual loading
- loading the data into your system

You wouldn't necessarily have to automate all these steps, but doing so ensures that your patron data is regularly updated with as little staff intervention as possible.

Also keep in mind that if you do automate all of these steps, you'll want to set up some type of ongoing reporting about the process. That enables you to keep tabs on the process and to monitor for any issues that may arise over time.

Augmenting Your Patron Data to Take Advantage of New Features

As time passes and you acclimate to using your new system, it's always a good practice to track any changes to the system that relate to patron data. You should be prepared to take advantage of new features or data fields that are added to the system. For example, if your system is updated to enable you to add information about students' majors or faculty departments, this can be useful information to track and leverage.

Different systems release updates at different times, and you'll want to develop a process for monitoring release notes on an ongoing basis. When an update occurs that sounds promising, you can explore it with other library staff as well as any staff (whether in the library or outside of it) who maintain your regular patron load process. Updating your ongoing process to take advantage of the new functionality or data fields is ostensibly the same as that you pursued when you first developed the process. The steps are pretty much the same: planning, development, testing, and then going live with the new process.

SETTING UP USER AUTHENTICATION

User authentication is both simpler and more complicated to set up than the process for migrating your patron data. Simpler, because you'll have fewer decision points than you do when migrating user data. More complicated, because issues may be difficult to uncover and complex to resolve, may involve trade-offs that compromise the user experience, and are often challenging to troubleshoot and resolve while working in the public eye (authentication has lots of stakeholders!).

In addition, when implementing authentication your campus IT and new vendor are probably going to do much of the setup and configuration work. So being able to communicate effectively with the various parties with whom you're working as well as your many stakeholders is perhaps the most critical element in implementing authentication.

Common Types of User Authentication

There is a small range of authentication types that are in use by ILS systems today:

- *Local*: This method utilizes user data that is stored in the ILS itself to authenticate patrons. Examples include users authenticating with last name and barcode, barcode and PIN, or barcode and a password stored in the ILS itself.
- *LDAP*: This stands for "Lightweight Directory Access Protocol." It is an authentication method that is typically offered by your campus IT department, which will employ a standard username and password combination that users will use when logging in to other campus systems (e-mail, learning management system, etc.). It's important to note that for security purposes, LDAP is often limited by firewall restrictions that prevent off-campus systems from communicating with it.

- *CAS*: This stands for "Central Authentication Service," and is a protocol for single sign-on (SSO) authentication. There are two principal benefits of SSO authentication methods, such as CAS: 1) when users have signed into one SSO service (e.g., campus e-mail), they will not be asked to sign in again when they access another SSO service, and 2) the SSO handles the actual user validation on behalf of the ILS, and simply indicates to the ILS that the user is valid (or not), which simplifies the user authentication process and provides greater security. The result is a streamlined and more secure user experience, and increased ease of access from one system to another.
- *SAML*: This stands for "Security Assertion Markup Language," which is a more recently developed protocol for SSO. When implemented, users will experience the same seamless sign-on experience that they do with CAS. The principal difference between SAML and CAS is that SAML relies on two separate components, an Identity Provider (IdP) and Service Provider (SP), which enables the federation of user information across platforms in a secure, standards-driven fashion. As a result, SAML has been widely adopted across academic settings. The most common form of SAML authentication is Shibboleth.
- *OAuth*: This is an authentication method that enables users to use a third-party account (e.g., their Google or Facebook accounts) to authenticate to another system. It works similarly to CAS and SAML, wherein the ILS relies on a separate OAuth-enabled system to do the actual authentication and does not store the user's username and password combination.

Figure 7.1 illustrates the different authentication flows that result when these different options are in place.

What Authentication Method(s) Are You Using Now?

The first step in setting up authentication for your new system is to assess the authentication methods that you are currently using, and how they are set up. Do this by first answering a few, simple questions:

1. Do you enable both campus and community patrons to sign in to your discovery system or catalog?
2. If yes, are you using one authentication method, or multiple methods? For example, do campus patrons authenticate using a campus authentication method (e.g., CAS), but community patrons use local authentication? Or are both groups using the same authentication method? In either case, make note of the method(s) that are in use now.
3. If no, and you are only authenticating campus users, what authentication method are you using?

FIGURE 7.1

Authentication workflows

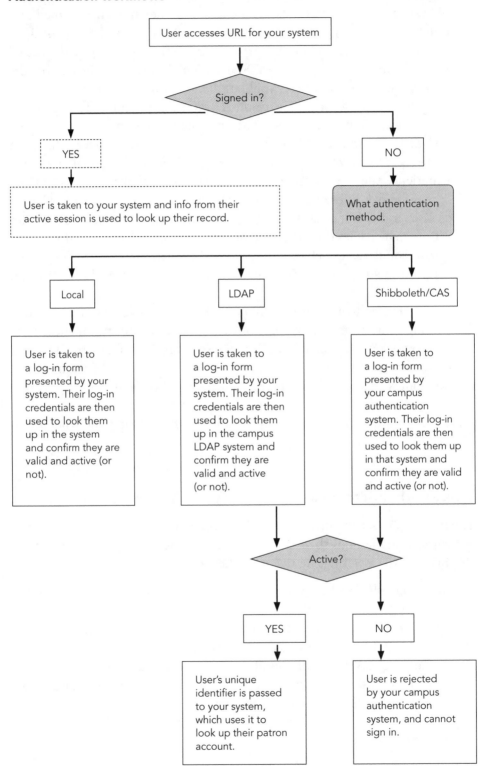

After identifying the authentication methods that are currently in place, you'll want to clarify how they are set up. For each method that you are using, determine:

- Is the method supported and maintained by your campus IT department? This will commonly be the case with LDAP, CAS, or Shibboleth. But local authentication will be specific to the ILS, and so likely managed by the library, whereas OAuth will be managing by a third party.
- What attributes or fields in the ILS's patron records are used by the authentication method(s)? For example, if you are using campus-supported authentication methods, you will likely only be relying on a single attribute in each patron record (username, campus ID, etc.) for supporting authentication. But if you are using local authentication, you will be using multiple attributes.
- Will (or do) these fields migrate to your new system as part of your patron data migration? For example, if you are using local authentication and a locally stored password, this attribute may not be included in the data that you migrate to your new system.

What Authentication Options Does Your Campus Support?

It's worth noting that in terms of authentication, where you are now does not necessarily provide an accurate picture of where you *could* be. Your current system may support authentication options that you do not use. For instance, it isn't unusual for the library catalog to be running on top of a legacy system that uses something such as last name and barcode for authentication. At the same time, there are often alternative, campus-supported authentication options used more broadly across campus, such as LDAP or CAS.

Therefore, an important step at this point in the process is to determine what authentication options your campus supports and what considerations apply to each. In many cases, multiple options are supported (e.g., LDAP and Shibboleth), though each will have benefits and limitations that will affect your decision to implement them. LDAP is often limited in terms of whether off-campus applications (e.g., vendor-hosted ILS or discovery systems) are allowed to communicate with them, which may prevent you from using it for your new system. Shibboleth may be supported by both your campus and vendor, but can be complex to set up and require a good deal of cooperation between both.

Ultimately, this is a moment where it is important to engage with the campus IT staff that manage the available authentication options. You'll want to identify whom they are, explain the nature of the project to them (if they don't know already), and share as much documentation about your new system's authentication architecture as you can find. The more thoroughly you engage with them at this point, the smoother your process is likely to be as you get farther in your implementation.

Understanding Your New System's Authentication Options

Now that you know what authentication mechanisms you are using for your current system and what mechanisms your campus supports, the next step in the process is to identify what authentication options your new system supports, how they work, and how they are set up.

As a quick primer, it's useful to revisit what the workflow is when a user attempts to sign-in to your system. Figure 7.1 lays out this workflow, illustrating the decision-points that are involved:

There are three decision points that your system makes when granting user access:

1. When users first access your system, it determines whether they are already signed in or not. If not, it will ask them to authenticate, and if they are already signed in, it will let them into the system.
2. Before the system can ask users to authenticate, it must determine how they should authenticate. Should they use local authentication, LDAP, Shibboleth, CAS, or something else? Depending on the answer to this question, the user is taken to an appropriate log-in form.
3. Once users' log-in credentials have been validated by the system they are signing into (i.e., the username and password match what the system is expecting), then the system determines if they are active users. In the case of local authentication this step is all part of the same sign-in process. With campus authentication, the campus system will first determine whether a user is active or not. If yes, the user's unique identifier will be passed to your system, where it will be matched up with an existing user (assuming one exists); then your system will check his status to confirm they are active and valid.

With this basic authentication workflow, you can turn your attention to evaluating what authentication mechanisms your new system will support. For each option, assess how it functions relative to the workflow diagrammed in figure 7.1. and to the patron records that you will be setting up. For instance, what fields in the patron record will be used to support authentication, and how does this vary by mechanism?

The answers to this question may vary significantly depending on whether you will be using local or campus authentication. Because local authentication means that your system will be handling the entire log-in process, it will depend on two elements in the patron record, and will likely be very specific about what they are. In most cases, one of these is a PIN or password, and the other will be something such as last name or barcode.

In contrast, when you use campus authentication, the actual sign-in process will be handled by whatever campus system you are using, and so the data elements that will need to be stored in your system are much more limited and typically include just a single unique identifying element. When the user successfully signs in via your campus authentication, a unique identifier will be handed off to your system, which it will use to look up his patron record.

It's also important to determine whether your new system supports the option of offering multiple authentication options. Many libraries enable both campus and community users to sign in to their system, with each group typically using a different authentication method. Whereas campus users will use either LDAP, CAS, or Shibboleth, community users will often be configured to use local authentication, because they don't exist as valid users in campus systems, which are intended to support students, staff, and faculty.

In this case, you will need to determine whether your new system supports configuring multiple authentication options. If so, what is the user experience like? How do patrons identify which option to choose? And are you limited in terms of what options can be set up to work in parallel like this? For instance, can you only set up LDAP and local authentication together? Or can local authentication be set up as an alternative to any campus authentication option?

The last question to consider is who will set up authentication for your system, you (along with your campus IT staff) or your vendor? This varies greatly from system to system, and is helpful to clarify before you get started with implementation. During an initial implementation, vendors will often provide a good deal of support for setting this up. But it is also likely that you will need to incorporate support from your campus IT staff at some point along the way, particularly if you are setting up any form of campus authentication. It is therefore useful to clarify with the vendor what the process is for setting up authentication, and to bring your campus IT into the process as early as possible.

Choosing Your Authentication Option(s)

Now that you have gathered all this information, you have determined the three key elements in setting up authentication for your new system:

1. The authentication options you are using now.
2. The options your campus supports.
3. The options your new system supports.

If you know these three items, you should be prepared to select the authentication options for your new system.

Will You Need to Set up Multiple Authentication Options?

There remains just one additional question that you will need to answer at this point: will you need to offer multiple authentication options to your patrons? As discussed above, this is commonly done in cases where libraries need to enable both campus and community patrons to sign in, and the two groups will need to use different authentication mechanisms.

In most cases, the two options will be local (ILS-specific) authentication for community patrons, and some form of campus-based authentication (e.g., LDAP, CAS, or Shibboleth) for campus patrons. But this could vary, because as OAuth-based forms of authentication become more common, they can often be used in place of local authentication for community patrons, and potentially even for campus patrons.

But as a first step in selecting your authentication options, you'll simply want to determine whether two authentication options are necessary.

Selecting Your Authentication Option(s)

The next step is to consider each authentication path. The easiest way to do this is to break down your users into two groups: campus users and community users.

Authenticating Community Users

If you'll be supporting community users signing into your system, and they will be using a different authentication method than campus users, begin by identifying what options exist. You will likely be limited to using either local authentication or OAuth, and the two directions offer a notably different experience for patrons.

If you opt for local authentication, then depending on how it is configured, community users may need to maintain a separate password for signing into your system. If so, there are obvious security implications for storing this information in your system, and you'll want to take this into consideration. It's especially useful to check with your campus IT staff to see if doing so would breach any campus security policies.

If you opt for OAuth authentication, because the sign-in process will now be handled by a third-party vendor, the need to set up and store usernames and passwords in your system is removed, as are the related security implications. That said, the potential downside is that this option requires that all community users who sign in to your system must have an account with one of the third-party OAuth vendors that your system supports. This is potentially a limiting factor in some scenarios.

You'll want to weigh the pros and cons of each option relative to your unique local considerations. These could include the nature of your population of community users, local security preferences or requirements, and library workflows.

Authenticating Campus Users

Selecting an authentication method for campus users may involve fewer decision points because even though there may be multiple options that are theoretically available for you to implement, your campus IT department is likely to prefer which one you *should* implement.

For instance, LDAP is widely supported in academic settings, though both CAS and SAML are increasingly common. The result is that in most cases where both LDAP and other forms of single sign-on (SSO) are available, your campus IT is likely to favor the latter over the former. This is because SSO offers both better security and a superior user experience relative to LDAP. Yet again, this is a case that illustrates the need to collaborate with your campus IT staff throughout this process to ensure that their priorities and concerns are considered.

It's also worth noting that if your campus offers an SSO method but your library has not yet taken advantage of it, this is the optimal moment to do so. SSO offers a far superior experience compared to any other form of authentication (LDAP, local, etc.), and this is especially true for library patrons. The seamless nature of the user experience that SSO can enable is particularly beneficial for library settings where patrons are typically traversing multiple systems throughout the research process. Not only will patrons be able to crosswalk from campus e-mail or learning management systems to the library's discovery system without having to repeatedly sign in, they will also be able to navigate from item discovery to access (EZProxy) and requesting systems (local holds via the ILS or interlibrary loan system) just as easily. SSO enables the library's ecosystem of separate-but-related systems to work as a unified, coherent whole.

In general, it is highly recommended that you take advantage of SSO for authentication if one of these methods is available on your campus. If not, LDAP still offers some of the benefits of SSO—in particular, that the library will not need to store and/or validate patrons' log-in credentials—but includes notable drawbacks as well.

Thus, there is essentially a hierarchy of authentication methods for campus patrons, and selecting the method you will implement should be as straightforward as starting at the top and working your way down the hierarchy until you find one that you can implement.

Campus authentication options ordered from most to least optimal include:

- SAML is the best method to implement because of its unique federation capabilities and the more seamless user experience it makes possible via single sign-on.
- CAS is the next best method to implement because even though it does not offer the federation capabilities of SAML, it still enables single sign-on.
- LDAP is the third-best option because even though it does not offer single sign-on, it at least pushes authentication to your campus's systems and enables users to make use of their campus log-in credentials.

Implementing User Authentication

Once you've selected the user authentication mechanisms that you will implement, and researched how they will work and how they are set up, you are ready
to begin implementation. As mentioned earlier, in some ways this will be the
simplest part of the whole process. Your new vendor and your campus IT staff
will be critical partners as you work forward, and will most likely be doing much
of the actual setup work with you. The bulk of your role while implementing
authentication will be to coordinate the process from start to finish and conduct
testing when necessary.

It's most likely that because setting up authentication will be part of the
overall process of migrating to your new ILS, your vendor will reach out to you
at some point. With the information that you will have gathered through the
preceding steps, you should be ready to move forward when they do.

It's not possible for a single chapter to provide a detailed step-by-step process that illustrates what you will experience while setting this up. Each library's
implementation will be a bit different; yours will vary based on the authentication
mechanisms that you have selected, to which ILS you are moving, how your
campus has configured its authentication mechanisms, and how successfully
you can work with both your vendor and your campus IT staff. That said, there
are essentially four principal components that are involved in the actual implementation process. You should focus on

- Coordinating the work of the vendor and your campus IT staff and determining how they will share information. You will be the hub via which the
  two groups communicate and get authentication fully up and running.
- Configuring and updating authentication-related settings in your ILS. This
  may be setting up test user accounts that mirror different types of patrons
  or updating settings for a specific authentication mechanism (if you have
  access to them) in your ILS.
- Testing, testing, and more testing. Spend enough time testing a wide range
  of scenarios related to authentication. (Can all staff sign in? Can different
  patron groups sign in to the discovery system? When patrons sign in to the
  discovery interface, is the system linking their ILS account properly?)
- Communicating with library stakeholders. It's critical to keep the stakeholders, particularly fellow staff, in the loop as authentication is implemented.
  Many potential topics will call for ongoing communication, including: letting
  them know how authentication works (or will work); enlisting them to help
  with testing; and working with them to inform patrons as appropriate.

Ultimately, setting up authentication for your new system is not necessarily a
difficult or complicated process. There are not that many options to pursue,
and how authentication works for any given system is typically quite specific.

Instead, setting this up is challenging simply because of the amount of back-and-forth communication that is involved, and the need to conduct thorough testing at each step of the process. In some cases, implementing authentication can sometimes feel like you are taking one step backwards for every two steps forward.

But the implementation process is very linear and straightforward when viewed from a high level. By following each of the steps laid out in this chapter, you can model an approach to implementation that will help navigate the challenges, both foreseen and unexpected, that will arise along the way.

RESOURCES

Resources for Learning XML

Ray, Erik T. *Learning XML (2nd edition).* Sebastopol: O'Reilly Media, 2003.

Ray, Erik T. *Learning XML (1st edition).* Sebastopol: O'Reilly Media, 2001. https://archive.org/details/OReillyLearningXML.

Harold, Elliott Rusty and W. Scott Means. *XML in a Nutshell.* Sebastopol: O'Reilly Media, 2004.

Whatley, Kay. "XML Basics for New Users." IBM developerWorks. Last modified February 24, 2009. www.ibm.com/developerworks/library/10-newxml/.

Parsing XML Using Common Scripting Languages

"PHP: Basic SimpleXML Usage." http://php.net/manual/en/simplexml.examples-basic.php.

"Ruby Nokogiri: Parsing an HTML/XML Document." www.nokogiri.org/tutorials/parsing_an_html_xml_document.html.

"Python: XML Processing Modules." https://docs.python.org/2/library/xml.html.

Common Authentication Methods

LDAP

"Lightweight Directory Access Protocol." https://en.wikipedia.org/wiki/Lightweight_Directory_Access_Protocol.

"The 10-Minute LDAP Tutorial—Automating System Administration with Perl." http://archive.oreilly.com/pub/a/perl/excerpts/system-admin-with-perl/ten-minute-ldap-utorial.html.

SAML

"Security Assertion Markup Language." https://en.wikipedia.org/wiki/Security
_Assertion_Markup_Language.
"Shibboleth." https://shibboleth.net.

CAS

"Central Authentication Service." https://en.wikipedia.org/wiki/Central_Authentication
_Service.

OAuth

"OAuth.net." https://oauth.net.
"OAuth." https://en.wikipedia.org/wiki/OAuth.
"An Introduction to OAuth 2." www.oreilly.com/pub/e/2184.

SERIALS

Elan May Rinck, Serials Technical Assistant, University of Portland

S erials are often considered a unique beast, and for good reason. Although serials share many of the same migration concerns as other resources, they also present their own challenges. It's crucial to devote the attention and planning they deserve when approaching a system migration at your institution. It's equally important to devote time to understanding how your new system handles continuing resources on a theoretical level prior to planning the practical aspects of your migration.

Striking a balance between determining functional requirements in the new system and maintaining data integrity during migration are crucial, although difficult. Involving individuals who understand the complexity of the migration process and individuals who understand the complexity of serials data and workflows can help accomplish this. If your situation allows it, involving serials staff in the vendor-review process can avoid potential pitfalls in serials migration by vetting a potential system's serials support capabilities.

It's best to take a pragmatic approach. Expect that the new serials infrastructure will be considerably different from your existing system. Because of the trend towards electronic resources, be aware that the new system may support less functionality for print resources than your old system. A major consideration with serials data is that migration is often a more manual process than with other resources. Serials acquisitions data and item data can present hurdles during migration, and it's worth mapping out a plan for dealing with these prior to making the move.

Your institution's serial workflows will be unique because they are based on your patron base and collection priorities. The purpose of this chapter is to help you explore the best way to translate these goals to a new system while undergoing a migration and effectively explore the potential serials infrastructure of a new system.

SCANNING YOUR ENVIRONMENT

Identify Data Sources

Many institutions utilize multiple tools to manage their serials collection, so you must identify which data sources are relevant to your situation. Your current integrated library system may contain useful information in bibliographic, holdings, item, acquisitions, and/or check-in records. Additionally, many institutions use outside electronic resource management systems (ERMS) to handle their serials efficiently. Exploring what role these third-party products currently play in your serials management and maintenance will help you identify what data you need to migrate to your new system and determine whether you need to maintain outside systems to manage your serials. Talk to relevant staff about all potential serials data sources, including:

- integrated library systems
- homegrown systems
- A-Z title lists
- knowledge bases
- link resolver products

Your library may have just a few of these or many. Make sure you identify what sources exist in your specific scenario, and define what purpose they serve in your serials resource management efforts. You will also want to investigate what data you wish to maintain from each source, and whether you will continue to use these products after migration.

Analyze Current Infrastructure

An important part of migrating serials data is looking back before you move forward. It is worth the time to sit down with staff who work with serials on a day-to-day basis and examine what workflows are being used in the current system. Fully understanding your current infrastructure and workflows will help you best take advantage of your new system's features. Although you should take the time to fully understand your existing cataloging workflow, some specific serials issues to look for include:

- *How are you handling serials acquisitions?*
  Aim to understand completely how your library is currently handling acquisitions records. For multi-format or multi-title subscriptions, do you have a single order record, multiple order records for each portion, or a combination? To what extent do you use order records for recording the history of that subscription (i.e., notes regarding vendor and publisher changes, publishing delays, or title changes)? Work with your staff to understand what your current procedures are for maintaining acquisition records as resources change.

- *What are your holdings records like?*
  Is your data clean and up to standard? Do you use any local field or other potentially difficult-to-map fields? What holdings data must be preserved?

- *How are you handling item records?*
  Does your institution check in individual physical items? Do you currently use predictive inventory functionality or check-in cards? Migrating this data to a new system can be particularly tricky, so it is worth investigating the value and purpose of your current practices regarding individual item records. This can help you determine how much effort you should allot to manual efforts when migrating item records to a new system (which will be discussed in depth later).

- *How does your library manage physical received items?*
  Investigate what current workflows your institution is using to manage physical resources. Look at your actual processing workflow. Who receives items: staff, student workers, or volunteers? Does the item move through separate locations before processing is completed? If your institution undertakes claiming, discuss the current system tools that are used for this process. Is claiming automated, semi-automated, or a manual process?

- *How do you handle electronic resources?*
  Is your ERMS incorporated within your main system, or are you using a secondary system? For more information on ERMS migration considerations, please review the next chapter.

- *What functions are handled by third-party systems, if any?*
  This is particularly relevant for libraries using ERMS to support serials management, and you should involve staff members that participate in electronic resource management. Identify what systems handle which functions, and why.

All these questions are individually important, but also serve as components of the larger question: How is your current infrastructure set up, and why? The main goal in investigating how you're currently handling your serials is to identify your greater philosophy. This is also the perfect time to investigate what you can't currently accomplish but wish you could. Ask your staff if there's any functionality or workflows they feel would improve serials management, and explore whether those would line up with your institution's philosophy.

Understanding the functionality you wish to maintain and what you're willing to let go will help you best take advantage of a new system's serials infrastructure, as well as prioritize pre- and post-migration cleanup efforts. Keep in mind that this exploration may involve parties who are not exclusively invested in serials management, such as staff involved in acquisitions and electronic resource management endeavors.

Analyze New Infrastructure

Now that you have a clear understanding of how your institution currently approaches serials management, it's time to analyze how your new system handles these resources. Establishing a clear understanding of how serials data is handled in the new system will allow you to develop a more complete plan for data mapping and post-migration cleanup. It's best to approach this task from a top-down approach.

How serials data is handled within the new system may be intimately related to the system structure. Looking at the general system structure will help you understand why and how it differs from your current system, and what translation may be necessary for migration.

The first thing to look at is how the new system treats serials in general. Is the serials infrastructure built off a generalized monographic infrastructure, or is it modular with unique serials features? Answering this question will help guide you in understanding the system's potential, as well as establishing a basis for how data is treated within the system—and what may pose a potential problem during migration.

As with your analysis of your institution's existing system, you should explore the following questions:

- How are acquisitions records handled? Will your existing order records migrate successfully, and will they remain open and usable?
- How does the system approach holdings records? Are there differences between the way monographic and continuing resources holdings migrate?
- How does the system handle item records? Does it support item check-in, automated inventory creation, and claiming?
- How does the system treat electronic resources?

- Is there the potential for internal usage data support?
- What, if any, third-party services will you need in addition to your integrated library system?

As much as possible, try to identify what analogous workflows are available in the new system. If the system is substantially different on a basic level, this may not be possible. Instead, work with staff to identify workflows that have a similar outcome, and remind them that the migration may come with substantial changes to current practices. You will likely identify workflows that cannot be replicated in the new system, such as claiming or automated inventory creation. Explore whether these are crucial to your serials management philosophy, and what alternative options there may be within and without the new system.

This is also a great time to explore what added benefits your new system can bring to serials management. Newer systems tend to have a more robust electronic resource management infrastructure, and can also provide a greater level of resource management automation. Depending on your current system and goals, you may also be able to consolidate some or all third-party system functionalities into your new system.

Develop a Plan for Migration

Developing a plan for serials data migration often means balancing the ideal with the possible. Because serials often encompass a large amount of data and large number of records, and migration time lines are often shorter than we would like, pragmatism is required to identify what data must be migrated, and what would merely be nice to have. Much of your serials data-migration plan will overlap with your larger data migration, but there are also special considerations for serials.

Selecting Data

Start by working with serials staff to identify what data should be prioritized in migration. This could include:

- acquisitions data
    - » renewal periods
    - » pricing history
    - » subscription notes
    - » vendor information
- summary holdings
- item holdings

- electronic resources data
  - » administrative access information
  - » licensing data
  - » addition access information
  - » check-in data

- check-in records
- check-in cards
- prediction patterns
- claiming information
- binding data
- circulation data

Some of this data will be treated the same as monographic data in your migration plan, but some will require special planning. Work with your vendor to confirm what your new system will support.

You will also need to create realistic migration specifications for serials data. Depending on your institution's serials collection size and individual migration process, you may be restricted in how many records you can migrate based on available labor (e.g., when manually creating linking numbers). Weigh your institution's labor costs, potential benefits, and system constraints when you develop migration specifications. This is highly variable depending on your library's situation. For some institutions, this may mean migrating only active subscriptions, check-in information after a certain date, or no item information at all.

Depending on your circumstances, it may be necessary to develop an archiving process for outstanding data that is not within your serial migration specifications (e.g., claims or payment history) if your legacy system will not remain online after migration. Work with your staff to identify what data and archiving method works best for your individual needs.

Mapping Fields

After selecting which data you want to migrate, you must develop a plan to map existing fields to the new system. Creating a schema crosswalk at the outset can be useful in determining how to handle trickier serials data (e.g., acquisitions information), and what data cannot be mapped appropriately. Your system vendor will likely handle the simpler fields, especially bibliographic and holding records. Existing MARC fields will be translated to those available within the new system. For fields that are less parallel, you will likely need to work with your vendor or on your own to identify how they should be mapped.

Serials and acquisitions records can be especially tricky to migrate due to the inconsistent nature of record formats between systems, so special care should be taken when mapping these fields. You may need to be flexible in how you handle acquisition notes, subscription notes, access notes, renewal dates, vendor information, and prediction patterns. If your new system does not have defined fields for this data, user-defined or free-text note fields may provide a solution. Keep in mind that free-text note fields often are not searchable, so are a less-than ideal solution to record, for example, renewal dates or vendor information. You may also find that data you would like to include, such as prediction patterns, cannot be mapped to your new system. In those cases, you may need to develop a post-migration work-around to maintain the functionality that data provided.

Testing Data

Ideally, your migration time line includes adequate time for testing data migration. You should involve both staff with serials knowledge and those with experience with the new system in this process. If your institution is undertaking centralized migration data testing, ensure that serials data—and staff—are adequately represented. Do your best to include as many record variations as possible in testing, including:

- formats
- frequencies
- retentions
- locations
- access types and platforms
- order types
- multiple vendors and acquisition funds
- statuses (e.g., active or ceased)

Including as many variations in testing as possible will help you determine if all data is behaving as expected, if data has loaded into the correct fields, and if it has been formatted correctly. It will also help you identify where post-migration cleanup efforts will be needed, and what projects will need to be prioritized once the system goes live.

Develop a Plan for Post-Migration

Working through the field-mapping and data-testing processes will likely highlight issues that will need to be addressed after migration. Most of these will be related to bugs or unexpected effects in system functionality, but some challenges might be more extreme. You may find data—such as prediction patterns or acquisitions data—that will need to be entered manually once your new system goes live. You may also identify functionality—such as claiming—that will need to be moved to an outside system.

To address functionality problems that appear post-migration, you should establish a reporting protocol that elevates issues to systems staff and the vendor if necessary. Staff should be trained to investigate and report on specific functionality, behavior, replicability, and effect. Serials staff may be the first to encounter major issues, especially those relating to electronic resource management and access, so establishing a course of action in these cases is important.

For data that needs to be entered into the new system manually, develop realistic plans and time lines for each project. Prioritize these projects according to urgency, based on staff and patron needs. If you're nearing your renewal period, this may mean choosing to fast-track a project focusing on acquisitions data over item data. Similarly, you may find it makes sense to prioritize certain parts of larger data input projects over others. As with your migration specification, identify clear limits for manual data entry and do your best to keep project scopes to a manageable size. It is almost certain that data entry will take longer than expected. You may also want to investigate the possibility of keeping your old system up and functioning, even without vendor support, during the initial post-migration period. This can substantially improve the quality and completeness of data entry. If that is not possibile, make sure you have pulled all the data you will need from your old system prior to migration.

When considering serials processes that need to be handled outside of the new system, weigh the value of those processes against the difficulty of implementing a local or third-party solution. Work with staff to determine whether the functionality is realistically worth preserving. If you determine it is, reach out to other users of your new system. If you think a system feature is worthwhile, it's likely others do as well—and they may have found a work-around within the system to accomplish it. If you determine that there truly is no system work-around, investigate other solutions that fit within your institution's budget, even if that means an old-fashioned spreadsheet. Work with staff to integrate this with new workflows.

Keeping Staff Sane during and after Migration

A full system migration is challenging for everyone in the library, and serials staff are faced with unique challenges during the process. However, the process needn't be painful. Keeping a focus on staff engagement, training, and communication can be incredibly helpful during the migration process. Involve staff in relevant investigation and decision making. Their expertise can help you catch problems early and plan effectively. Create a comprehensive training program that spans pre- and post-migration to keep things running smoothly. Work with your vendor to identify appropriate training opportunities and resources. Additionally, providing clear lines of communication can help identify needs, issues, and opportunities. All these efforts lead to greater staff flexibility and response, which will make your migration more successful.

ELECTRONIC RESOURCES MANAGEMENT

Todd Enoch, Head of Serials and Electronic Resources,
University of North Texas

In the world of electronic resources (ER), libraries often find themselves struggling to stay on top of the intricacies of these resources. Although we no longer live in the veritable Wild West of the late 1990s, when every vendor appeared to be making up the rules as it went along, there is still a wide range of variance among providers in the licensing and permissions of databases, ejournals, ebooks, and streaming media platforms. The electronic resource management system (ERMS) can serve a vital role in providing libraries a space to gather and maintain all the data they need to manage their ER work-flows effectively; however, the amount of data that needs to be gathered and input into these systems can prove intimidating.

DATA TYPES

There are many types of data that can be housed in ERMS. At the most basic, an ERMS will contain a resource record that contains descriptive information about the ER itself. The resource record can be for something as broad as a publisher platform, or as narrow as a single reference work. The decision for what deserves its own resource record and what can exist as a subset of another resource is up to the discretion of the library. Much of this data can mirror that found in bibliographic records in the main catalog:

- title/alternate titles
- coverage dates
- connection and proxy information
- subject headings
- format (HTML, PDF, media, etc.)
- product description
- author/access providers

In addition, the resource record may contain resource-specific information that is more suited for internal library use:

- renewal and expiration dates
- trial information
- administrative usernames and passwords
- issue logs

The ERMS can also contain holdings data for individual titles housed within the larger resource. These holdings are often a result of data imported from a knowledge base, and will allow a user to see the titles and dates available for all titles provided by a database or platform. These holdings lists may or may not be visible on the main resource record, depending on the ERMS and its settings.

Many libraries find it useful to track usage data provided by vendors in their ERMSs. Most vendors format usage data using the Counting Online Usage of NeTworked Electronic Resources (COUNTER) standard. When preparing to migrate your usage data, make sure you know what types of reports your ERMS is set up to receive, because there are multiple types of COUNTER reports for different formats (ejournals, ebooks, databases, multimedia, etc.). Probably the common report is the JR5 report, which measures the number of full-text downloads for ejournals. Usage data can either be downloaded manually by you from vendor websites, or if the vendor utilizes the Standardized Usage Statistics Harvesting Initiative (SUSHI) protocol. the statistics can be sent to you automatically. The SUSHI protocol is specifically designed to work with COUNTER-compliant usage statistic. Of course, some vendors may provide usage statistics in non-COUNTER compliant formats that might not be compatible with your ERMS. If the ERMS allows financial data to be entered, then it may be able to generate Cost Per Use figures for the resources as well.

One of the most useful aspects of the ERMS is to track license data. The license record in an ERMS can include information such as

- authorized users
- ILL permissions

- archival rights
- reproduction rights
- performance rights
- authorized locations
- indemnification
- warranty
- renewal/cancelation windows

Finally, an ERMS may allow you to store vendor data such as names and contact information for your customer-service representatives, e-mail addresses for technical support, and remit addresses for payment. In the III ERM, these contact records are also used to populate fields in the resource records, allowing for easy tracking of which entity is responsible for various aspects of a resource such as access or copyright. You can also use the contact records to store information about any consortial memberships or affiliations, which by extension can be linked to the resource records of products purchased through consortial deals.

STEP 1 INVESTIGATION

If you are implementing an ERMS for the first time, your initial data migration might pull from various sources. In fact, even if you are migrating from one ERMS to another, you might need to expand your data collection sources if the new ERMS contains features not present in your previous system. For example, when the University of North Texas (UNT) was forced to migrate to its current ERMS, we had to pull in data not only from the defunct ERDB, but also from our Integrated Library System (ILS), knowledge base (KB), and various spreadsheets and text files containing administrative and usage information. To ensure your migration goes as smoothly as possible, your first steps should be to fully explore the capabilities of your ERMS.

The first capability to consider is the types of fields available for entering data in your ERMS. They may be fixed fields that only allow a narrow list of options to be selected; free text or variable fields that allow any text to be entered; or text fields that have a combination of the former two. For example, the III ERM module allows you to create a standard list of subjects you can select from a drop-down menu, but you may also input freestanding text into the subject field. Knowing what fields are available, and how customizable they are, will help you later when you need to create a map between the ERMS and the data you wish to migrate. These fields can also serve to inspire you to migrate data you may not have previously considered. For example, the III ERM contains a fixed field for consortia information that we hadn't thought to include in the ERDB, but which has been extremely helpful in letting us keep track of our consortial purchases.

Another capability to investigate is the ability to store files such as PDFs or other documents in your ERMS. If your ERMS has this ability, then you may wish to attach copies of your ER license agreements in the ERMS for easy retrieval; if your ERMS does not have this ability, then it becomes more important to transfer the information accurately from these documents into license records.

TIP: You may wish to determine a way to point to the location of the actual documents on your network from the ERMS license record if possible. Inputting complex legal language into a license record is time-consuming, and possibly confusing to the layperson; better to express the ideas in layman's terms in the record, and then go to the original document when exact language needs to be consulted

One aspect to pay close attention to during your initial research into your ERMS is how different fields and record types interact with each other. This could determine the best order to migrate your data. For example, in the III ERM resource records there are multiple fixed fields that are populated from data pulled from the vendor contact records. If the vendor information is not input first, these fields must remain blank. Along similar lines, if your ERMS is designed to regularly interact with another product, such as your ILS or knowledge base, then certain pieces of data migration may involve setting up links between the two products instead of moving data. Order records with financial information in the III ILS may be linked to resource records in the III ERMS so that the information is available in both modules without having to copy or move the data manually.

Finally, perhaps the most important capability to discover before proceeding with the data migration is the data-import capabilities of your ERMS. You need to discover what types of data will be easy for your staff to import and what types will need to be input manually. For the importable data, getting a good grasp of file format is recommended. Although MARC may be the standard for bibliographic records in an ILS, I've found that tab and comma separated file formats such as TXT, TVS, and CVS appear to be the lingua franca for ERMS. Knowing what can and can't be imported will be critical information as you gather your data. Most likely a large portion of your data will need to be input manually, rather than loaded automatically, but do your due diligence to make sure that everything that can be automated will be.

TIP: If there is some data you'd like to import but nothing in the documentation indicates that it is possible, feel free to reach out to your ERMS's technical support staff to see if there's anything they can do behind the scenes. They might not be able to help, but if there's even a slight possibility that you can send them a data file to process rather than having your staff input data manually, it's worth asking.

STEP 2 DETERMINING PHILOSOPHY AND FOCUS

As you review the capabilities of your ERMS, it is also valuable to review your philosophy behind implementing the system and determine what areas you wish to focus on. Some questions to consider include:

- Is the ERMS going to be used primarily as a behind-the-scenes product that allows staff to keep track of ER workflows?
- Is it going to be used to supplement or replace the ER records of the online catalog?
- What information should be publicly available and what should be accessible only by library staff?
- What types of resources warrant full resource records?
- What types of agreements, licenses, amendments, order forms, etc. warrant full license records?

These questions can help determine the basic settings for your ERMS, and where particular pieces of data should be entered. For example, the III ERM has both private and public note fields available, so it is best to decide which data fits in each category before migration begins.

STEP 3 IDENTIFYING DATA SOURCES

Once you have explored the capabilities of your ERMS and solidified your philosophy, it's time to determine the sources of your data. As mentioned earlier, there can be a myriad of sources to choose from, depending on how your ER data is currently managed.

The best-case scenario is migrating data from one ERMS to another, because both should nominally contain the types of data discussed above. In the best-case scenario, this data would also be easily exportable into a format that your new ERMS could import. This format is typically a tab- or comma-separated text file. These file types are easily edited and manipulated in a spreadsheet program such as Excel; just be sure to save as the correct file type once you're done making changes.

Even if your two ERMS speak the same basic language, watch out for possible speed bumps. Understanding how your new ERMS reads the file it imports is crucial. Take the following holdings data derived from a comma-separated file as an example. The display is how the data appears when opened in Excel. The first row contains the field names, and the second row contains the data to import.

RESOURCE NAME	ISSN	JOURNAL TITLE	START DATE	END DATE
Gallica Publishing	0755–8333	Accusateur public	1795	1797

For some programs, all that is important is the order in which the data is presented. In these cases, you need to make sure that there is a space allocated for any fields for which the importing program might be looking. For example, if the new ERMS expects there to be a space for an eISSN, you would need to create a column for that value, even if you have no information to input.

RESOURCE NAME	ISSN	EISSN	JOURNAL TITLE	START DATE	END DATE
e1432423	0755–8333		Accusateur public	1795	1797

Other programs may match on field names, so it doesn't necessarily matter if you have a column for blank data; what's more important is that you know that what your old ERMS called a Resource Name is known as a Resource ID in your new ERMS.

RESOURCE ID	ISSN	JOURNAL TITLE	START DATE	END DATE
Gallica Publishing	0755–8333	Accusateur public	1795	1797

You will also want to investigate how any import function of your ERMS handles data from repeatable fields such as subject headings or alternate titles. They may be contained in the same field separated by a piece of punctuation the system recognizes as an indicator that there are two pieces of data present. Or the system may not play well with repeatable fields, and your data will need to be entered manually after the initial importing is complete.

If your former ERMS is not set up to easily export the data you need, then exploring other data sources might be preferable. That was the case for UNT; what little information we could pull from the defunct ERDB was useful only in terms of double-checking that all our resources were represented after importing from other sources.

Your ILS can be a prime source of data for your ERMS, especially if your ILS and ERMS are provided by the same vendor. For the UNT migration, we were able to create a list of our ERs in the ILS, which III then converted into resource records in the ERM. However, even if your ILS and ERMS are provided by two different vendors, you will most likely be able to export a good amount of data about your ERs from your ILS. Typically, data from your ILS will be bibliographic data such as title, author, subject headings, and URLs, but you may also be able to glean financial data if you have utilized an ILS acquisitions module for ER payments.

If you currently use a knowledge base such as EBSCO A-to-Z, Serials Solutions, or SFX to assist with OpenURL linking or web scale discovery, getting its data into your ERMS is essential. As with the ILS, if your knowledge base is provided by the same vendor as your ERMS, data migration will be greatly simplified, but most knowledge bases allow for exporting holdings data into tab- or comma-separated files. For the initial data migration, this data is most helpful for ensuring that every database and platform active in your knowledge base has a corresponding resource record in your ERMS. This is especially important if your ERMS allows you to import holdings data from your knowledge base. For example, the III ERM coverage load matches an ID field in the resource record to the resource name from the knowledge base; if there isn't a match, the load fails.

We now move into the area where tracking down sources of data can be more time-consuming. If you've never used an ERMS before, it's likely that much of the data you'd like to migrate is housed in an assortment of spreadsheets in a variety of locations on your library's network. At UNT, we had multiple spreadsheets to track our ER workflow, maintain our administrative passwords, store usage statistics, describe the various processes for downloading MARC records for each vendor, monitor license terms for streaming video, and so on. Many of these were stored in different folders on our network, and some were even maintained only on a single staff member's personal drive. Migrating all this data into the ERMS has been a huge help, but it has taken a lot of time to get it all in place.

Last, but certainly not least, are your ER licenses. As daunting as tracking down various spreadsheets can be, it pales in comparison to the task of compiling data from years of licenses that have never been entered electronically. And in some cases, even if you do have the basic license information in one of the formerly mentioned sources, you may find that the capabilities of your ERMS allow you to input data in new ways that make the task of digging out the old licenses worthwhile.

STEP 4   MAPPING FIELDS

After you've identified your data sources, you need to figure out how to map the data you want to migrate onto the fields you identified earlier, a task that is often easier said than done. For the first step of UNT's ERMS migration, the most basic mapping was largely out of our hands, because the bulk of our resource records were imported from ILS bibliographic records and transformed into ERMS resource records. The vendor took the appropriate MARC fields and translated them into the closest corresponding fields available in the resource record. You may find that your ERMS vendor can do something similar. But the odds are good that even in that eventuality, there's a large amount of data that only you can adequately map, or that cannot be easily mapped in a 1:1 ratio for one reason or another. For example, if you are trying to map data from a 245 field in a MARC record to a title field in a resource record, there may be extraneous bits of information such as author names or general material designators that fall outside of the strict title category. UNT had to do a large amount of resource title cleanup due to unwanted information being transferred from the MARC records. Another instance of mapping difficulties can be found in migrating basic author and publisher information, as it could conceivably map to a wide range of other fields such as access provider, copyright holder, data provider, etc. Mapping might tell you which of the fields where such data could conceivably go, but making the determination of whether a publisher is also a copyright holder or merely an access provider is going to be a case-by-case decision.

For the fields with fixed terminology, it's very important to come up with strict definitions of the terms before you begin migration, especially if you have multiple people inputting and interpreting data from a source with no such terminology. One person's "reference source" may be another person's "data set," and without some sort of authority control the muddled usage will become worse than if no data was entered at all. You may be able to edit this fixed terminology to some degree, and should take full advantage of that capability if it exists to create a more fully rounded set of choices instead of cramming everything into a small set of broad categories.

As you begin your mapping, you may find that some pieces of data do not easily fit into any of the preexisting ERMS fields. In some cases, your ERMS may also provide you with a series of fields that can be user-defined. For example, UNT has utilized user-defined fixed fields in the resource and license records to indicate the source of MARC records, availability in our discovery layer, and whether streaming video is licensed for hosting on internal servers.

If your ERMS does not allow for user-defined fields, or you find that these fields still cannot accommodate all the data you wish to include in your ERMS, then you are in the unenviable, but perhaps inevitable, position of having to construct work-arounds to fit your desired data into the ERMS schema. The easiest solution is to take advantage of any free-text note fields available in the ERMS, but that can quickly lead to an overabundance of notes that are difficult to sort, search, or parse. Another option is to co-opt a field that seems useless to your library's needs; if your library never makes any consortial purchases, then perhaps a field regarding consortia may be turned to a better use. The danger here, of course, is that co-opting an unused field may be confusing to anyone learning the system in the future. Plus, what if your library suddenly becomes part of a consortia? Balancing current needs with the those of the future can be a tricky business, and one you should be mindful of when trying to game the system.

INSTITUTIONAL REPOSITORIES AND DIGITAL COLLECTIONS

Kyle Banerjee, Digital Collections and Metadata Librarian, OHSU

D igital asset management (DAM) systems and institutional repositories (IRs) are often described as a single type of system. However, they are alike in the same sense that dogs, clams, and spiders are all animals. Each platform is designed to meet specific needs. Some are established to publish articles and others are designed to create visual exhibitions. Some are intended to serve as an integral part of the creative workflow, while others are created to preserve finished objects so they cannot be changed. Some are designed to manage resources centrally, and others assume objects and metadata will be managed in a distributed environment. Some systems are designed to be as open as possible, whereas others were designed with powerful granular controls to address security, privacy, or other concerns. Many are optimized for specific types of assets such as textual articles, images, video, sound, archival books, geographical data, or specific types of scientific data sets.

The differences between DAMs and IRs are not important for migration purposes. IRs are used to preserve and disseminate the digital collections and intellectual output of institutions. DAMs focus on digital assets that might be actively used and modified. For example, a marketing department might use a DAM to keep track of photos, releases, licensing information, and the like. DAMS and IRs vary dramatically in scope, content, capabilities, and configuration, so migrating one may be a simple task that junior staff could easily execute, but it could also be a major project that challenges a team of experts. However, all DAM/IR migrations share certain elements in common, and the article and image repositories common to libraries present relatively few conceptual or technical challenges.

The process of selecting a DAM/IR is outside the scope of this chapter. Likewise, specific systems will not be discussed because there are too many to provide even cursory details, and rapid technology cycles render information obsolete within months. Rather, the focus of this chapter is on performing the actual migration using tools and skill sets available at most libraries. No programming knowledge is assumed, but certain migration tasks require coding or data skills. When special skills are necessary, you'll receive guidance that helps you identify individuals who can help.

The key to migrating a DAM/IR is understanding what users need it to do and having a plan for migrating functionality that users depend on—the goal is more about migrating an effect than it is about migrating data. Librarians tend to focus on transferring objects and metadata, but if users deposit materials in a DAM/IR because of the statistics they're provided, they might seek alternatives if the new system doesn't offer that functionality. If search functionality is provided by a separate discovery system, you'll need to ensure that system still receives the data it needs. You'll need to confirm that the many links that point to your existing system point somewhere useful after the migration.

The major steps in migrating a DAM/IR is provided below, followed by an explanation of what those steps are. The specific systems, resources, or needs may require additional steps, so the list provided here should only be considered a guide.

STEPS INVOLVED IN MIGRATING A DAM/IR

- Determine nature of collections.
- Understand metadata in the DAM/IR.
- Determine access controls in place.
- Identify import and export methods supported on old and new systems.
- Identify required fields in new system.
- Verify exported metadata and objects.
- Identify and address schema differences.
- Verify metadata and object transfer.
- Configure system.
- Integrate with other systems.
- Update entries to handles, DOIs, and PURLs.

- Transition statistics.
- Update URLs in catalogs, websites, documentation, and marketing.

DETERMINE THE NATURE OF COLLECTIONS

The first step in planning a successful migration is to make sure you fully understand what you need to migrate. Questions that need to be answered include but are not limited to:

- What resources do you need to migrate? Books, articles, images, video, data sets, sound files and other resources each present their own challenges.
- Do collections or objects exist in complex structures or hierarchies? For example, are multiple files associated with single objects? Are articles and books stored as single objects or as single pages that are linked together? Is each image a stand-alone object, or are some intended to be used together (e.g., photos of an item taken from different angles)? When multiple objects are associated with a record, what determines how they are presented? Are they organized into collections and subcollections, and can one object belong to multiple collections?
- What metadata schemes and elements are present? Do values contain embedded code or values designed to exploit system-specific behavior? Are there any special characters, and if so, how are they represented?

UNDERSTANDING METADATA IN A DAM/IR

A successful migration requires that metadata be transferred completely and accurately. There are too many metadata standards to list, but as of this writing, the most widely supported standards within library applications are Dublin Core, MARCXML (MAchine Readable Cataloging eXtensible Markup Language), MODS (Metadata Object Description Schema), and OAI-PMH (Open Archives Initiative Protocol for Metadata Harvesting). However, the systems you are migrating from and to might not support any of those standards, but all systems have some provision for getting data in and out of the system.

When exporting data, the easiest way to work with standards you are unfamiliar with is to simply look at the data. Similarly, when importing data into a new system, seek and copy simple examples. These methods are generally much more effective than reading technical specifications because "supporting" a standard means very different things in different contexts. Even if the old and new systems nominally support the same standards, the systems may not implement the standards in a compatible way. Significant configuration or custom programming may be necessary.

> Just because the old and new systems nominally support the same standards does not mean the systems implement the standards in a compatible way.

Regardless of where and how it is stored, all metadata can be described in terms of one or more of three basic metadata types. *Descriptive* metadata is information that helps people identify and access resources. Descriptive elements include titles, authors, subjects, and notes, and common library standards including Dublin Core and MARC (MAchine Readable Cataloging). Descriptive metadata is usually the easiest type to transfer because different systems use it in similar ways. *Structural* metadata describes the physical and logical relationships between objects. For example, EAD (Encoded Archival Description) can describe which file contains a letter and which box contains a file. Likewise, an XML file that describes the relationships between pages and chapters of a digitized book is an example of structural metadata. Structural metadata is normally more difficult to transfer than descriptive metadata because systems use different mechanisms to associate objects. However, when collections consist of individual metadata records associated with individual files, it may be a nonissue. *Administrative* metadata is used to manage resources. Such metadata includes license information, provenance, when the item was created, what size it is, and technical information necessary for rendering a file. The administrative section containing rights and preservation information of a METS (Metadata Encoding and Transmission Standard) document is an example of administrative metadata. For simple collections, administrative metadata may be mixed with descriptive metadata and the difficulty of transferring it depends on both the old and new systems.

A few things to know:

1. If metadata is readable, it is migratable. The container used for export—delimited, Dublin Core, METS, MARC, and so on—is largely unimportant because it can be put into a different container for import if necessary.
2. Most import/export APIs are easy to use. Retrieving, updating, or adding a record can often be done with a single line of code.
3. Each metadata standard is optimized for certain uses. Except when transitioning from a simple standard such as Dublin Core to a more complex one such as MARCXML or MODS, there is usually data loss.
4. Some standards are designed to be used with a specific format but others define elements that can be transmitted in several formats. For example, OAI-PMH uses XML (eXtensible Markup Language) but Dublin Core metadata can be expressed in XML, RDF (Resource Description Framework), XHTML (eXtensible Hyptertext Markup Language), JSON (JavaScript Object Notation), delimited, and other formats.

5. Standards are sometimes containers for other standards. OAI-PMH is often used to transmit Dublin Core in XML, but it can be used to transmit information in a wide variety of standards. As well, a single METS record can contain different sections expressed using different standards.
6. Generally speaking, sophisticated implementations of standards are difficult to transfer to a new system.
7. Metadata must often be obtained using multiple mechanisms—you probably can't use a single metadata standard to transfer all information and objects.
8. Custom programming is almost always necessary whenever more than one file is associated with a record or more than one record is associated with an object.
9. It's rarely possible to migrate a DAM/IR without significant data manipulation.
10. System specific metadata is inherently problematic and some may not be transferrable.
11. If you run into trouble, seek online communities where you can ask for direct assistance with specific problems. Such help is often fast and free for both open source and vended products.

DETERMINE ACCESS CONTROLS IN PLACE

It's important to ensure access controls are enforced after migrations to prevent copyright, privacy, and legal violations. Severe financial penalties can result from HIPAA (Health Insurance Portability and Accountability Act), FERPA (Family Educational Rights and Privacy Act), or rights-protected materials are inappropriately made available after a migration, so it's critical to verify that such materials are protected after the migration.

Transferring access control information is sometimes difficult because:

- The new system cannot fully utilize access control metadata from the old system.
- The old system does not export access control metadata.
- Access control works differently in the old and new systems.

If access control metadata cannot be transferred, it is best to use a separate process to load controlled materials to prevent materials from being inappropriately available. If certain types of access controls can be transferred (e.g., embargo dates), the controlled materials can be transferred in groups. In all cases, controls should be thoroughly tested before the new system goes live.

IDENTIFY IMPORT AND EXPORT METHODS SUPPORTED ON OLD AND NEW SYSTEMS

Most systems support a variety of formats and methods for importing data and objects. The basic methods are harvesting, delimited or formatted file transfer, and API (Application Programming Interface). Most likely, you will need to use multiple methods to extract the data you need. For example, if a digitized book is stored as a compound object, the process used to retrieve the metadata for the book and the individual pages might be very different. The process for extracting structural and administrative metadata is often not straightforward. When this is the case, contacting the vendor for hosted systems or performing data dumps for locally managed services is usually the best option.

When you identify formats and standards for extracting data, make sure that you have enough information to associate metadata with actual objects—it does no good to download the metadata for an object if you can't associate it directly with files.

Harvesting

There are numerous protocols that can be used for harvesting, in a library context the most useful ones are OAI-PMH (Open Archives Initiative Protocol for Metadata Harvesting) and SRU (Search/Retrieve via URL). OAI-PMH is a simple protocol that allows you to list collections and records in a repository. For example, to view the collections in the Library of Congress Memory project it is only necessary to point a program or browser at https://memory.loc.gov/cgi-bin/oai2_0?verb=ListSets, which retrieves:

```
<OAI-PMH xmlns="http://www.openarchives.org/OAI/2.0/" xmlns:xsi="http://www
.w3.0rg/2001/XMLSchema-instance" xsi:schemaLocation="http://www.openarchives
.org/OAI/2.0/ http://www.openarchives.org/OAI/2.0/OAI-PMH.xsd">
  <responseDate>2016-06-17T19:02:26Z</responseDate>
  <request verb="ListSets">http://memory.loc.gov/cgi-bin/oai2_0</request>
  <ListSets>
    <set>
      <setSpec>coll</setSpec>
      <setName>
        Collections of historical content with digitized items
      </setName>
      <setDescription>
        <oai_dc:dc xmlns:oai_dc="http://www.openarchives.org/OAI/2.0/oai_
        dc/" xmlns:dc="http://purl.org/dc/elements/1.1/" xmlns:xsi=
        "http://www.w3.0rg/2001/XMLSchema-instance"xsi:schemaLocation=
```

```
    "http://www.openarchives.org/OAI/2.0/oai_dc/ http://www.openarchives
    .org/OAI/2.0/oai_dc.xsd">
      <dc:title xml:lang="en">
        Collections of historical content with items digitized by, or
        in partnership with, the Library of Congress
      </dc:title>
        [fields omitted for brevity]
    </oai_dc:dc>
  </setDescription>
</set>
<set>
  <setSpec>drwg</setSpec>
  <setName>Drawings (documentary)</setName>
  <setDescription>
    <oai_dc:dc xmlns:oai_dc="http://www.openarchives.org/OAI/2.0/oai_
    dc/" xmlns:dc="http://purl.org/dc/elements/1.1/" xmlns:xsi=
    "http://www.w3.0rg/2001/XMLSchema-instance"xsi:schemaLocation=
    "http://www.openarchives.org/OAI/2.0/oai_dc/ http://www.openarchives
    .org/OAI/2.0/oai_dc.xsd">
      <dc:title xml:lang="en">
        Records for Digitized Documentary Drawings from LC's Prints &
        Photographs Division
      </dc:title>
        [fields omitted for brevity]
    </oai_dc:dc>
  </setDescription>
</set>
[rest of output omitted]
```

To list the records in the first set in Dublin Core, it is only necessary to look at https://memory.loc.gov/cgi-bin/oai2_0?verb=ListRecords&meta dataPrefix=oai_dc&set=coll

The beginning of the output looks like:

```
<OAI-PMH xmlns="http://www.openarchives.org/OAI/2.0/" xmlns:xsi="http://
www.w3.0rg/2001/XMLSchema-instance" xsi:schemaLocation="http://www.openarchives
.org/OAI/2.0/ http://www.openarchives.org/OAI/2.0/OAI-PMH.xsd">
  <responseDate>2016-06-17T18:59:32Z</responseDate>
  <request verb="ListRecords" metadataPrefix="oai_dc" set="coll">http://
  memory.loc.gov/cgi-bin/oai2_0</request>
```

```
<ListRecords>
  <record>
    <header>
      <identifier>oai:lcoa1.10c.gov:lccn/00528551</identifier>
      <datestamp>2010-113-29T15:56:33Z</datestamp>
      <setSpec>coll</setSpec>
    </header>
    <metadata>
      <oai_dc:dc xmlns:oai_dc="http://www.openarchives.org/OAI/2.0/oai_
      dc/" xmlns:dc="http://purl.org/dc/elements/1.1/" xmlns:xsi=
      "http://www.w3.0rg/2001/XMLSchema-instance"xsi:schemaLocation=
      "http://www.openarchives.org/OAI/2.0/oai_dc/ http://www.openarchives
      .org/OAI/2.0/oai_dc.xsd">
        <dc:title>
          African-American sheet music, 1850-1920 selected from the col-
          lection of Brown University.
        </dc:title>
        <dc:creator>
          Library of Congress. National Digital Library Program.
        </dc:creator>
        <dc:subject>African Americans-Music.</dc:subject>
        <dc:subject>Minstrel music.</dc:subject>
        <dc:subject>
          United States-History-Civil War, 1861-1865-Songs and music.
        </dc:subject>
        <dc:subject>Popular music-United States.</dc:subject>
        <dc:subject>Music-United States-19th century.</dc:subject>
        <dc:subject>Music-United States-20th century.</dc:subject>
        <dc:subject>sheet music; African-American</dc:subject>
        <dc:description>
          Selected from the Sheet Music Collection at the John Hay
          Library at Brown University. Consists of 1,305 pieces of
          American-American sheet music dating from 1850 through 1920.
          Includes many songs from the heyday of antebellum black face
          minstrelsy in the 1850s and from the abolitionist movement
          of the same period. Numerous titles are associated with
          the novel and the play Uncle Tom's Cabin. Civil War period
          music includes songs about African-American soldiers and the
          plight of the newly emancipated slave. Post-Civil War music
          reflects the problems of Reconstruction and the beginnings of
          urbanization and the northern migration of African Americans.
          African-American popular composers include James Bland, Ernest
          Hogan, Bob Cole, James Reese Europe, and Will Marion Cook.
```

```
    </dc:description>
    <dc:description>
      Copyright and other restrictions: Permission to copy in any
      form or to publish material from the Collection must be ob-
      tained from Brown University Library.
    </dc:description>
    <dc:description>Title from home page as viewed on Nov. 9,
    1999.</dc:description>
    <dc:description>
      Offered as part of the American Memory online resource
      compiled by the National Digital Library Program of the
      Library of Congress.
    </dc:description>
    <dc:description>"LC/Ameritech Award Winner"</dc:description>
    <dc:publisher>
      [Washington, D.C.] : Library of Congress, American Memory
    </dc:publisher>
    <dc:date>19910-</dc:date>
    <dc:identifier>http://hdl.loc.gov/loc.gdc/collgdc.gc000019</
    dc:identifier>
    <dc:language>eng</dc:language>
  </oai_dc:dc>
    </metadata>
  </record>
[rest of output omitted]
```

OAI-PMH servers usually limit the number of records returned; therefore, tokens are issued so data can be downloaded in chunks. Those with scripting abilities may want to write their own OAI harvesters because the data can be cleaned as it's downloaded, or they could use MarcEdit (see chapter 4) and clean it using other means.

OAI-PMH is widely supported within applications deployed in the library community. However, it is often not a viable export mechanism because:

- OAI-PMH may prove too lossy for migration purposes because the OAI server often remaps the metadata in the repository onto a simpler scheme such as Dublin Core. Fields might be remapped or missing entirely.
- OAI-PMH does not convey structural or administrative metadata that can't be expressed in a bibliographic record.
- The OAI-PMH metadata might only provide enough information to identify the landing page for resources when the objects themselves must be retrieved.

It is worth seeing if the old and new systems support OAI-ORE (Open Archives Initiative Object Reuse and Exchange). OAI-ORE retrieves objects as well as metadata, so the transfer could be very simple. If collections and/or metadata are complex, significant configuration will be required in both the old and new systems to use OAI-ORE. OAI without ORE can sometimes be used, though object pointers are typically to a landing page rather than the actual object and additional programming is required to retrieve them.

SRU is another protocol to look for because it is easy to work with, and SRU servers can sometimes be configured to provide full availability and access information. As is the case with OAI without ORE, SRU object information may point to a landing page rather than the object itself. Like OAI, SRU does not express structural or administrative metadata that is not already in the bibliographic record. SRU was designed to be a search rather than harvest protocol, so it does not provide a direct mechanism to download an entire database. Rather, you must start with a list of identifiers, which are then individually queried.

Remember that the purpose of protocols such as OAI and SRU is to expose publicly available information. Therefore it might not be possible to use these protocols to assist with migration of access controlled resources.

"Screen scraping"—that is, using a program to parse web pages designed for humans—is a form of harvesting that should be avoided because it is more difficult and less reliable than working directly with data or an interface designed for machines. However, screen scraping is sometimes the best or even the only way to obtain information and objects. Screen scraping requires strong programming and analytical skills and is more time consuming to implement than other data transfer mechanisms.

> The purpose of protocols such as OAI and SRU is to expose publicly available information. It might be impossible to use these protocols to assist with migration of access-controlled resources.

Delimited File Transfer

Delimited files are an old and simple method for structuring data. Such files use a single character—typically a comma or a tab—to separate fields with records separated by line breaks. The advantage of delimited files is that they are widely supported and easy to use in most situations. However, delimited data is more complex than it appears on the surface because there is no standard way for dealing with situations when the fields contain the delimiter or line breaks.

Delimited data is the easiest transfer mechanism for simple data. However, database and/or programming skills are often necessary to migrate complex data in delimited formats because information from multiple files must be combined.

Chapter 3 discusses working with delimited files in detail as well as cleaning data in any kind of file.

XML (eXtensible Markup Language)

XML is one of the most widely supported formats, and most modern systems support some form of XML import and export. Despite its name, XML is not a language; instead, it defines a syntax for markup languages. Most newer library metadata standards are usually expressed in XML—for example, Dublin Core can be expressed in a variety of ways, but is normally expressed in XML as in the OAI example above—and some such as MARCXML, OAI, METS, EAD (Encoded Archival Description), and SRU (Search and Retrieve via URL) are required to be expressed in XML.

❚ **XML is not a language. Rather, it defines a syntax for markup languages.**

XML is human-readable and can be manipulated using a wide variety of tools including Word processors. Even if the old and new systems support the same XML standard, such as Dublin Core or MARCXML, it will probably be necessary to modify it using a tool such as OpenRefine (chapter 3) or MarcEdit (chapter 4). Sophisticated XML manipulation requires significant programming skills.

API (Application Programming Interface)

Using an API to extract data is a form of harvesting. For migration purposes, APIs extract, insert, and modify data. As the name implies, using an API requires programming. However, many APIs are simple enough that they can be used by a nonprogrammer. Generally speaking, people who can write scripts or manipulate data files can use an API, even if they have never done so previously. Often only a single line of code is required to retrieve, update, or add records.

❚ **Anyone who can write scripts or manipulate data files can use an API, even if he or she has never done so before. It is often possible to retrieve, update, or add records with a single line of code.**

Most DAM/IR APIs are REST- (REpresentational State Transfer)-based. That's a fancy way of saying they work a lot like a web form. In fact, they are so similar that you can use a regular web browser to interact with many APIs. With a RESTful API, you typically read data from a DAM/IR using an HTTP (HyperText Transfer Protocol) GET command—the same method used to retrieve a web page—and you add data using HTTP POST—the same method your browser uses to submit information via web forms. You can interact with RESTful APIs using any modern programming language. However, coding experience is often not necessary to use an API.

A good way to understand how simple using an API can be is to download the free cURL command-line tool, which works on any platform. from https://curl.haxx.se/download.html. cURL simulates a web browser, and it can be used with any RESTful API. Typically, the way to insert data into a repository is a variation of:

```
curl -H 'Content-Type: text/xml; charset=UTF-8' -d @myfile.xml -X
POST https://my.server.org/api
```

where myfile.xml contains the data that will be inserted into a DAM located at https://my.server.org. In this example, the -H designates the specific HTTP headers that tell the server what kind of data to expect (in this case XML) to be contained in myfile.xml. Different APIs may require different or additional parameters such as a username and password, but the process is conceptually simple.

Many DAM/IRs have their own APIs, but some support standards such as SWORD (Simple Web-service Offering Repository Deposit). Standards like SWORD are neither inherently easier nor more difficult to work with than application-specific APIs. In all cases, it is a matter of supplying information the way the system expects.

Embedding Metadata Directly in Objects

For some migrations, the best option may be to embed metadata in the headers (the beginning of the files) themselves. For example, rich image metadata is often difficult to migrate via harvesting or delimited formats. However, EXIF (EXchangeable Image File) metadata is already present in images and conveys virtually all technical metadata a library might wish to migrate, IPTC (International Press Telecommunications Council) metadata conveys a range of descriptive metadata, and XMP (eXtensible Metadata Platform) can be used to embed any metadata within images. Many platforms read EXIF and IPTC metadata natively, and some platforms can be configured to read any XMP fields you wish to transfer.

Be aware that IPTC and XMP metadata can only be used for migrations if your current platform has the ability to write these fields, because such metadata within existing files will be inaccurate unless it was specifically maintained. EXIF metadata is normally generated automatically by programs and devices that create or manipulate images, but you should still verify that it hasn't been tampered with before trusting it.

Writing metadata directly to images does not cause them to degrade because they are not part of the image itself. However, doing so will cause checksums to change, so you will need to generate new checksums if that is part of your preservation strategy.

Other Export Options

Most other export options require programming skills. The fastest and most reliable way to extract data from a system is usually with a full database dump or a direct database connection, but these methods require programming expertise. Database dumps and calls are easy to perform, but depending on the complexity of the underlying data structure, they might or might not represent a feasible migration path.

Your existing DAM/IR may be able to export AIPs (Archival Information Packages) or use BagIt, a hierarchical format for packing objects and metadata. BagIt typically requires modest programming skills but is easy to implement. However, its simplicity also prevents it from conveying complex relationships or administrative metadata. AIPs allow much more flexibility, but the learning curve for using them in a practical setting is steep, and they involve complexities that all but guarantee a need for sophisticated programming skills.

VERIFY EXPORTED METADATA AND OBJECTS

Before loading exported data into the new system, ensure they are loadable and complete. Don't assume the old system exported everything correctly. Migrating out of systems is rarely a development priority, so this area is often buggy and lacking in functionality. Some widely used systems are known to generate syntactically invalid XML, systematically corrupt certain fields, alter character encodings, and introduce other problems.

Chapters 2 and 3 describe tools and methods that are useful for identifying problems and correcting data. If your data export is in delimited format, verify that each record contains the correct number of fields, that all records contain expected fields, and that the field values don't contain field or record delimiters.

Regardless of the format of the data export, closely examine the data for:

- *Integrity*: Make sure the export is syntactically valid and all metadata and objects are present. The export process may not transfer all metadata. Information about relationships between objects might not be exported. Some DAM/IR systems modify metadata and object files by design or because of bugs.

- *Format*: Verify all fields are in a format that the new system expects. Different systems have different requirements for how names, dates, and other fields are structured. Make sure that fields do not contain program code the new system won't use.
- *Encoding*: Some systems convert character encodings upon export, which makes special and non-Latin characters look like garbage. Look for HTML and program code within fields because some systems allow storage of such values, but your new system might escape the codes rather than let them be interpreted.
- *Identifiers* Most systems have a concept of a primary identifier. If your records contain multiple identifiers, develop a mechanism to ensure these are loaded into the new system in the way that allows your identifier system to function as intended.

It's best to analyze one field at a time. For example, extract and examine the date fields from all records to make sure they comply with the new system's requirements. Inspect the title fields for encoding issues. Make sure subject fields are structured as expected. Inspect description and note fields for embedded code. Ensure that you've captured all variations of fields that you need to map to new values, and verify that mappings based on complex logic will work.

The objects themselves must also be inspected. Verify checksums if these are available. If not, as many files as practical should be inspected because intermittent technical issues could corrupt object files. Make sure the export process does not perform unwanted modifications such as adding cover pages to objects.

| Don't assume the old system exported everything correctly.

IDENTIFY AND ADDRESS SCHEMA DIFFERENCES

In addition to rectifying format differences as explained above, you must address differences in how the DAM/IRs are structured. Most systems are optimized to do a specific task well, for example, publishing, managing documents or media, creating visual exhibitions, serving as a preservation system for binary objects and metadata. Some are designed to be maintained using a community model, whereas others presume centralized control. If the old and new systems were designed with different core uses in mind, migrations can be complicated if the objects and metadata are not simple. Also be aware that repositories may be based on totally different technical infrastructures. For example, if the old IR/

DAM stored information in relational database tables and the new one keeps it in an RDF (Resource Description Framework) triple store, both the structure of the information and the mechanisms to get it in and out of the system will be very different.

Even if the old and new systems are designed with the same purpose in mind and depend on the same underlying technologies, specific areas that complicate migrations include:

- *Different field definitions.* Some fields with the same name may be defined or used differently. For example, the old system might use free text for a field whereas the new one might require a code.
- *Different fields.* A field that is required and performs an essential function in one system might not exist in the other. For example, if the old system contains embargo dates or access controls and the new system doesn't support this functionality directly, you must find a way to make sure these resources are transferred in a way that does not violate agreements. Functionality might depend on different combinations of fields in the old and new systems. This is especially problematic when the field definitions are different.
- *Different record structures.* Some record types are nearly universal but others exist only in specific systems.
- *Differences in how relationships between objects are expressed.* There are many ways this can manifest itself, but an example would be how individual pages and chapters are related to a digitized book. The systems may not have the same capabilities in terms of the relationships they can express, and even when they do, the methods used to express those relationships could vary significantly.

VERIFY IMPORTED METADATA AND OBJECTS

A wide variety of issues may occur when importing metadata and objects. Unresolved schema differences may cause missing data and functionality as well as unpredictable side effects. System limits in terms of file sizes, time-outs, or bugs could cause items to import improperly. The preferred method of confirming that objects and metadata migrated correctly is to export them from the new system and verify that they are the same as what was added.

> The best way to ensure objects and metadata migrated properly is to export them from the new system and verify they are the same as what was added.

CONFIGURE SYSTEM

The process for configuring systems varies significantly, but most systems require the following:

User Accounts and Authentication

Even simple systems need administrators as well as staff who can add, delete, modify, and view content. Sophisticated systems may contain hundreds of separately defined permissions, so it's important to make sure all individuals working on the system have the authority to perform their duties. If outside programs must access your system via API, be sure to configure these accounts with appropriate permissions.

If your system contains protected content, you may need to integrate with an outside authentication system. Chapter 7 discusses user and authentication details.

Look and Feel

Configuring systems so that they integrate with the overall look and feel of your other services might be as simple as copying some files and/or modifying some templates, but it can be also very difficult. Web frameworks for user displays vary widely, so if the new system is based on a different technology than your other services, a major project requiring strong web development skills may be necessary.

Collections, Metadata, and Vocabularies

Before loading objects into the new system, collections, metadata profiles, and supported vocabularies must be configured. If your old system contained collections with different types of objects, configuration might be extensive because each collection might have its own look and feel, metadata schema, and vocabularies.

Specialized metadata schema can be especially challenging during migrations. Unless schema and vocabularies can simply be imported, specialized elements may require custom programming as well as configuration to achieve desired search, display, and system behavior characteristics. Vocabularies are generally simple to transfer when they are just lists of terms. However, migrating true authority files and ontologies can be another matter entirely. Significant programming expertise will most likely be required for migrations involving Linked Open Data (LOD).

Integrating with Other Systems

If your DAM/IR is integrated with an external search mechanism, utilizes cloud storage, provides or relies on harvesting services, or otherwise integrates with other systems, this will need to be set up with the new system. For systems integrations based on widely supported standards, configuration might only require providing credentials and/or connection information. However, integrations with local systems might require custom programming.

Update Entries to Handles, DOIs, and PURLs

Handles, DOIs (Digital Object Identifiers), and PURLs (Persistent Uniform Resource Locators) use an unchanging identifier to direct users to a resource, so the entries must be changed to point to the new URL. Hopefully, resources in your old repository were referenced using one of these mechanisms because all links to system-specific URLs will be permanently broken following a migration unless your library can indefinitely maintain a custom resolution service.

If resources were accessed using system-specific URLs, this is a good time to implement handles, DOIs, or PURLs to avoid having all links go bad the next time there is a migration. PURLs point to a resolver that directs people to a URL where a resource resides, handles provide permanent identifiers via a resolution service, and DOIs are a specific implementation of a handle service. For maximum future flexibility, handles or DOIs are better than PURLs because the latter are inherently tied to a specific domain.

Associating the existing handles, DOIs and PURLs with the new URLs usually requires importing all the objects with accompanying metadata and then performing an export that includes the handle, DOI, or PURL as well as the new location. However, if your new system allows you to determine canonical URLs, it's easiest to define the URLs in terms of existing persistent identifiers. Once your URLs can be associated with persistent identifiers, the respective resolution services can be updated. This will require programming expertise.

Transitioning Statistics

Libraries rely heavily on statistics for internal and external reporting, so it's essential to understand what statistics were generated from the old system and how they were used. Ideally, the migration team should determine how to produce the same statistics. If this is impossible because of inherent differences in how the systems function, determine how to best meet the needs served by the old statistics and document differences in how metrics are collected to help others understand reporting discrepancies.

Update URLs in Catalogs, Websites, Documentation, and Marketing Materials

The URL for your old DAM/IR will be listed on websites as well as in documentation and marketing materials. There may be links to resources in catalogs, bibliographic utilities, or even on business cards. All these sources must be updated, and you'll need a CNAME (Canonical Name) DNS (Domain Name Service) entry to forward people from the old web address to the new one.

If your old URL was hosted on a vendor site and the service was accessed using the vendor's domain name, you will need the vendor's assistance to automatically forward users to the new site. For this reason and others, it's best practice to have all services hosted on your own organization's domain, which is possible even when a vendor provides the service off-site.

RESOURCES

Common Descriptive Metadata Standards in Library DAM/IRs

Dublin Core—http://dublincore.org/documents/dces/
MODS—www.loc.gov/standards/mods/
MARCXML—www.loc.gov/standards/marcxml/
VRA Core (Visual Resources)—http://core.vraweb.org/
Darwin Core (Biology)—http://rs.tdwg.org/dwc/index.htm
PBCore (Media)—http://pbcore.org/
EAD (Archival Finding Aids)—https://www.loc.gov/ead/

Transmitting Administrative and Structural Metadata

BagIt Specification—https://wiki.duraspace.org/display/DPNC/BagIt+Specification
METS Documentation—www.loc.gov/standards/mets/
Archival Information Packages—www.iasa-web.org/tc04/archival-information
    -package-aip

Harvesting and Content Transfer

OAI-PMH—https://www.openarchives.org/pmh/
OAI-ORE—https://www.openarchives.org/ore/
SWORD—http://swordapp.org/

MIGRATING TO SHARED SYSTEMS

Al Cornish, Program Manager, Orbis Cascade Alliance

Migrating to a shared library management system requires addressing a range of technical and project management issues. In this chapter, the scenario addressed in greatest depth is of a consortium or group migrating to a shared management system. It is understood that groups will choose between commercial and open source management systems; this chapter will focus on the former approach. But even with open source systems, vendors are frequently contracted to provided supporting services.

The successful implementation and use of a shared management system is founded on policy agreements between the libraries using the system. The ideal is to have an agreed-upon set of policies in areas such as technical services practices, data sharing, and (if appropriate) discovery service configuration prior to the acquisition and implementation of a shared system.

The shared system migration process itself can benefit greatly when project management principles are applied to it. The vendor will bring its skill and expertise, but following project management fundamentals on the consortium or group side will improve the chances of migration success.

SHARED BIBLIOGRAPHIC STANDARDS AND POLICIES

Beyond the systems level, it's strongly beneficial for a group migrating to a shared system to put in place policies for working in the shared environment prior to the migration. For example, in the case of the Orbis Cascade Alliance consortium (US Pacific Northwest region), the group implemented a set of technical services mandates prior to the Request for Proposal (RFP) process and the later selection of a shared system vendor. These requirements included:

- designation of a single bibliographic utility—namely OCLC—for the group
- cataloging work by group members be performed at the network level, in this case directly on OCLC WorldCat
- definition of floor standards for bibliographic records
- member libraries use separate bibliographic records for each format of a single title

The last requirement is one that should be carefully considered, because it directly impacts user resource discovery. In a shared catalog in which records come from many sources, the use of single records for each format greatly simplifies batch load and maintenance procedures. Also, a group (or individual institution) that manages multiple formats of items on a single bibliographic record may find that its ability to employ faceted search by format is compromised in the discovery system.

This kind of policy development could extend to areas such as circulation loan policies and to data sharing.

Additionally, policies and practices should be set for restricted bibliographic records or bibliographic records limited to use by a member institution through a contract with a vendor. For a consortium migrating to a shared system for the first time, the restricted record sets should be inventoried, and vendors contacted to attempt to gain permission to use them in the shared system. It's likely that some vendors will agree to share and others will not. For the latter case, access to the records will need to be restricted to the institution in the shared system. This capability should be included in the RFP for the shared system.

DATA SHARING

Before migrating to a shared system, group members should have a clear mutual understanding of acceptable data sharing and the limits on data sharing among members. This is most important in the sharing of Personally Identifiable Information (PII) among members. Given the linkage between user data and library services (for example, adoption of a visiting user by another institution using the shared system; data reporting in the shared system that includes user and user transaction data; and central configuration of the shared system), the ability of group members to share data with one another will be a major determinant in the efficient use of the shared system. If possible, this understanding should be encoded in a legal agreement that is implemented prior to the migration to the shared system. For a new institution joining a shared system, the same need exists for the group and the incoming institution to have a clear mutual understanding of acceptable data sharing.

> **Group members should have a clear mutual understanding of acceptable data sharing and the limits on data sharing between members before migrating to a shared system.**

With institutions tightening data security management, defining the data that must be shared among members to support services has never been more challenging. One method of achieving an agreement between members is to define as specifically as possible the data items that must be shared and the staff who will have access to the data items.

CONTRACTUAL AGREEMENT WITH VENDOR
(Commercial Shared System)

Migration Scope

Through an RFP, sole source, or other acquisitions process, the consortium or group needs to come to an agreement with a vendor on migration scope for the shared system. The scope could include any one of the following:

- management service
  - » print-based management system (supported by format-specific systems)
  - » unified resource management services
- management and discovery services, integrated migration

The decision of whether to pursue an integrated management and discovery solution (from a single vendor) is one of the most important that a group will consider. Both approaches have significant strategic pros and cons that each group may weight differently.

Nonintegrated management and discovery services (different vendors for the two services):

- *Pros*: More flexibility in price negotiations with vendors; possibility of integrating "best in breed" solutions for two very different library service functions.
- *Cons*: Bandwidth required (consortium- or group-side and vendor-side) to make the solutions work together.

Integrated management and discovery services (same vendor for the two services):

- *Pros*: Increasing interdependencies of discovery and management functions (including knowledge bases) and the ability to focus the consortium or group's efforts on communication with a single primary vendor (for example, through user group work).
- *Cons*: Potential lack of strategic flexibility through overdependence on one primary vendor.

System Infrastructure

If possible, the library or group should have its shared management system hosted by the vendor in a networked environment. This may require additional contractual terms among the group and its institutions and the vendor hosting the data (when compared to hosting the management system on a local server). Also, the negotiation of security- and service-level agreements for employing a cloud-based system may be significant. Nevertheless, the labor savings achieved by off-loading server hardware, software, database, and server security management are so compelling that a locally hosted management service should be implemented only if absolutely needed.

Implementation Methodology

For a group migrating to a shared system, a key methodology decision will be to employ a single-cohort (all institutions migrating in one group) or multiple-cohort approach. The advantages of a single-group approach are significant, particularly in terms of configuration alignment for libraries migrating to the management system. Having consistent configuration will both reduce the amount of effort required for migration and position the shared system as a collaborative work environment when the migration is complete.

Conversely, with multiple cohorts, it's inevitable that the consortium must manage live transactions in multiple systems. This creates numerous complications, including workflow complexity because staff are working in, at minimum, two different management systems. This adds to the complexity of training and communication tasks for the group. Also, the reporting task is complicated because staff must retrieve data and reconcile data from multiple management systems.

However, there are some advantages to a cohort-based migration to a shared system. With this model, libraries in the consortium are divided into groups, which migrate to the shared system in chronological sequence. Staff from the earliest cohort(s) can perform training and support migration work in libraries in the later cohort. Additionally, configuration problems found in the earlier group can be corrected for the later libraries and institutions.

The implementation methodology should be described by the vendor during the RFP process. Vendors marketing so-called "next-generation" library management services are increasingly able to migrate large groups into a shared system in a single group.

Number of Data Loads

The number of data loads performed during the migration is an important point to negotiate with the vendor prior to the start of the migration process. At an absolute minimum, two data loads are needed: one of test data that can be reviewed by staff for a significant period of time (at least one month), and a second load to support the cutover to production.

The number of data loads is closely related to the implementation time line discussed in detail in the next section. A third data load (i.e., two test and one production) in the time line will allow an improved level of data quality at cutover to production, provided that adequate review time (at least one month following each test load) is available for an institution's staff to review data and to identify and correct problems.

THE MIGRATION PROCESS

Like data-sharing parameters, the work practices needed to support the shared system should be defined as early in the migration process as possible. For a group migrating from one shared system to another, this process may be straightforward—many of the management work practices from the legacy system will be carried forward to the new system. For a group migrating to a shared system for the first time, careful planning of the tasks described in this section will improve the chances for efficient and collaborative use of the system.

Support Request Submission

The submission of support cases and follow-up work on the cases represents one of the most direct relationships with the product vendor. For a group implementing a shared system, there are three different models to consider:

- *Central*: Support requests, including migration-related requests, are triaged by central consortium/group staff prior to submission to the vendor. This has the advantage of using the expertise of central staff and area experts who perform the triage work. From the vendor standpoint, the triaging of support cases should improve its efficiency and reduce duplicative work.

- *Distributed*: Support requests are submitted by staff at libraries in the group with no central triaging. For groups with small central support operations, this may be an appealing model. Some degree of coordination can be achieved through the vendor's use of a Customer Management System (CMS) that supports viewing requests among the group and through group e-mail list communication. Central staff submit requests specific to the group or consortium as a whole.
- *Hybrid*: Support requests are submitted both by central staff as well as staff at libraries in the group, with some degree of coordination in this work. The capabilities of the vendor CMS may aid in this coordination (e.g., for a migration request submitted by an institution, the CMS may enable central staff to provide information in the request that could aid in resolution, along with the support being provided by the vendor). As in the distributed case, central staff submit requests specific to the group or the whole consortium.

Other Pre-Migration Work

Prior to migration, as much data cleanup as possible should be performed in the legacy system of each library or for the group. For those groups that rely on OCLC as a bibliographic utility, this could include performing a reclamation project and reloading data to the legacy system prior to migration.

Team Structure

This area is critical, because the effectiveness of the human resources dedicated to the project (i.e., from the vendor, consortium, and library) is one of the most important factors determining both the efficiency of the migration project and the long-term success of the shared system.

Vendor-Side

The project manager and product experts can be expected to make up the vendor-side team for the migration project.

- *Project manager*: This position is the most crucial in terms of project success. The manager will be the group's advocate in the vendor organization during the migration project, in addition to the organizational lead on the vendor side. The group should state its expectations for this position to the vendor, including that the manager has completed formal project management training. Additionally, the group should have the opportunity to meet the designated manager as early as possible, ideally before the start of the project time line events.

- *Product experts*: During the migration, the group will be working with product and workflow experts on the vendor side. To the staff of the group and its libraries, these experts will be, to a great degree, the face of the vendor. They will perform migration-related support work and participate in vendor-group project meetings.

Shared System Group/Consortium-Side

The project manager and functional area leads should make up the group-side team for the migration project.

- *Project manager*: Like the vendor-side manager, this position is crucial to the success of a migration project. Each group needs to decide what it wants in this position. Some important attributes include experience with the group's libraries and workflows, integrated knowledge across functional areas, and project management experience.
- *Functional area experts*: This is the customer-side migration team. It's important to identify the most-qualified experts with the greatest knowledge of library and group workflows to serve in these leadership positions.

Project Milestones

These are some key events that each group and vendor need to consider for inclusion in a shared-system migration project plan:

- Kickoff event
  Given the complexity of the migration project, an early, in-person meeting with both consortium and library staff and vendor staff is highly advantageous. The face-to-face contact will make the follow-up project work easier, and the forum will provide an opportunity for the vendor and group to present the project plan and to field questions from the group and library staff impacted.

- Submission of sample data and configuration for loading
  The vendor will require the submission of sample data (full or complete data from integrated library system[s] used by the group) and from other related systems, such as link-resolver services. This, along with basic information provided by the group and its libraries, will support the initial provisioning of the shared system for testing and training use.

- Management system and service training
  Training is one of the most important components of a migration project. The group and vendor should work together on the development of a training

plan that balances the vendor's knowledge of and experience with the product with the workflows and use cases. Issues to consider include:

» *Method of delivery*: Web and/or online, in person, or a blend of both.
» *Roles of group or library staff in training*: Having group and library specialists lead training sessions was mentioned during discussion of the cohort implementation model. There are numerous benefits of a "train the trainer" approach, including having training delivered by people recognized and trusted by staff at the group's libraries.
» *Realism of systems being used*: The group should strive, whenever possible, for training to be conducted in an environment mirroring the shared system to which it will be migrating.

For migration to a shared management system, training support should be split between the vendor and the group. The vendor will take the lead on product training, including basic functionality sessions and certification training. However, the group has the expertise in applying the system to workflows. Additionally, library staff members tend to respond positively to training conducted by colleagues with whom they work. There are benefits to conducting blended workflow training, in which both vendor and group staff bring their expertise to the training task. Records should be saved from these sessions, which may include presentation slides, notes taken by a recorder, and, when feasable, session recordings.

- **Third-party integration implementation**
  These integrations cover a significant part of the migration process work. Successful completion of integrations often require work with stakeholders including each institution's Information Technology Services (ITS) unit and third-party vendors.
  These integrations include:

  » Bursar system (export of fines and fee information, potentially import of payment information)
  » Finance system (invoice and purchase order export)
  » Self-check stations
  » Student Information System (user imports)
  » Management service authentication
  » Discovery service authentication
  » Discovery service integration (when third-party discovery is used)

- These integrations must be carefully prioritized in the milestones plan, with go-live blockers clearly marked in the plan. Additionally, even prior to the migration, the group and individual institutions must establish contacts and share information with the external units needed to make the third-party integrations successful. For example, if the management system vendor makes its Student Information System required data formats available online (e.g., for user data), this information should be shared with the university's ITS as early as is possible—optimally as soon as the contract is signed.

> » *Creation of cutover plan.* The consortium or group needs to work with the vendor in the development of a cutover plan. This includes designating the go-live date for cutover to the shared management system (or the new system). The plan provides a granular breakdown of events leading to and following the transition to production use of the shared management system. Tasks that should be calendared and tracked include:
>> – submission of any final configuration forms to the vendor
>> – submission of any final or cutover data loads to the vendor
>> – freezing activities (technical services work, circulation work) in the legacy system
>> – final library data checks before going live, which should include problem records and scenarios identified during the test data review period
>> – For OpenURL services, verifying that all institutional data sources point to the correct service page

- The cutover plan will serve as a map for the later steps of the migration, defining the sequencing, start date, and end date for each task, along with the responsible party (on the vendor, library, or group side).

LESSONS LEARNED

Based upon the recent migrations of other groups to shared management systems, four key lessons stand out.

Need for Sustainability in Human Resources

One of the key challenges in management service migration is the limit on skilled staff expertise. This is true on the consortium or library side as well as the vendor side. For the migration to a shared library management system, the skilled technical demands are significantly higher than for single-institution migration. Additionally, the number of staff required to support the shared system following the migration must be fully considered. Recommended approaches for addressing this include:

- Ensuring that the consortium-side project manager has strong project management, library data, and technology skills.
- Conducting a library- or consortium-side inventory of human resources available to the migration project and for post-migration use of the system prior to engaging with the vendor on the project.

- Ensuring that library or consortium administrators are aware of any gaps between the on-the-ground project needs and the inventory, both during and after the migration period.
- Conducting regular meetings between the group's migration leaders and the vendor-side project manager, starting as early in the project time line as possible, and provide ongoing feedback to the manager on her performance.

The shared management system provides challenges in terms of identifying tasks to be performed at the group level and at the institution level, and in building sustainability into the group-level system support. This group-level work is critical to the success of any institution. In some ways, the migration project is easier to plan for, given that by definition it is a temporary endeavor with specific goals. Still, groups need to avoid single points of failure in terms of expertise whenever possible, and account for the need to replace staff who provide project support. The longer-term, post-migration management of the system can be more challenging. For this programmatic work, it may be valuable to inventory tasks and divide them into those done by the group's staff, tracked and balanced tasks that are done by member staff that's, and tasks that are performed without tracking.

❙ Group-level work is essential to the success of all institutions.

Access to Legacy Management System(s) Post-Migration

Retaining access to legacy management systems in a staff-access-only mode following the migration will be extremely beneficial to the library or group. This may or may not be possible, depending on the contract with the system vendor and the legacy system hosting arrangements (hosted locally or hosted on a cloud server by the vendor). Keeping this system available to library staff will enable statistics retrieval and review of configurations (e.g., circulation locations and loan rules) following the migration to the shared system.

Benefits of Single-Group Migration

While there are some advantages to a cohort-based migration plan, including a learning curve that benefits downstream cohorts and support for a "train the trainer" model, they are outweighed by the advantages of migrating to a shared system in a single group.

These benefits include:

- avoiding the scenario of having some institutions in migration to the shared system with others in production use (which greatly adds to project complexity)
- support for a more standardized shared system configuration when migration is completed

Importance of Local Project Management Skills

As noted above, the library- or consortium-side project manager should have strong project management skills. This is frequently a challenge for library organizational managers, given the fact that library and information science programs do not emphasize project management training. Optimally, the library- or consortium-side project manager will have gone through training based on the Project Management Institute's *PMBOK* standard and will have been certified as a Project Management Professional. Short of this, the manager should have some formal project management training to help provide effective project leadership.

CONCLUSION

The migration to a shared system touches a number of technical, human, organizational, and legal issues. This chapter emphasizes the importance of preplanning, to the greatest extent possible, even prior to the acquisition of the shared system.

It's important not to go it alone. Consortia or institutions considering migration to a shared system can gain practical advice on product and service options by engaging with like-minded groups such as the International Coalition of Library Consortia (ICOLC) and through vendor or product-user groups.

WORKING WITH LIBRARY VENDORS

Kate Thornhill, Repository Community Librarian, OHSU

his chapter focuses on navigating vendor relationships throughout the process of a successful data migration. It focuses on the example of migrating a digital library out of a legacy system into a managed platform. The concepts discussed apply to migrations into vended solutions, because other types of migrations involve technical and organizational dimensions that are difficult to generalize. Although the focus is on working with vendors, the ideas and methods also apply to working with other organizational entities such as a campus's central IT department.

Note also that this chapter does not focus on vendor partnerships that support eresource content platforms, socioeconomic or ethical issues that may emerge when outsourcing digital library solutions, or the relationships between libraries and vendors who monitor services.

THE THREE-LEGGED DIGITAL LIBRARY CHAIR

Imagine a scenario where faculty, students, and staff want you to change the aesthetics and behaviors of the digital library you manage. Meeting such challenges requires addressing several factors, including how the technical infrastructure operates, what resources are available, and how your institution is organized.

These three core components, which are adapted from the Digital Preservation Management: Implementing Short-Term Strategies for Long-Term Problems workshop hosted by the MIT Libraries in 2016 (www.dpworkshop.org/), symbolize a three-legged chair that represents programmatic pillars (figure 12.1). Like chairs, digital libraries come in different shapes and sizes, and as the field continues to grow and change, new materials and solutions help librarians coordinate policies, procedures, people, software, hardware, secure environments, maintenance, and funding. Although this chair metaphor was designed to describe digital libraries, it is applicable to a wide range of library systems.

FIGURE 12.1

Three-legged digital library chair

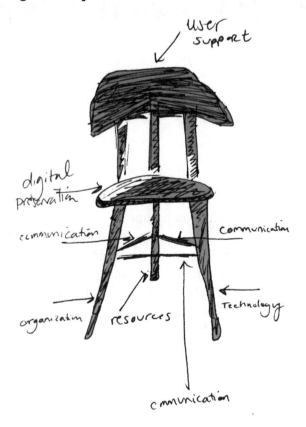

Illustration created by Kate Thornhill, adapted from Digital Preservation Management: Implementing Short-Term Strategies for Long-Term Problems (www.dpworkshop.org/).

Figure 12.1 shows a three-legged chair that represents the conceptual components for a digital library. Together these design elements reinforce digital library reliability and trustworthiness using construction materials standardized for digital library management and a variety of use cases. Starting from the bottom, the chair legs symbolize the library's organization, resource, and technology infrastructure. The triangular spindles represent support and communication between each leg. Above these structural supports is a seat for digital preservation and chair back for user support. You may have noticed this metaphor does not only apply to technical stacks, but to the entire digital library social and technological infrastructure. The chair we will work with in this chapter needs its technology leg replaced to have digital library services continue to run.

Let's break down our problem into a high-level scenario to help us think about making decisions about digital library sustainability. Suppose our goal is to migrate digital library data from the old system to a new one within the next year. One potential solution would be software as a service (SaaS) digital libraries.

This means we will have to replace the entire technology leg. Regardless of whatever technical support we may or may not have, there will still be certain aspects that will need to be done in-house. These include digital preservation media management, metadata schema, and authority best practice standards.

SAAS VENDOR RELATIONSHIPS AND COMMUNICATION

SaaS is a third-party model for software distribution in which a vendor hosts applications and makes them available to customers over a network. SaaS data migration is highly coordinated, and its success is dependent on business relationships, librarian abilities, available resources, vendor personnel, system capabilities, and user needs. Returning to the chair metaphor, SaaS is part of our technology leg. User support and digital preservation are integrated in the spindle communication lines.

SaaS collaborations are complicated. Digital collections librarians must set realistic data-migration goals and outcomes that connect vendor business exchanges, data curation, data interoperability, and user expectations. For the project to succeed, the vendor must be capable and predisposed to perform functions that match the library's needs. For example, contracted support is a good solution when you do not have sufficient capacity or personnel with the needed skills. Working with vendors offers other potential advantages. But in contrast to the SaaS model, to host applications locally you might need to invest energy and time, and build relationships to implement systems managed by your university's central IT unit. However, communication can be complex with the SaaS vendor, particularly because the vendor is unlikely to possess knowledge of local practices and policies (table 12.1).

TABLE 12.1

Pros and cons of working with SaaS vendors

PROS AND CONS OF WORKING WITH SAAS VENDORS

Pros	Cons
• Vendor supports service as well as all technologies on which it depends.	• Library's back-end access to data is usually more limited than on-site systems.
• Vendor has expertise with all areas of system.	• Sales representative versus implementation technician versus system administrator information communication relays can cause confusion about library's needs.
• Vendor upgrades software and hardware for you.	
• Vendor can more easily provided storage and disaster recovery.	• Library's legally and organizationally mandated security and data requirements are often more difficult to meet.
• Library staff can communicate directly with other customers who use identical systems.	

> The key to any relationship with a library vendor is clearly communicating your expectations to the vendor.

Financial considerations often complicate service partnerships between libraries and vendors. It is critical to define your needs and to translate them so that the vendor will understand and execute them—otherwise, frustration will be the inevitable result. The relationship you establish with a vendor sets the tone for how your organizations will work together. Migrations into a proprietary digital library system are rarely a one-time collaborative initiative. In fact, the business agreement specified in your contract's terms and conditions can forge a years-long relationship with the vendor.

Vendor-supported platforms require you to work with sales representatives, product managers, project implementers, systems administrations, and others who support SaaS digital repositories.

Sales representatives are your first point of contact. They guide clients through system acquisitions and contracts. Technical implementers teach clients how to use the system and ingest and manage data. They serve as liaisons between you and the systems administrators who work on back-end solutions to your problems. Often you won't interact directly with systems administrators because the technical implementer is your designated contact.

It is essential to work well with your technical implenter. Technical implementers typically have technology, technical services, or related library and information science backgrounds. Partnering with technical implementers requires give and take. Communication, respect, and stating priorities form the foundation of vendor collaborations.

> Your relationship with the technical implementer is crucial for data-migration success.

As in any team relationship, you cannot depend on a single person to accomplish everything. A professional and respectful rapport with a vendor leads to benefits that will continue throughout your business relationship. Some benefits to a good working relationship include your needs being assigned a high priority, learning how to best utilize support, and receiving favorable contract terms on future services.

To maintain a healthy business relationship and ensure vendors are responsive to your needs, it's important to treat them well. A partnership may be strained when technical implementers don't understand the problems you describe. This can be due to communication errors or gaps in either party's knowledge. When this occurs, try using different terms and metaphors to get your point across diplomatically. As well, there is always the chance that vendor representatives are unresponsive because they are overworked or focused on issues more critical than yours. Regardless, always begin work with a vendor as if you will be collaborating with her as you would any other work colleague. Remember that even though you are a customer, your conduct influences your library's reputation; therefore, you should always maintain a professional demeanor.

SaaS vendors become part your digital library infrastructure once you decide to migrate into their systems. Table 12.2 lists typical vendor expectations about what work they will and will not do for your migration. If you need to convert and normalize massive amounts of metadata and you do not have someone to do it in-house, then you will need to contract the work to another party.

TABLE 12.2

What SaaS vendors will and will not do during a data migration

WILL DO	WILL NOT DO
• Setup	• Transform your data
• Talk you through configuration	• Talk to your users as digital collections managers
• Supply training and documentation	
• Troubleshoot issues	• Advertise your services
• Assist you with user support needs	• Catalog your digital materials

MIGRATION STRATEGY FOR WORKING WITH A VENDOR

Communicate expectations clearly and in advance to avoid confusion and pitfalls. A great deal of planning and preparation must be done before greenlighting a migration, including

- pre-assessment
- selecting a system
- assigning migration tasks and responsibilities
- system setup and administration training
- data structure conversion
- data validation and verification
- post-migration testing

Reviewing your three-legged chair leads to efficiency and effectiveness. Our goal is to rebuild the technology leg to continue digital library service. Knowledge of

- staffing
- funding
- data
- the legacy system
- user information-seeking and use behaviors

will prevent data information loss, security breaches, unnecessary system down times, and the endless headaches surrounding data cleanup after migration. A comprehensive plan is essential to avoid long-term data curation problems.

Before researching vendors or planning collaborative migration workflows, it's critical to assess your data as well as fiscal, staff, and technical resources. Assessment aids in deciding how to plan, delegate, and realistically determine feasible migration paths. So how do you determine what constitutes vendor work? Vendors are unlikely to be digital collections managers. Unlike librarians and archivists, they seldom specialize in data curation. Their role is to supply us with services to help us do our jobs when our institutions cannot support digital library technical infrastructure.

PRE-MIGRATION ASSESSMENT

The first stage of a SaaS data migration is conducting a pre-migration assessment that clearly outlines your capabilities to manipulate and transfer data (figure 12.2). You should focus on which metadata and digital files the library staff need from the new system while ensuring data are transferred correctly and completely, and meet user experience expectations. This phase of migration strategy forces you

FIGURE 12.2

SaaS digital library migration strategy cycle

Illustration by Kate Thornhill.

to identify and establish roles, responsibilities, and overall work and decisions that must be completed. As you review the list of questions in table 12.3 that describe what vendors will and will not do for you, think about how these will interface with your staffing, data, legacy system, users, and funding.

Assessment gives baseline information for migration strategy evaluation, including how to research library vendors. Digital library systems are optimized to meet specific sets of criteria, so questions asked during selection should map directly to your library's needs. For example, systems designed for ease of access may not support data curation, statistical analysis, or batch maintenance functions. If one of the latter items is important, they should guide your decision-making processes.

> Digital library systems are optimized for to meet specific sets of needs, so questions asked during selection should map directly to your library's needs.

TABLE 12.3

Pre-Migration Digital Library Assessment Questions

PRE-MIGRATION DIGITAL LIBRARY ASSESSMENT QUESTIONS

Library Staffing

- What is the full-time staff effort?
- What are the staff roles and experiences?
- What are current staff priorities?
- What technical skills do staff have for a migration?
- Why is your staffing in its current organizational form?

Data

- How much data do you have and where does it live?
- What shapes and sizes does your data come in? What file types do you have?
- What metadata standards are you using?
- How should you prepare data for the new system?
- What data doesn't have to go into the new system?
- Is your data interoperable?

Legacy System

- What system are you using?
- What type of system do you need to migrate into to support user and library service needs?
- Where is data stored and how easy will it be to get out of the current system?
- How is the data secured?
- Who currently oversee your system administration?
- How easy is it to get data out of the legacy system?

Users

- How are they accessing and discovering information in the current system?
- What would happen if the system goes off-line during migration?
- How will new system features and capabilities affect user workflows?

Funding

- How much money do you have in the fiscal year budget for migrating library data? Is the funding continuous in case the migration goes over deadline?
- Is funding only allowed to be spent in specific ways according to your institution's policies?
- What are the continuous funds to maintain the new system you migrate into?

Communicating with other libraries may help you determine if a SaaS solution is right for your library. Conversations with library colleagues will help you understand what does and does not regarding data curation and user scenarios. Through colleagues and cold calls to other institutions, you can find out how libraries have set up workflows and identify problems not discussed by vendors. It is also an opportunity to discover how vendors form and maintain relationships with institutions like your own.

Once you have identified your needs and capabilities and selected a system, you must work with technical implementers to determine who is responsible for what tasks and to define expectations for strategy, workflows, and system support. SaaS vendors have standard plans for library data migrations and should be asked outright for overviews of past migration projects, as well as points where challenges came up. Talk to the vendor about the state of your data and your library staff's abilities. By this stage, you should already know the vendor's support commitments, but it's still better to articulate them, especially in the context of active migration.

System setup begins after migration roles and responsibilities are established. Think of system setup as the technology leg's attachment to your chair before it is secured and ready for prime time. The vendor's systems administrator is the representative who sets up the application environment and system configurations before you start any administrative digital collections work. Depending on the system, the vendor should ask questions about URI setup, basic system templates, and administrative access. Digital collection management functions are not yet performed at this point in the migration.

Once the digital library is set up, training on the system's administrative features should begin. Training should also cover how to ingest digital materials and configure metadata behaviors to support user information-seeking behaviors, to leverage data curation capabilities, and include instruction about how the user interface setup works and how to determine which limitations need to be addressed.

After system setup and training, you can configure metadata to support workflows and user needs. Metadata configuration is often the most challenging aspect of migration, especially when the SaaS system's configuration is not robust enough to capture desired schemas and vocabularies. Think of our digital library chair. The spindle connecting the technology leg should communicate with the chair's organizational leg whenever there are decisions to be made about metadata schema, authority control definitions, and field validations. This is helpful for data validation and verification, future migrations, and describing digital materials as standards for data and system performance evaluation.

Major choices about complex digital object descriptions need to be strategically managed by the digital collections librarian rather than the vendor. Most likely, you will lose some information when migrating to a new digital library because of how the database was constructed and due to human error. However, you can learn how to mitigate such issues by working with the technical implementer or other libraries that have migrated to the same system.

Once your metadata has been configured in the new system, you must determine how to ensure they are valid and can be maintained. Data can be validated manually or automatically, depending on your system's analytical features. SaaS digital libraries usually come with built-in basic validation functions. The

functions that digital collections managers tend to use most are field-level validations that minimize human data-entry error. The validations are also used to
figure out what fields are missing data upon batch or individual content ingest.
Common database field-level validations include the validation rule property,
which requires data entry to be written following a specific rule; data types
requiring fields to be formatted in specific ways like date and time; and required
property, which forces data entry.

Once an approach to data structure definitions and validation is documented
and configured, the next migration stage is performing data validation and verification. Envision this as a quality check to assess how secure the chair's technology
leg is to the rest of the chair. You need to make sure spindle connections work,
and if digital materials are described and discoverable. Remember, data cleanup
is in your hands. The technical implementer is only there to support glitches
or answer system questions. For this reason, it's best to ingest data in small,
diverse test loads to verify validation techniques on the back end and front end
of your system.

Once data is validated and verified, it is time to load your entire collection
and begin post-migration testing. This is another stage in which the vendor
does not participate because it is framed around your specific digital library use
cases. Your goal is to discover if the system does what users need by conducting
usability testing and data cleanup. Think of this stage as someone sitting down
in your metaphorical chair to see if it is functional. Do all the fields function
as expected? Do users like the look and feel? Post-migration is also the time to
train library staff and digital production assistants how to use and process digital
collections before launch.

As the end of migration approaches, all that remains is to launch the service.
Once this happens, the vendor takes a back seat but continues to support system
inquiries. The vendor will reach out to you occasionally, usually to communicate
about system downtime and upgrade periods, new function releases, or how the
system is working out. As figure 12.2 indicates, system launch is not the final
migration stage. In fact, the migration cycle never ends

CONTINUOUSLY MANAGING BUSINESS RELATIONSHIPS WITH VENDORS

When you collaborate with vendor representatives, it will take time to build meaningful and mutually beneficial relationships. Open communication, likeability,
respect, and professionalism will take you far when managing these business
relationships. Your flexibility, patience, and interest in the vendors as people, as
well as their services, will benefit your library. Think about these partnerships as
means to build a personal network. Business relationships with vendors could

be lasting engagements that follow you throughout your career. I have met librarians who have built career-long partnerships with vendor representatives that have endured for twenty years. It is important to remember SaaS digital library migrations are not purely about managing technology to benefit library services. Once your digital library chair's technology leg is secured and the chair is being used, always remember other people have joined you, and library staff, and users as part of the ecosystem.

13

TESTING AND GOING LIVE

Bonnie Parks, Collections Technology Librarian, University of Portland

 our library staff spent months preparing for this day. Now it's time to see all the hard work and preparation pay off. Your library probably won't shut its doors just because you're migrating to a new system—users still need to use resources and check out materials. It therefore makes sense to begin post-migration testing with functions that directly affect your users, especially those standing in front of you at the service desk.

This chapter walks you through the process of testing each of the components of your new library management system (LMS) to ensure your first day runs as smoothly as possible. The recommendations in this chapter are a set of guidelines to help you get up and running with essential library activities as soon as your new system is live. These will need to be tailored to meet your library's specific needs.

💡 **PRO TIP**

Prior to conducting testing, create test users and e-mail addresses to verify that each of the steps works correctly.

CIRCULATING LIBRARY MATERIALS

Data Integrity

Your first step should be to verify existing information. Examine your patron records and confirm that the records migrated as you expected. Look for and correct migration anomalies such as multiple barcodes or e-mail addresses in a single field. Then perform the following tests:

Create and Modify Users

- Search and browse for existing users.
    - » Last name
    - » First name
    - » Last, first
    - » Barcode/card ID number

- Create a staff user.
    - » Assign permissions for each of the various areas of your system (Circulation, Acquisitions, Cataloging, etc.)
    - » Modify permissions for the user
    - » Modify data associated with the user (expiration date, internal or external notes if applicable)

- Create a new public user.
    - » Include all essential fields (name, address, type of user, etc.)

> Depending on your library, you may have many different user types that include, but are not limited to, faculty, staff, undergraduate, graduate, and community users. Your library may employ different loan periods depending on the type of user as well as the type of material. Different systems handle the relationships among user types, material types, and loan periods very differently; therefore, it is crucial that you test every combination of user, material type, and loan period associated with your library.

- Modify user data associated with the user (address, phone, e-mail, internal or external notes, etc.).
- Block a user or the user's record.
- Delete a user.

Check out, Return, and Renew Materials

- Check out materials to each of your patron types. Don't just check out books. Check out all types of materials in your collection that circulate—books, DVDs, CDs, journals, multipart items, educational kits, and so on.

 PRO TIP

This activity becomes complicated very quickly! Create a spreadsheet that contains all your patron types, material types, and loan periods. Work through the spreadsheet one step at a time and be sure to test every combination.

  » Change the due dates. Make sure you change one of the dates to be overdue so you can test the functionality when you check in materials.
  » Place an item on hold for a test user. Then check out the material.
  » Place multiple holds on a single item.
  » Place a recall on an existing item that is checked out.
  » Mark a checked-out item as lost.

- Check in those materials.
  » Check in an item not yet due.
  » Check in an overdue item.
  » Check in an item with a hold and verify that the patron with the hold is notified.
  » Check in an item owned by another branch or library if applicable.
  » Backdate a check-in.
  » Check in an item that was marked as lost.

- Renew checked-out materials.
  » Renew items individually, and if the system permits, renew all materials at once. Verify that the renewal period is correct.
  » If you have configured your system to allow a maximum number of renewals, test the maximum by renewing the item again.

- Try to check out an item that should not circulate.

Additional Circulation Functions

- Select an item that has circulated several times and determine whether the circulation history migrated correctly.
- Request an item that is on the shelf and ask for it to be picked up at your service desk. If you have more than one desk, place multiple holds for multiple items and test pickup at each location.

- Once you've set up your patron notifications, test them. Include:
  - » Courtesy notices.
  - » Overdue notices.
  - » Lost notices.
  - » Holds and recalls.
  - » Any other notices or notifications used by your library.

- Once you've set up your fines and fees, test them. If your system is configured to print or e-mail receipts, verify that the functionality is working correctly and that the users' accounts are updated appropriately.
  - » Manually create a fine.
  - » Test system-generated fines.
  - » Waive a fine.
  - » Reduce a fine.
  - » Pay a fine.
  - » Mark an item as lost and then generate a replacement fee for that item.

- If your new system includes physical course reserves functionality that you plan to employ, do not forget to give it a thorough testing.
  - » Create a new course.
  - » Add library items to the course.
  - » Add a personal copy to the course.
  - » Remove material from the course.
  - » Delete a course.
  - » Add material to an existing course.
  - » Add multiple copies to a course.

- If your system is configured to print or e-mail circulation receipts, test the functionality.

 PRO TIP

Don't forget that any off-line circulation functions that were performed during your system freeze and cutover period must be reconciled. You should have a record of these activities.

Systems Administration

Now that your LMS is up and running and you can circulate materials to your users, it's time for a systems check. Your library staff rely on seamless integrations among the libraries various platforms and servers to perform their day-to-day activities, so taking this crucial step may help save time and frustration in the long run. During your library's initial migration preparation, your system lead or delegate shared your migration strategy and time line with your IT department and other campus stakeholders. Therefore, it shouldn't come as a surprise to anyone that you will need to verify all functionality once you're in production. Keep your campus partners in the loop and know that you may need to call on their expertise if something doesn't go as expected.

Integrations with Other Systems

Integrations with other systems that require input from IT and other campus partners include:

- Testing link resolver software.
- Ensuring bibliographic utilities (e.g., OCLC Connexion, SkyRiver, etc.) are configured correctly.
- Checking bursar transfer processes for fines and fees.
- Importing and exporting users to and from student information systems (Banner, PeopleSoft, etc.).
- Verifying proxy implementation and authentication for both on- and off-campus users.
- Testing SFTP server functionality. Be sure to test both upload and download capability.
- Confirming connections to networked printers including label printers.
- Checking interfaces with resource-sharing systems.

Other System Functions

Locations and internal codes play an important role in LMS systems. As you spot-check the records in your new system, don't forget to

- Verify that each location you have defined for your library has migrated as it should.
- Confirm that system codes have mapped correctly.

Acquisitions and ERM Functionality

Now that you're back in business, make sure your acquisitions staff can perform basic acquisitions tasks. Examine and verify the integrity of the data that migrated to your new system. It is best to run through the checklist before resuming with your ordering and receiving workflows.

Data Integrity

- Open orders in your legacy system should migrate as open orders in your new LMS.
- Closed orders in your previous system should remain closed.
- Fund ledger structures are as you've laid them out.
- Vendor files should migrate correctly.
- If you have an ERM, verify that your licenses have migrated properly.
- If your ERM is linked to your order records, verify the links.

Create and Update Information

- Place an order for a serial, standing order, and firm order. (If you order through a vendor system, test whether you can import Electronic Order Confirmation Records [EOCR]) from your vendor.
- Cancel an order for a serial, standing order, and firm order.
- Create an invoice both manually and through import.
- Export an invoice.
- Receive physical material including serials, standing orders, and firm orders.
- Activate an eresource.
- Transmit orders to your vendor. This is crucial if your system utilizes EDI (Electronic Data Interchange).
- Create a vendor record.
- Create a new license record and link appropriately.
- When ordering, paying, or cancelling invoices, verify the integrity of the fiscal information (e.g., when you order a book for $100, make sure the system encumbers the correct amount).

Finally, run standard acquisitions and collections reports (budget, new items, etc.) and look for anomalies.

 PRO TIP

Keep in mind that if you migrate after fiscal close, you may have to build the ledger for the new fiscal year.

Cataloging

Bibliographic metadata may include records for tangible, electronic, and in some cases digital resources. Test materials in all formats. As with other components in the new system, cataloging staff must also be able to perform essential cataloging functions. Pick a record or two to play with and test the following:

Data Integrity

- Did your MARC fields map correctly?
- Have your system control numbers mapped to where they should be?
- If you use a single-record approach for print and electronic resources, did the information for the print and electronic locations and holdings migrate properly?

Importing and Exporting

- Test whether you can export from your bibliographic utility and import to your new system without errors.
    - » Individually
    - » Batch

- If you maintain an authority file, export an authority record from your bibliographic utility and import into your new system.
    - » Individually
    - » Batch

- If you receive vendor MARC records, make sure your system is configured to import the records correctly.
    - » Test individual record import.
    - » Test a batch import.

- Make sure you can merge or overlay brief bibliographic records with full records upon export from your bibliographic utility and/or vendor record sets.
- If you use Z39.50 to search and retrieve MARC records, make sure that your settings are configured properly and test the functionality.
- Verify all fields are indexed and displayed as expected.

Create and Update Information

- Create a new bibliographic record in your new system. It can be brief. Perform the following tasks:
    - » Add a single item record.
    - » Add multiple item records.
    - » Delete an item record.
    - » Move an item record to another bibliographic record.
    - » Add a new field.
    - » Delete a field.
    - » Verify indexed fields display as expected.

- Modify an existing record using the same tasks listed above.

- Suppress a record from discovery.
  - » Bibliographic
  - » Item
  - » Holdings

- Delete a bibliographic record. Depending on your system, you may not be able to delete a bibliographic record that has items or holdings attached. Follow the instructions set forth in your system's documentation to ensure that you can remove the record from your system.
  - » Delete a single record.
  - » Perform a batch delete.

- Create a set of records and test whether you can perform a global update to one of the fields in the record set.

A FEW WORDS TO THE WISE

No matter how thoroughly you planned and tested your migration, things will go wrong and it will take time to correct these things. Get into the mindset of a user and prioritize correcting issues that impact users the most. Common problems that cause significant disruption to services include:

- Some of the data didn't migrate. This may cause resources, patrons, or items to mysteriously disappear.
- Ebooks lack URLs and/or other issues prevent access to electronic resources.
- Fields in some records did not migrate properly. For example, summary holdings information on journals may be missing, locations may be missing or incorrect on items, call numbers might not be stored properly, or patron records containing multiple barcodes might contain all barcodes in a single field or the wrong barcode might be in the primary.
- Configuration errors may cause a wide variety of issues that affect patrons and staff alike.

Keep your legacy system running as long as possible to help resolve questions that arise. Before shutting down your legacy system, dump any data that you can if it is not already included in the migration files.

Document everything. The new system works differently than the old one, and libraries tend to build workflows around their functionality and idiosyncrasies, so be sure to evaluate tasks and determine workflows, which must then be documented.

Leverage the experience of others. Join discussion lists and forums frequented by others who use the system. Ask questions. And don't be afraid to call or e-mail people out of the blue. If you don't already use this technique, you might be amazed how often and how well it works. Many people are flattered to be identified as authorities and will take time to help people who contact them.

Don't forget to update your web page links on go-live day to direct users to your new system. If the URL of your new system differs from that of your legacy catalog, you should redirect because many of your users will have bookmarked the page for your previous system. General redirects will be necessary for links to specific records or pages in your system, but certain pages such as new books lists may require special redirects.

Migrations are challenging for many reasons. You must move data designed for one system into a new one that works differently. All your staff suddenly have to change how they perform tasks in the system—and in some cases, must change the tasks themselves. The entire nature of a migration is that it requires coordinating many people at your library, your organization, and your vendor partners. This may be your first migration, but it probably won't be your last. The good news is that although systems change, the basic task facing migration planners remains the same—you are connecting the past to the future.

ACRONYMS

AIP	Archival Information Package
API	Application Programming Interface
ASCII	American Standard Code for Information Interchange
CLI	Command Line Interface
CMS	Content Management System
CNAME	Canonical Name
CR	Carriage Return
CRLF	Carriage Return and Line Feed
CSV	Comma Separated Values
DAM	Digital Asset Management
DNS	Domain Name Service
EAD	Encoded Archival Description
EDI	Electronic Data Interchange
EDIFACT	Electronic Data Interchange for Administration, Commerce, and Transport
ERM	Electronic Resources Management
ERMS	Electronic Resource Management Systems
EXIF	EXchangeable Image File
FERPA	Family Educational Rights and Privacy Act
FTP	File Transfer Protocol
HIPAA	Health Insurance Portability and Accountability Act
HTML	HyperText Markup Language
HTTP	HyperText Transfer Protocol
ILL	InterLibrary Loan
ILS	Integrated Library System
IM	Instant Messaging
IPTC	International Press Telecommunications Council
ISBN	International Standard Book Number

ISSN	International Standard Serial Number
IT	Information Technology
JPEG	Joint Photographic Experts Group
JSON	JavaScript Object Notation
KB	Knowledge Base
LF	Line Feed
LMS	Library Management System
MARC	MAchine Readable Cataloging
MARCXML	MAchine Readable Cataloging eXtensible Markup Language
METS	Metadata Encoding and Transmission Standard
MODS	Metadata Object Description Schema
MP4	Moving Picture Experts Group 4 part 14 player
NCIP	NISO Circulation Interchange Protocol
OAI	Open Archives Initiative
OAIS	Open Archival Information System
ONIX	ONline Information eXchange
OPAC	Online Public Access Catalog
OREL	OpenRefine Expression Language
Perl	Practical Extraction and Reporting Language
PMH	Protocol for Metadata Harvesting
PREMIS	Preservation Metadata: Implementation Strategies
REST	REpresentational State Transfer
RFP	Request for Proposal
SGML	Standard Generalized Markup Language
SIP	Submission Information Package
SWORD	Simple Web-service Offering Repository Deposit
TIFF	Tagged Figure 3-File
URI	Uniform Resource Indicator
URL	Uniform Resource Locator
UTF-8	Unicode Transformation Format 8 bit
UTF-16	Unicode Transformation Format 16 bit
XHTML	eXtensible HyperText Markup Language
XML	eXtensible Markup Language
XMP	eXtensible Metadata Platform
XSLT	eXtensible Stylesheet Language Transformations

ABOUT THE
CONTRIBUTORS

AL CORNISH is a program manager at the Orbis Cascade Alliance, where he managed a project to migrate thirty-one institutions to a shared ILS. Previously he served for more than twenty years as an automation and systems librarian at three ARL institutions, most recently as head of library systems at Washington State University.

TODD ENOCH obtained his MLS from the University of North Texas (UNT) in 2005. He served as the electronic publications librarian for the UNT Libraries for two years before assuming his current position as head of serials and electronic resources in 2008. The two positions have provided him with a decade's worth of experience in electronic resource management systems.

DAVID FORERO has more than two decades of experience helping people solve problems using technology in environments including higher education, K-12, nonprofit, Fortune 500, and even a tech startup. In 2015 he completed an MLIS and is now the technology director for the Library at OHSU.

KATE HILL is currently the electronic resources librarian at the University of North Carolina at Greensboro (UNCG). She fell in love with data transformation tools when she began her library career at North Carolina State University, where she migrated and transformed data to fit into the new Global Open Knowledgebase project (GOKb). She teaches other librarians about the joys of data transformation outside of Excel through presentations at library conferences and training at her own library and the broader UNC system. She also is using OpenRefine to continue the migration of data into OCLC Worldshare at UNCG and attempts to still contribute to the GOKb project in her free time.

KELLEY MCGRATH is the metadata management librarian at the University of Oregon. Previously, she worked as the cataloging and metadata services librarian (audio-visual) at Ball State University. She was a member of the Orbis-Cascade

Alliance's Shared ILS Cataloging Working Group during its migration to a consortial catalog and coordinated the preparation of the University of Oregon's bibliographic, holdings, and item records for migration to Alma.

NATHAN MEALEY is the manager of library technologies at Portland State University Library, where he served as the institutional lead for its migration to the Alma and Primo integrated library system in 2014, which was part of the Orbis Cascade Alliance's overall migration to a shared integrated library system.

TERRY REESE is the head of digital initiatives at The Ohio State University Libraries. Over the past seventeen years, his primary research interests have been related to the changing nature of library metadata and the ways in which this data can be reused and transformed in different contexts. He is the author and creator of MarcEdit, a cross-platform library metadata-editing tool designed to lower the technical barriers for users working with various forms of library metadata.

ELAN MAY RINCK is a serials technician who also has paraprofessional experience in access services at the University of Portland. She participated in the University of Portland's 2014 systems migration from Millennium's III to Ex Libris's Alma.

SIÔN ROMAINE is an acquisitions librarian for the University of Washington Libraries. He also served as the Alma Library Management System coordinator following the Libraries' migration from a locally hosted Millennium system to the Orbis Cascade Alliance's shared Alma Library Management System.

KATE THORNHILL is a repository librarian who works at OHSU, where she leads digital assets management and institutional repository assessment and outreach. Over the past ten years, Kate has built her digital library expertise through her work in digital humanities, e-science, and special collections digital initiatives, as well as from communicating with repository vendors. She is a graduate of Simmons College.

INDEX